PANKAJ MISHRA

INDIA IN MIND

Pankaj Mishra was born in north India in 1969 and
now lives in London and India. He is the author of
The Romantics, which won the *Los Angeles Times*'s Art
Seidenbaum Award for First Fiction, and *An End
to Suffering: The Buddha in the World*. He is a regular
contributor to *The New York Review of Books*, *Granta*,
and *The Times Literary Supplement*.

INDIA IN MIND

INDIA IN MIND

AN ANTHOLOGY

Edited and with an Introduction by

Pankaj Mishra

VINTAGE DEPARTURES

VINTAGE BOOKS

A DIVISION OF RANDOM HOUSE, INC.

NEW YORK

 A VINTAGE DEPARTURES ORIGINAL, JANUARY 2005

Copyright © 2005 by Pankaj Mishra

All rights reserved under International and Pan-American
Copyright Conventions. Published in the United States by
Vintage Books, a division of Random House, Inc., New York,
and simultaneously in Canada by Random House
of Canada Limited, Toronto.

Vintage is a registered trademark and Vintage Departures
and colophon are trademarks of Random House, Inc.

Permissions acknowledgments can be found at the end of the book.

Library of Congress Cataloging-in-Publication Data
India in mind : an anthology / [edited and with an introduction
by Pankaj Mishra]
p. cm.
ISBN 0-375-72745-0 (pbk. : alk. paper)
1. India—Literary collections. 2. India—Description and travel.
I. Mishra, Pankaj.
PN6071.I514I43 2005
808.8'03254—dc22   2004051764

Author photograph © Nicola Dove
Book design by Jo Anne Metsch

www.vintagebooks.com

Printed in the United States of America
10 9 8 7 6 5 4 3 2 1

CONTENTS

INTRODUCTION

In his great *History*, the Greek historian Herodotus mentions India, briefly and inaccurately. It is the first known reference to India in western literature; and what should surprise us now is not how little but how much Herodotus, who is supposed to have traveled only as far as Egypt, knew about lands farther east of Greece's great rival, Persia. Much of the world was then a mystery, as much for Herodotus, the father of western history, as for anyone living around the Mediterranean in the fourth century BC. India, where the Buddha was then teaching his subtle philosophy, existed for Herodotus at the extremity of the inhabited world—he could not believe that Asia could be bigger than Europe. He also thought that gold-digging ants existed in India and produced the tribute he imagined Indians paying to Persia. He did get some things right, however. "The tribes of India are numerous," he wrote, "and do not at all speak the same language."

In around 400 BC a Greek critic of Herodotus, Ctesias of Cnidus, became the first writer to produce a separate work on India. But he had even fewer facts. To him Indians were satyrs and the Indian sun was hotter and ten times bigger than it was elsewhere. Xenophon spoke of the fabulous wealth of India in his historical novel, *Cyropaedia*. Plato and Aristotle made half-informed guesses about the country east of Persia. India was, from its first references in western literature, a blend of fact and fantasy in the European imagination.

The precise shape of India was unclear even to the Macedonian conqueror Alexander, who reached as far as the Punjab in north India in 326 BC before turning back, exhausted, and returning to an early death in Babylon. But Alexander managed to bring the West closer to the East than it had been at any other time before. Megesthenes, the Greek envoy to the court of the great Indian emperor Chandragupta Maurya (320–297 BC), soon provided the first firsthand account of India. He described a society in which honor, virtue, and wisdom were prized above all. He noticed the Brahmins and the ascetics. He painted an idyllic picture of peasant life. His accounts fed the fantasies of the geographer Strabo (64 BC–AD 24) and of the Roman writer Pliny (AD 24–79), who thought that India covered one-third of the earth's surface. These general ideas about India—its great population and wealth, the caste system—also showed up in the work of the influential Greek historian Arrian.

More people traveled to India during the first centuries of the Roman Empire when trade between the Mediterranean and Asia flourished. But the Roman historians show little advance over their Greek predecessors in their knowledge of the region. During the Middle Ages, a time of intellectual torpor in the West, India became even more remote. Islam, rising fast in the eighth century across Arabia, Mesopotamia, and North Africa, came to form another barrier between the West and India. During this time, Arab travelers—al-Beruni in the tenth century and Ibn-Batutah in the fourteenth—wrote the greatest accounts of India.

Medieval Europe invested its own fears and fantasies in the

remote unknown land; myth and legend flourished in the absence of information. The cult of Alexander the Great came to be propped up by imaginary tales of his exploits in India. India was where St. Thomas had preached and found converts soon after the death of Christ. India was also the home of Prester John, the fabulously wealthy Christian king, who was going to help Europe decisively defeat the Muslims.

This embroidered veil of ignorance lifted in the sixteenth century, when Jesuit missionaries penetrated India farther than anyone before them and sent back detailed reports to Europe. The opening of the sea route to India in the late fifteenth century brought European traders to India; they studied carefully the native cultures they encountered. The new impulse of curiosity and learning that inspired the Renaissance and led to the Enlightenment took many more Europeans to India. Among the more famous of these were the French travelers Francois Bernier and Jean-Baptiste Tavernier, whose seventeenth-century accounts of India were analyzed closely by Voltaire, among other philosophers of the Enlightenment, and formed the persistent European view of India as an Oriental despotism.

The judgments on India were much less harsh before the days of European empires, when the inferiority of native peoples became an article of faith. Travelers from Europe did not deny that they had in India come up against a culture much older, and in many ways more sophisticated, than the one they belonged to. Voltaire, for instance, often invoked the virtues of India and China in order to show up the inadequacies of eighteenth-century France.

But the nineteenth century brought new attitudes. A series of scientific, economic, and political revolutions gave Western

Europe a new idea of itself. India, and more generally, Asia, became a place against which the traveler from the West measured his own society, and usually found it superior; it became the gigantic but often invisible backdrop to understanding his emotional state, and the refining of his moral and philosophical vision.

The nineteenth century also saw the British complete their conquest of India and become the paramount power in the world. Unlike the Persian and Central Asian conquerors of India before them, the British never looked as if they meant to stay on in India and make it their home. They either went home or died young. India remained, despite a veneer of modernity, a profoundly foreign country; and travelers from the West continued to record its alienness and their own sense of difference and bewilderment.

In E. M. Forster's *A Passage to India* (1924), the elderly Mrs. Moore, looking for the "real India," visits the dark Marabar caves—the caves where the mysterious "rape" of Mrs. Quested later takes place, and which in the novel represent the deeply unsettling ambiguities of India. There is a crush of people inside. Mrs. Moore can't breathe. She tries to leave, but fails, and panics. She cries out for help, but the answer she receives is only a meaningless echo, "Boum."

The cave is famous for the echo, which is produced by just about any sound. As Forster writes, "The crush and the smells she could forget, but the echo began in some indescribable way to undermine her hold on life." It reveals to her the void that lies beneath her experience of India. It is as if India is telling her that "pathos, piety, courage—they exist but are identical, and so is filth" and that although "everything exists, nothing has value." "If one had spoken vileness in that place," Forster adds, "or quoted lofty poetry, the comment would have been the same— 'oum-boum.' "

Mrs. Moore's reaction may seem exaggerated to us. But it is the reaction of many an exhausted visitor from the West who despairs of ever making rational sense of the vastness and diversity of India. The same response can be found in the visitor who discovers in India an exact complement to his inner emptiness and seeks oblivion in drugs or a spurious form of spirituality.

But occasionally India receives confident, well-prepared travelers. In his memoir, *Tristes Tropiques* (1955), the French anthropologist Claude Lévi-Strauss describes his visit to a Buddhist village in the hills of northeastern India. Lévi-Strauss was an admirer of the Buddha. And so he walked barefoot through mud; he followed the "prescribed ablutions" before entering the temple. But he did not join his companion in prostrating himself four times on the ground before the altar. As he explains, he didn't hesitate out of embarrassment.

> It was not a question of bowing down in front of the idols or of adoring a supposed supernatural order, but only of paying homage to the decisive wisdom that a thinker, or the society which created his legend, had evolved twenty-five centuries before, and to which my civilization could contribute only by confirming it.

Lévi-Strauss will pay homage in the way he knows best: through the mind and sensibility that have been shaped by Europe. He will analyze the rites; he will describe the temple as accurately as possible. He will attempt to draw analogies between Buddhism and western philosophy. Most of the contributors to this volume—mostly writers from Europe or America—resemble Lévi-Strauss more than Forster's Mrs. Moore. They traveled to, and wrote about, India in the last century; they took their ideas and habits of rational analysis from a successful western civilization. By attempting to understand India through their own cultural and intellectual inheritance, they reveal honestly a variety of assumptions and prejudices whose history goes back to Herodotus, to the earliest images of India in the West.

Such continuities, extending over two millennia, may seem odd. After all, you are told by conventional history that during the last century—the time span covered by this volume—India moved from being a backward British colony to a modern democratic nation-state. But these changes often seem superficial to the outsider, and so they are to a large extent. After more than fifty years of modernization, India is far from being made over in the image of a western country. It remains too poor and populous and bewilderingly diverse. Its history lies in obscure ruins, not in museums, its religions proliferate in everyday life, not in grand organized churches, and its food is best had at homes, not in restaurants. Its heat is severe, its rain unending. It rarely inspires pure affection or admiration in the way Italy or Greece, other sites of great civilizations, do. It often poses hard challenges. The reactions it evokes are complex, ranging from awe and wonder to repulsion and rejection. They tell us as much about the traveler as the world he describes.

INDIA IN MIND

J. R. ACKERLEY

(1896–1967)

J. R. Ackerley was born in England. His father was a business tycoon and secretly maintained two separate households. Ackerley himself was no less unconventional and was certainly franker about his homosexuality and the greatest love of his life: his dog Tulip, who was brilliantly commemorated by Ackerley in *My Dog Tulip* (1956). He fought at Somme in World War I and saw his brother killed there. After serving eight months as prisoner of war in a German camp, he studied at Cambridge University where he met, among other furtive gay men, E. M. Forster, who had visited India in 1922 and had spent some time at the court of a campy Maharajah. As it turned out, the Maharajah was then looking for a secretary and had even written to H Rider Haggard for help in locating someone who resembled Olaf, a character in Haggard's *The Wanderer's Necklace*. The Maharajah wasn't impressed by Ackerley's good looks but fell for his poems. Ackerley later described his five months at Chhokrapur ("City of Boys"), his jokey name for the Maharajah's capital, in *Hindoo Holiday* (1932), which is one of the more witty products of the Anglo-Indian encounter. Ackerley shared none of the racial and political prejudices of the Englishmen of his class; the five months were, on the whole, great fun. As this excerpt shows, he and the Maharajah were perfectly matched as eccentrics.

from HINDOO HOLIDAY

January 7th

I spoke to His Highness yesterday about a tutor for myself (he is very anxious for me to learn to speak Hindi), and taking advantage of some remark of his on Zeus and Ganymede, asked whether I might not have his valet to teach me.

"I suppose he is indispensable to you?" I asked.

"No, he is not indispensable to me. I will send him to you if you wish. I will send him to you tomorrow morning."

"Do you think he will be pleased to come?"

"Oh, he will be very pleased—especially if you pay him two or three rupees a month."

After this neither of us said anything for some time, and then His Highness remarked with finality:

"No, he is not at all indispensable to me."

But this morning a tonga arrived at the Guest House bearing two men I had never seen before, with a letter from His Highness. It ran as follows:

"Dear Mr. Ackerley,—Here are two men who know English and Hindi very well. The bearer of this is called Gupta, he is my assistant librarian of Hindi books; and the other called Champa Lal, he is my icemaker. You can choose any one of them, and they will do for preliminary work well. Perhaps they might ask for some wages, and I think two rupees per month will do. Excuse pencil and paper."

To which I replied:

"*Dear Maharajah Sahib,*—Your messengers have arrived, but I do not know quite what to do. Indeed they have both uttered remarks in English, but neither of them appears to understand my replies. I thought to myself, there is nothing to choose between them in looks; I will take the one who is the sharper in wits. So I returned to them and said:

'I only want one of you. Which of you speaks the better English, for I will engage him?'
The silence was at last broken by the icemaker, who said:—
'I do not understand.'
—and then by the assistant librarian, who said:
'Your English is very high.'
I return them both, and hope I may still be allowed to have the dispensable valet, this morning or at 2:30 P.M., for even if he cannot teach me Hindi, I should like to make a drawing of him."

The valet came this afternoon. I was lying on my sofa reading, when the light flicked across the page, and looking up I saw him standing in the curtained doorway. He bobbed a nervous salaam; I beckoned him inside, and throwing a rapid glance over his shoulder, he shuffled his laceless European shoes from his bare feet, pulled the curtain right back so that the open doorway was unveiled, and came a few paces further into the room. I indicated a chair, but it was too near me; he took the first at hand, and moved it back so that it stood in the doorway.
I had already learnt a few Hindi phrases by heart: "Good day," "How are you?" "It is a nice day," "Don't talk so fast"; but I found I did not now believe in their pronunciation as much as

when I had addressed them to myself; and since he only nodded to the first three, or uttered a throaty monosyllabic sound, I had no opportunity to air my "Don't talk so fast" composition, which therefore remains in my memory as the only phrase I got right. He was clearly very ill at ease, and anxious to please; but I soon realized that he did not really understand anything I said and was trying to guess from my expression what his response should be, so that most of the time a timid smile trembled on his lips and eyes, ready to vanish at the slightest sign of severity. And whenever I looked for a moment to consult my dictionary, his head went round at once, I noticed, to the open door, through which he could see across the gravel space the usual crowd of servants drowsing in the shade of the *neem* tree in front of the kitchen. So I gave it up at last and said I was going to draw him, but the moment I rose to get my sketchbook he was out of his chair and watching me in apparent alarm. I tried to convey with smiles and gestures that my intention was quite harmless, but although I got him to sit down again, I could not get him to sit still, and at length, in despair, told him to close the doors, for I could not go on if he kept turning round to look out of them. He began immediately to talk to me very rapidly, and since I did not know what he was saying, I got up to close them myself; but again he sprang up and barred my way, still chattering and gazing at me in what seemed to be a pleading manner. I stood still, wondering what was the trouble, and he at once began beckoning, in great agitation, to one of his friends outside, throwing me, at the same time, nervous, placating smiles. Soon the friend arrived, the young clerk who called on me the other day.

"What is the matter with your friend?" I asked.

"He say I must stay with him," said the clerk.

"Why?"

"He is much frightened."

This was all I could get. He did not know why his friend was frightened, or if he did know he would not say. But at any rate it was clear enough that I must have both or neither, so I told the clerk he had better stay, though I did not want him—being a shy and, as will perhaps already have been noticed, a rather inexpert artist.

A little later, forgetting the valet's fear, I asked his friend, who had access to the storeroom, if he would get me some more cigarettes, for I had run out of them; but the moment he moved the valet caught hold of his hand, and, even when the mission was explained, would not let him go.

The drawing was indeed not good, and Narayan did not scruple to say so. Narayan is the name of the clerk; his friend, the valet, being called Sharma.

January 8th

Tom-tom Hill is my favorite walk because of the view. There is a ruined shrine with a fallen idol on its summit, and it is called Tom-tom Hill because a drum used to be beaten there years ago to assemble the people or to notify them of certain times and events. From the backyard of my house the stony slope climbs steadily up to a pretty white temple in its cluster of cypresses. The temple is dedicated to Hanuman, the Monkey-headed God of Physical Power, and the worshippers are often to be seen and heard on its terrace; but I have not yet found courage to enter it, being still ignorant of customs and observances, and afraid of making mistakes. Indeed I have never even ventured close to it, but, at a discreet distance, have always dropped down the western slope of the ridge, and clambered round through the brambles beneath its walls and up again on the other side.

As a matter of fact, this also is the only way of getting on, for the temple occupies the whole breadth of the ridge's back and cannot be otherwise passed.

It overlooks the town and is reached from that side by means of a long straight staircase of wooden steps which runs steeply up the eastern slope from the Rajgarh-Deori road.

Having skirted the temple in this way, walking becomes more difficult, for the ridge continues in a long narrow arête, scattered with huge boulders, many of which have to be clambered over; but beyond this it widens and rises gently to the foot of Tom-tom Hill, and the walk up to the ruined shrine is easy, though the gradient is rather steep. Usually I sit there and rest on one of the stones of the shrine, looking down upon the white town, thickly planted with trees; the Palace, imposing at this distance, in its center, the Sirdar tank immediately below. But today I saw smoke rising again from among the trees and bushes at the base of the hill on the far side, and descended to verify His Highness's information that this was a crematorium. This slope of the hill had an even steeper gradient, and as I zigzagged down I was able to keep the fires in sight, and took no precautions against observation, believing myself to be the only person about. But soon I perceived two Indians squatting on their heels by the nearer fire, apparently extinguishing the last embers and collecting some of the grey ashes in a metal pot. Realizing now that the King had probably been right, and fearing that I might be intruding upon sacred ground, I took cover behind a large boulder and watched them for a little from this shelter. Then I noticed that the other fire, which was a little further down, seemed unattended, so, as quietly as I could, I made a detour and approached it.

It was clearly a funeral pyre. The charred skull of the corpse, which was toward me, was split open, for it is customary, I believe, to break the skull of the dead when the body is being consumed, so that the soul may have its exit; and curving out of the center of the pile, like wings, were the blackened ribs which, released by the heat, had sprung away from the vertebrae. In all directions I noticed the remains of earlier cremations. As I returned home I passed the other fire and saw that the two Indians had just finished and were disappearing among the bushes; but their place had already been taken by two evil-looking vultures with yellow beaks which were picking scraps from among the extinct and smokeless ashes.

His Highness sent the carriage for me again this evening to bring me to the Palace. He was extremely interested in my meeting with his valet, Sharma, the barber's son, and put me through such a cross-examination about him that I began to feel rather uncomfortable. I had been quite expecting such questions as to how I had liked him, and what had occurred, and how long he had stayed, but could not understand why he should require such accuracy as to the time of the boy's arrival and the manner of his dress, or why, when I replied to this last question that Sharma had worn a very becoming long-skirted blue serge coat with velveteen cuffs and collar, he should have said "Ah!" with an appearance of such immense satisfaction.

I had brought my drawing with me, but he did not look at it. He was untouchable again, and bade me leave it on the table by my chair. Narayan's name was apparently known to him, and evoked another volley of questions the significance of which I was unable to understand; but, remembering Narayan's request a few days previously not to repeat something he had said, I answered with cautious vagueness, in case I should unintentionally get either of the two young men into trouble, and, as soon as I could, diverted his attention a little by remarking on Sharma's timidity.

"Yes, he spoke to me," said His Highness. "He told me he was frightened. He saw you closing the doors and thought you were going to confine him."

"But frightened of what?" I asked.

"That you would beat him."

"Beat him!" Nothing had been further from my thoughts, and it took me some moments to get hold of this.

"Do you beat him much?" I asked.

"Oh yes! I have to. I beat him very much!"

"But, Maharajah Sahib, didn't you explain to him that, apart from anything else, your guests were hardly in a position to beat your servants?"

"Yes, I did, I did, and he said, of his own accord, that he would come and see you tomorrow."

He went on to speak of some friend of his, the wife of an English officer, who had told him that she was convinced, after long experience of India, that no servant could be expected to be faithful to his employers until he had cuts on his back two fingers deep; and, from her, passed on to another English friend of his—this time a man. I do not now remember the connection between the two friends, but cannot refrain from expressing a hope that it was matrimonial.

"He was a very strange man," said he. "He used to say to me, 'Maharajah! do you see those clouds together up there?' 'Yes, I see those clouds.' 'Do you see my dead wife's face looking down from them?' 'No, I don't.' 'Damn!'

"Then again, when we were sitting together here, he said to me, 'Maharajah, do you see this wall over here by me?' 'Yes, I see that wall.' 'Well, it is talking to me. All the stones are talking. They are telling me everything that has passed in this room. Put your ear here. Do you hear them?' 'No, I don't hear them.' 'Damn!'"

For a few moments His Highness was shaken with laughter, then—"He suicided himself," he concluded.

January 9th

"And how are the Gods this morning, Maharajah Sahib?"

"They are very well."

"Where did you get them all from?"

"Mostly from Chhokrapur."

"And where did the others come from?"

"My dear sir, there are only five, and three are from Chhokrapur."

"Then where did the other two come from?" I persisted. "Did they fall off Olympus, or were they a Christmas present?"

"No, no, no," he spluttered, shaking with laughter; "I bought them. They were not very expensive."

He then embarked upon a long story about a twelve-year-old

boy he had seen dancing in some traveling company of players which had visited Chhokrapur.

"He is very beautiful—like Napoleon the Third."

"Napoleon the Third?" I asked, mystified. "Do you mean Napoleon the Second?"

"No, no; Napoleon the Third; I have a picture of him in a history book in my library. I will show you."

He had been so taken with this boy's appearance that he had wanted to buy him, and had asked how much he was. But the manager of the company, who was the boy's uncle, had demanded too much—fifty rupees a month for the boy's life, for he was irreplaceable.

"I said it was too much," concluded His Highness; then, after a pause—"But I want him. Should I pay it? Please advise me."

"What about the boy's parents?" I asked.

"Both dead," said His Highness promptly.

"Well, if you want him so much and can afford him, you'd better buy him."

"What would a European do? An Englishman?"

"The same thing, no doubt."

"And an ancient Greek?"

"I believe they sternly discountenanced such transactions," I said.

His Highness seemed to ponder this for a moment, then, "He's black, not fair," he observed. "Do you like black?"

"I prefer fair."

"Ah!" he breathed, nodding his head in agreement.

The sun was setting in front of us in a blaze of pink and golden light. His Highness waved a regretful hand toward it.

"I want a friend like that," he said.

January 10th

Perhaps His Highness was not pleased with the answer I returned him by his icemaker and assistant librarian; at any rate neither of them came back to me, and he never alluded to it, but placed the matter in the hands of Babaji Rao, who sent me a very alarming young man, the son of a pundit, who seemed to think the letter of introduction he bore was a letter of engagement, for almost before I had finished reading it he had begun to teach me Hindi, shouting pronunciations at me in an abrupt metallic voice that was actually hurtful, and jumping and gesticulating about the room as though he were composed of steel springs.

He was clearly bent upon making an impression on me (which indeed he did), and tried very hard to conceal the fact that he didn't in the least understand me; for whatever I said struck him at once, in the middle of some gesture, into a state of marionettelike immobility, an injured expression on his face. He would then complete his gesture and make a little rush at me with another staccato sentence, as though no interruption worthy of notice had occurred.

As is always the case when I have a visitor, he had been conducted into my room by curious sightseers—the waiter Hashim and two small boys, all Mohammedans. Hashim is easy to dismiss; one can do it with a nod, for he is accustomed to Europeans; though he would prefer to stay.

But the boys are very difficult and very exasperating. They stand about, quite quiet and expressionless, their wide gaze fixed upon me. A nod or gesture is quite useless. "Jao!" (Go!) moves them slightly, and may drive the older of the two out on to the verandah, where he will linger, rather bewildered, looking back;

but the younger and smaller, whose name is Habib (Lover), might almost be under some hypnotic influence; he moves his thick lips a little . . . and remains. The other day, all else having failed, I made a threatening advance toward him, and then he went, but slowly, reluctantly, rearranging the door curtains as he left, and staring at me all the time with large astonished eyes as though to say "This Sahib is certainly peculiar." But to return.

When the son of the pundit had given me a headache I managed to convey to him that I had had enough instruction in Hindi for one day and would call him if I wanted more, intending to do so if I could not find someone more efficient and less mercurial; but this morning I received another candidate. My new visitor was a grave, tall, thin-featured Mohammedan, not unhandsome, with a long aquiline nose and a slight black moustache.

His dress was that odd mixture of European and Indian garments which all the educated men here affect. A red tarbush was set squarely on his close-cropped skull, and from beneath an Army drill tunic, stained green, the tails of an ordinary European shirt hung down over narrow white cotton trousers. He wore no collar. Socks, patent leather slippers, and a long gold watch chain round his neck completed his attire. He carried an umbrella.

Holding himself very erect, he said that his name was Abul Haq, and that he had heard I was looking for a tutor, and had come to present himself. I began to explain that I already had a tutor, but he interrupted me, almost apologetically, to say that he had heard that also, but that—although he did not wish to speak ill of any man—the pundit's son was not nearly as well qualified to be my tutor as he himself was, and would not give such satisfaction.

This I felt might be true, and such self-assurance was disarming.

"I am very interested in you, gentleman, and will teach you well."

He smiled at me, compressing his lips, his head on one side, his chin drawn in, very persuasive, very smooth, very confident, his umbrella beneath his arm, his toes turned out, and one foot a little in advance of the other as though he were about to begin a prim, decorous dance.

I engaged him, and he said, "Thank you, Mr. Ackerley" three times and thrust out a clawlike hand; but I felt, while I grasped it, that he was really shaking hands with himself. He went, and rather dubiously I watched him down the drive, a thin, stiff figure with toes turned out, twitching back his shoulders, his left arm stiff down his body, his right sweeping the handle of the umbrella in expansive circles. Every now and then he jerked a swift, rather haughty, glance from side to side, so that the tassel on his cap leapt and swung.

It appears that Napoleon the Third is once more in the vicinity of Chhokrapur. The traveling players have returned, His Highness said, but he said it with so little emotion that I cannot help wondering whether they ever really left. At any rate they have not lowered the price of Napoleon, though they now make an alternative offer for a lump sum of two thousand rupees, which is about one hundred and fifty pounds. This is absurd. His Highness has never before paid more than about five shillings for any God. Moreover, for performing in Chhokrapur they now want fifty rupees a night, instead of fifty for the whole visit. They are robbers . . . wolves . . .

"What must I do?" he asked. "Should I buy him? Thirty years I have dreamed of that face, it is entangled in my heart, and then (he clapped his hands together) suddenly I see it! Why did I see it? How do these things happen? Did God put it before me? Is it God's wish that I should buy? If it is not God's wish, then He is a very wicked man! What must I do?"

"Do you suppose his mind, too, is like Napoleon the Third's?" I asked.

"No, like a donkey's!" he retorted emphatically, and then began to laugh silently, shielding his face with a letter he had just received from the Acting Governor-General of the Province. For some time, it appears, he has been angling for a decoration. All the neighboring potentates have, at one time or another, been honored with the K.C.S.I. or K.C.I.E. on the King Emperor's birthday, but so far His Highness of Chhokrapur has been passed over, which is a source of continual irritation to him. He said he could not explain the reason for this neglect, but went on at once to tell me that, at the time of his son's birth, one of his enemies had written an anonymous letter to the Political Agent, stating that the child was illegitimate and not his son at all, and further hinting that an investigation of His Highness's private amusements would prove instructive.

Apparently some sort of investigation had been made, but nothing had been discovered—nothing, that is to say, except the "Gods," whose number had been forthwith curtailed. This His Highness called "political interference with my luxuries." No doubt it is this suspicion that is operating still against his chances of a decoration; but he does not admit it, nor abate his efforts on his own behalf. The A.G.G. himself has recently been knighted, and His Highness, while congratulating him, had not scrupled to inquire again in the same letter when he himself was to be remembered. The letter that he had brought out today to show me was the answer to this, in which the A.G.G. assured His Highness that he would do his best to settle favorably the matter of which His Highness had spoken. The letter seemed sincere and cordial, so he was in a good humor—or would have been if it weren't for Napoleon the Third.

"I cannot afford two thousand rupees," he repeated. "It is the boy's uncle who makes the demand. I should like to poison him."

January 14th

For some time past His Highness has been cherishing a desire to erect a "Greek Villa" where, wrapped in a toga, he may hold symposia with his European friends and his Indian Gods; and today a Mr. Bramble, an English architect, friend to the A.G.G., arrived in Chhokrapur to stay for a few days in the Guest House. There are some other guests here as well, two women and their children; and we were all present when His Highness drove up this afternoon. A chair and cigarettes were put ready for him in front of the fire, and as soon as he was seated he addressed himself at once to Mr. Bramble.

"How old are you, Mr. Bramble?"

"Well, Maharajah Sahib," said the architect good-humoredly, His Highness's peculiarities having already been explained to him by the women, "I tell my bearer that I'm a hundred, and he believes me."

This caused general amusement, in which the King joined;

but he obviously did not quite understand the joke, for did not Mr. Bramble, with his silver hair, look very old indeed? So as soon as the laughter had ceased, he asked politely:

"Are you seventy-six?"

"Well—er—no," said Mr. Bramble, rather taken aback. "Let me think . . . when was I born? In sixty-six. That makes me sixty-four."

"And where is your wife?" asked His Highness, without the slightest pause—and also without the slightest knowledge of Mr. Bramble's domestic affairs; but then surely he must have a wife. There was an awkward silence.

"I'm very sorry to say that . . . Mrs. Bramble is . . . no more . . . no more."

He was clearly distressed; but His Highness did not appear to notice it.

"Dead?" he asked briefly.

"Yes," said Mr. Bramble sadly.

"And have you children?" continued His Highness, without pause.

"One boy."

There was a silence after this, and I awaited, with considerable apprehension, the King's next association of thought. But it was quite harmless.

"And where is he?"

"Well—at the moment he's in Portsmouth, I believe."

"Ah, yes—Portsmouth. Where is Portsmouth?"

Mr. Bramble was by now so confused and intimidated that he was quite unable to remember where Portsmouth was; so I came to his rescue.

"It's in the south of England, Maharajah Sahib."

"Near the Isle of Wight," said Mr. Bramble, with presence of mind.

"Which," I added, "is not the Isle of Man, you know, Maharajah Sahib."

His Highness at once looked very intelligent, and I knew I had succeeded in diverting his attention from Mr. Bramble's personal history.

"Have you read Hall Caine, Mr. Bramble?" he asked.

"Hall Caine? Yes, I think I have—something or other."

"*The Eternal City*?" asked His Highness enthusiastically. "A *very* good book. You *must* read it. He is Manx. Are you Manx, Mr. Bramble?"

"No, no, I'm not Manx," said the architect, laughing.

His Highness seemed disappointed.

"Ah, I like Manx," he said, nodding his head. "They have a separate Parliament, you know. The House of Keys. Do you know Edward Carpenter?"

"Yes, I know Edward Carpenter," said Mr. Bramble fatiguedly, and began to talk about the weather to one of the women. But their conversation was at once interrupted. His Highness had remembered the "Greek Villa," and, as always when he has an idea to impart, was far too impatient to wait quietly for an opening.

"You mean you want a villa in the Classic style, isn't that it?" asked Mr. Bramble. "Yes, I could do it for you certainly; but we shall have to talk about it first. You will have to show me the proposed site, and tell me how many rooms you want and how much you are prepared to spend, and then I'll make a design for you."

The King nodded sagely, but he had left off listening; he was groping in his mind after something else, which in a moment or two he triumphantly produced.

"Parthenon! Like Parthenon!" he cried; and then, rather dimly: "What is Parthenon?"

PAUL BOWLES

(1910–99)

Born in New York City and trained initially as a composer, Paul Bowles moved to Tangier, Morocco, in 1952. His novels *The Sheltering Sky* (1949) and *Let It Come Down* (1952) and many of his short stories and novels depicted Americans traveling in alien societies. The abrupt and violent endings Bowles contrived in his fictions spoke of an unrelentingly grim vision of Americans failing to survive the clash of cultures. But Bowles himself was a keen and oddly good-humored traveler, and his judgments were cautious. He first saw India in the 1940s. Traveling through eight thousand miles gave him, as he wrote, "a somewhat more detailed and precise idea of my ignorance." He recorded a second visit in *Their Heads Are Green and Their Hands Are Blue* (1963) from which the following excerpt is taken. In south India, Bowles was arrested for spying and interned for a few days. It was a situation as awkward as any faced by his doomed American travelers. But Bowles managed to escape and recovered enough to note the cow's centrality to the Hindu vision of a good life.

NOTES MAILED AT NAGERCOIL

CAPE COMORIN

I have been here in this hotel now for a week. At no time during the night or day has the temperature been low enough for comfort; it fluctuates between 95 and 105 degrees, and most of the time there is absolutely no breeze, which is astonishing for the seaside. Each bedroom and public room has the regulation large electric fan in its ceiling, but there is no electricity; we are obliged to use oil lamps for lighting. Today at lunchtime a large Cadillac of the latest model drove up to the front door. In the back were three little men wearing nothing but the flimsy dhotis they had draped around their loins. One of them handed a bunch of keys to the chauffeur, who then got out and came into the hotel. Near the front door is the switch box. He opened it, turned on the current with one of the keys, and throughout the hotel the fans began to whir. Then the three little men got out and went into the dining room where they had their lunch. I ate quickly, so as to get upstairs and lie naked on my bed under the fan. It was an unforgettable fifteen minutes. Then the fan stopped, and I heard the visitors driving away. The hotel manager told me later that they were government employees of the State of Travancore, and that only they had a key to the switch box.

Last night I awoke and opened my eyes. There was no moon; it was still dark, but the light of a star was shining into my face through the open window, from a point high above the Arabian Sea. I sat up, and gazed at it. The light it cast seemed as bright as that of the moon in northern countries; coming through the window, it made its rectangle on the opposite wall, broken by the shadow of my silhouetted head. I held up my hand and moved the fingers, and their shadow too was definite. There were no other stars visible in that part of the sky; this one blinded them all. It was about an hour before daybreak, which comes shortly after six, and there was not a breath of air. On such still nights the waves breaking on the nearby shore sound like great, deep explosions going on at some distant place. There is the boom, which can be felt as well as heard, and which ends with a sharp rattle and hiss, then a long period of complete silence, and finally, when it seems that there will be no more sound, another sudden boom. The crows begin to scream and chatter while the darkness is still complete.

The town, like the others here in the extreme south, gives the impression of being made of dust. Dust and cow dung lie in the streets, and the huge crows hop ahead of you as you walk along. When a gust of hot wind wanders in from the sandy wastes beyond the town, the brown fans of the palmyra trees swish and bang against each other; they sound like giant sheets of heavy wrapping paper. The small black men walk quickly, the diamonds in their earlobes flashing. Because of their jewels and the gold thread woven into their dhotis, they all look not merely prosperous, but fantastically wealthy. When the women have diamonds, they are likely to wear them in a hole pierced through the wall of one nostril.

The first time I ever saw India I entered it through Dhanushkodi. An analogous procedure in America would be for a foreigner to get his first glimpse of the United States by crossing the Mexican border illegally and coming out into a remote Arizona village. It was God-forsaken, uncomfortable, and a little frightening. Since then I have landed as a bona fide visitor should, in the impressively large and unbeautiful metropolis of Bombay. But I am glad that my first trip did not bring me in contact with any cities. It is better to go to the villages of a strange land before trying to understand its towns, above all in a complex place like India. Now, after traveling some eight thousand miles around the country, I know approximately as little as I did on my first arrival. However, I've seen a lot of people and places, and at least I have a somewhat more detailed and precise idea of my ignorance than I did in the beginning.

If you have not taken the precaution of reserving a room in advance, you risk having considerable difficulty in finding one when you land in Bombay. There are very few hotels, and the two or three comfortable ones are always full. I hate being committed to a reservation because the element of adventure is thereby destroyed. The only place I was able to get into when I first arrived, therefore, was something less than a first-class establishment. It was all right during the day and the early hours of the evening. At night, however, every square foot of floor space in the dark corridors was occupied by sleepers who had arrived late and brought their own mats with them; the hotel was able in this way to shelter several hundred extra guests each night. Having their hands and feet kicked and trodden on was apparently a familiar enough experience to them for them never to make any audible objection when the inevitable happened.

Here in Cape Comorin, on the other hand, there are many rooms and they are vast, and at the moment I am the only one staying in the hotel.

It was raining. I was on a bus going from Alleppey to Trivandrum, on my way down here. There were two little Indian nuns on the seat in front of mine. I wondered how they stood the heat in their heavy robes. Sitting near the driver was a man with a thick, fierce moustache who distinguished himself from the other passengers by the fact that in addition to his dhoti he also wore a European shirt; its scalloped tail hung down nearly to his knees. With him he had a voluminous collection of magazines and newspapers in both Tamil and English, and even from where I sat I could not help noticing that all this reading matter had been printed in the Soviet Union.

At a certain moment, near one of the myriad villages that lie smothered in the depths of the palm forests there, the motor suddenly ceased to function, and the bus came to a stop. The driver, not exchanging a single glance with his passengers, let his head fall forward and remain resting on the steering wheel in a posture of despair. Expectantly the people waited a little while, and then they began to get down. One of the first out of the bus was the man with the moustache. He said a hearty good-bye to the occupants in general, although he had not been conversing with any of them, and started up the road carrying his umbrella, but not his armful of printed matter. Then I realized that at some point during the past hour, not foreseeing the failure of the motor and the mass departure which it entailed, he had left a paper or magazine on each empty seat—exactly as our American comrades used to do on subway trains three decades ago.

Almost at the moment I made this discovery, the two nuns had risen and were hurriedly collecting the "literature." They climbed down and ran along the road after the man, calling out in English: "Sir, your papers!" He turned, and they handed them to him. Without saying a word, but with an expression of fury on his face, he took the bundle and continued. But it was impossible to tell from the faces of the two nuns when they returned to gather up their belongings whether or not they were conscious of what they had done.

A few minutes later everyone had left the bus and walked to the village—everyone, that is, but the driver and me. I had too much luggage. Then I spoke to him.

"What's the matter with the bus?"

He shrugged his shoulders.

"How am I going to get to Trivandrum?"

He did not know that, either.

"Couldn't you look into the motor?" I pursued. "It sounded like the fan belt. Maybe you could repair it."

This roused him sufficiently from his apathy to make him turn and look at me.

"We have People's Government here in Travancore," he said. "Not allowed touching motor."

"But who *is* going to repair it, then?"

"Tonight making telephone call to Trivandrum. Making report. Tomorrow or other day they sending inspector to examine."

"And then what?"

"Then inspector making report. Then sending repair crew."

"I see."

"People's Government," he said again, by way of helping me to understand. "Not like other government."

"No," I said.

As if to make his meaning clearer, he indicated the seat where the man with the large moustache had sat. "That gentleman Communist."

"Oh, really?" (At least, it was all in the open, and the driver was under no misapprehension as to what the term "People's Government" meant.)

"Very powerful man. Member of Parliament from Travancore."

"Is he a good man, though? Do the people like him?"

"Oh, yes, sir. Powerful man."

"But is he *good*?" I insisted.

He laughed, doubtless at my ingenuousness. "Powerful men all rascals," he said.

Just before nightfall a local bus came along, and with the help of several villagers I transferred my luggage to it and continued on my way.

Most of the impressively heavy Communist vote is cast by the Hindus. The Moslems are generally in less dire economic straits, it is true, but in any case, by virtue of their strict religious views, they do not take kindly to any sort of ideological change. (A convert from Islam is unthinkable; apostasy is virtually nonexistent.) If even Christianity has retained too much of its pagan decor to be acceptable to the puritanical Moslem mind, one can imagine the loathing inspired in them by the endless proliferations of Hindu religious art with its gods, demons, metamorphoses, and avatars. The two religious systems are antipodal. Fortunately the constant association with the mild and tolerant Hindus has made the Moslems of India far more understanding and tractable than their brothers in Islamic countries further west; there is much less actual friction than one might be led to expect.

During breakfast one morning at the Connemara Hotel in Madras the Moslem head waiter told me a story. He was traveling in the Province of Orissa, where in a certain town there was a Hindu temple which was noted for having five hundred cobras on its premises. He decided he would like to see these famous reptiles. When he had got to the town he hired a carriage and went to the temple. At the door he was met by a priest who offered to show him around. And since the Moslem looked prosperous, the priest suggested a donation of five rupees, to be paid in advance.

"Why so much?" asked the visitor.

"To buy eggs for the cobras. You know, we have five hundred of them."

The Moslem gave him the money on condition that the priest let him see the snakes. For an hour his guide dallied in the many courtyards and galleries, pointing out bas-reliefs, idols, pillars, and bells. Finally the Moslem reminded him of their understanding.

"Cobras? Ah, yes. But they are dangerous. Perhaps you would rather see them another day?"

This behavior on the priest's part had delighted him, he recalled, for it had reinforced his suspicions.

"Not at all," he said. "I want to see them now."

Reluctantly the priest led him into a small alcove behind a large stone Krishna, and pointed into a very dark corner.

"Is this the place?" the visitor asked.

"This is the place."

"But where are the snakes?"

In a tiny enclosure were two sad old cobras, "almost dead from hunger," he assured me. But when his eyes had grown used to the dimness he saw that there were hundreds of eggshells scattered around the floor outside the pen.

"You eat a lot of eggs," he told the priest.

The priest merely said: "Here. Take back your five rupees. But if you are asked about our cobras, please be so kind as to say that you saw five hundred of them here in our temple. Is that all right?"

The episode was meant to illustrate the head waiter's thesis, which was that the Hindus are abject in the practice of their religion; this is the opinion held by the Moslems. On the other hand, it must be remembered that the Hindu considers Islam an incomplete doctrine, far from satisfying. He finds its austerity singularly comfortless, and deplores its lack of mystico-philosophical content, an element in which his own creed is so rich.

I was invited to lunch at one of the cinema studios in the suburbs north of Bombay. We ate our curry outdoors; our hostess was the star of the film then in production. She spoke only Marathi; her husband, who was directing the picture, spoke excellent English. During the course of the meal he told how, as a Hindu, he had been forced to leave his job, his home, his car, and his bank account in Karachi at the time of partition, when Pakistan came into existence, and emigrate empty-handed to India, where he managed to remake his life. Another visitor to the studio, an Egyptian, was intensely interested in his story. Presently he interrupted to say: "It is unjust, of course."

"Yes," smiled our host.

"What retaliatory measures does your government plan to take against the Moslems left here in India?"

"None whatever, as far as I know."

The Egyptian was genuinely indignant. "But why not?" he demanded. "It is only right that you apply the same principle. You have plenty of Moslems here still to take action against. And I say that, even though I am a Moslem."

The film director looked at him closely. "You say that *because* you are a Moslem," he told him. "But we cannot put ourselves on that level."

The conversation ended on this not entirely friendly note. A moment later packets of betel were passed around. I promptly broke a tooth, withdrew from the company, and went some distance away into the garden. While I, in the interests of science, was examining the mouthful of partially chewed betel leaves and areca nut, trying to find the pieces of bicuspid, the Egyptian came up to me, his face a study in scorn.

"They are afraid of the Moslems. That's the real reason," he whispered. Whether he was right or wrong I was neither qualified nor momentarily disposed to say, but it was a classical exposition of the two opposing moral viewpoints—two concepts of behavior which cannot quickly be reconciled.

Obviously it is a gigantic task to make a nation out of a place like India, what with Hindus, Parsees, Jainists, Jews, Catholics, and Protestants, some of whom may speak the arbitrarily imposed national idiom of Hindi, but most of whom are more likely to know Gujarati, Marathi, Bengali, Urdu, Telugu, Tamil, Malayalam, or some other tongue instead. One wonders whether any sort of unifying project can ever be undertaken, or, indeed, whether it is even desirable.

When you come to the border between two provinces you often find bars across the road, and you are obliged to undergo a thorough inspection of your luggage. As in the United States, there is a strict control of the passage of liquor between wet and dry districts, but that is not the extent of the examination.

Sample of conversation at the border on the Mercara-Cannonore highway:

"What is in there?" (Customs officer.)

"Clothing." (Bowles.)

"And in that?"

"Clothing."

"And in all those?"

"Clothing."

"Open all, please."

After eighteen suitcases have been gone through carefully: "My God, man! Close them all. I could charge duty for all of these goods, but you will never be able to do business with these things here anyway. The Moslem men are too clever."

"But I'm not intending to sell my clothes."

"Shut the luggage. It is duty-free, I tell you."

A professor from Raniket in north India arrived at the hotel here the other day, and we spent a good part of the night sitting on the window seat in my room that overlooks the sea, talking about what one always talks about here: India. Among the many questions I put to him was one concerning the reason why so many of the Hindu temples in south India prohibit entry to non-Hindus, and why they have military guards at the entrances. I imagined I knew the answer in advance: fear of Moslem disturbances. Not at all, he said. The principal purpose was to keep out certain Christian missionaries. I expressed disbelief.

"Of course," he insisted. "They come and jeer during our rituals, ridicule our sacred images."

"But even if they were stupid enough to want to do such things," I objected, "their sense of decorum would keep them from behaving like that."

He merely laughed. "Obviously you don't know them."

The post office here is a small stifling room over a shop, and it is full of boys seated on straw mats. The postmaster, a tiny old man who wears large diamond earrings and gold-rimmed spectacles, and is always naked to the waist, is also a professor; he interrupts his academic work to sell an occasional stamp. At first contact his English sounds fluent enough, but soon one discovers that it is not adapted to conversation, and that one can scarcely talk to him. Since the boys are listening, he must pretend to be omniscient, therefore he answers promptly with more or less whatever phrase comes into his head.

Yesterday I went to post a letter by airmail to Tangier. "Tanjore," he said, adjusting his spectacles. "That will be four annas." (Tanjore is in south India, near Trichinopoly.) I explained that I hoped my letter would be going to Tangier, Morocco.

"Yes, yes," he said impatiently. "There are many Tanjores." He opened the book of postal regulations and read aloud from it, quite at random, for (although it may be difficult to believe) exactly six minutes. I stood still, fascinated, and let him go on. Finally he looked up and said: "There is no mention of Tangier. No airplanes go to that place."

"Well, how much would it be to send it by sea mail?" (I thought we could then calculate the surcharge for air mail, but I had misjudged my man.)

"Yes," he replied evenly. "That is a good method, too."

I decided to keep the letter and post it in the nearby town of Nagercoil another day. In a little while I shall have several to add to it, and I count on being able to send them all together when I go. Before I left the post office I hazarded the remark that the weather was extremely hot. In that airless attic at noon it was a wild understatement. But it did not please the postmaster at all. Deliberately he removed his glasses and pointed the stems at me.

"Here we have the perfect climate," he told me. "Neither too cold nor too cool."

"That is true," I said. "Thank you."

In the past few years there have been visible quantitative changes in the life, all in the one direction of Europeanization. This is in the smaller towns; the cities of course have long since been Westernized. The temples which before were lighted by bare electric bulbs and coconut oil lamps now have fluorescent tubes glimmering in their ceilings. Crimson, green, and amber floodlights are used to illumine bathing tanks, deities, the gateways of temples. The public-address system is the bane of the ear these days, even in the temples. And it is impossible to attend a concert or a dance recital without discovering several loudspeakers in operation, whose noise completely destroys the quality of the music. A mile before you arrive at the cinema of a small town you can hear the raucous blaring of the amplifier they have set up at its entrance.

This year in south India there are fewer men with bare torsos, dhotis, and sandals: more shirts, trousers, and shoes. There is at the same time a slow shutting-down of services which to the Western tourist make all the difference between pleasure and discomfort in traveling, such as the restaurants in the stations (there being no dining-cars on the trains) and the showers in the first-class compartments. A few years ago they worked; now they have been sealed off. You can choke on the dust and soot of your compartment, or drown in your own sweat now, for all the railway cares.

At one point I was held for forty-eight hours in a concentration camp run by the Ceylon government on Indian soil. (The euphemism for this one was "screening camp.") I was told that I was under suspicion of being an "international spy." My astonishment and indignation were regarded as almost convincing in their sincerity, thus proof of my guilt.

"But who am I supposed to be spying *for*?" I asked piteously.

The director shrugged. "Spying for international," he said.

More than the insects or the howling of pariah dogs outside the rolls of barbed wire, what bothered me was the fact that in the center of the camp, which at that time housed some twenty thousand people, there was a loudspeaker in a high tower which during every moment of the day roared forth Indian film music. Fortunately it was silenced at ten o'clock each evening. I got out of the hellhole by making such violent trouble that I was dragged before the camp doctor, who decided that I was dangerously unbalanced. The idea in letting me go was that I would be detained further along, and the responsibility would fall on other shoulders. "They will hold him at Talaimannar," I heard the doctor say. "The poor fellow is quite mad."

Here and there, in places like the bar of the Hotel Metropole at Mysore, or at the North Coorg Club of Mercara, one may still come across vestiges of the old colonial life; ghosts in the form of incredibly sunburned Englishmen in jodhpurs and boots discussing their hunting luck and prowess. But these visions are exceedingly rare in a land that wants to forget their existence.

The younger generation in India is intent on forgetting a good many things, including some that it might do better to remember. There would seem to be no good reason for getting rid of their country's most ancient heritage, the religion of Hinduism, or of its most recent acquisition, the tradition of independence. This latter, at least insofar as the illiterate masses are concerned, is inseparable not only from the religious state of mind which made political victory possible, but also from the legend which, growing up around the figure of Gandhi, has elevated him in their minds to the status of a god.

The young, politically minded intellectuals find this not at all to their liking; in their articles and addresses they have returned again and again to the attack against Gandhi as a "betrayer" of the Indian people. That they are motivated by hatred is obvious. But what do they hate?

For one thing, subconsciously they cannot accept their own inability to go on having religious beliefs. Then, belonging to the group without faith, they are thereby forced to hate the past, particularly the atavisms which are made apparent by the workings of the human mind with its irrationality, its subjective involvement in exterior phenomena. The floods of poisonous words they pour forth are directed primarily at the adolescents: it is an age group which is often likely to find demagoguery more attractive than common sense.

There are at least a few of these enlightened adolescents in every town; the ones here in Cape Comorin were horrified when, by a stratagem, I led them to the home of a man of their own village named Subramaniam, who claims that his brother is under a spell. (They had not imagined, they told me later, that an American would believe such nonsense.) According to Subramaniam, his brother was a painter who had been made art director of a major film studio in Madras. To substantiate his story he brought out a sheaf of very professional sketches for film sets.

"Then my brother had angry words with a jealous man in the studio," said Subramaniam, "and the man put a charm on him. His mind is gone. But at the end of the year it will return." The brother presently appeared in the courtyard; he was a vacant-eyed man with a beard, and he had a voluminous turkish towel draped over his head and shoulders. He walked past us and disappeared through a doorway.

"A spirit doctor is treating him . . ." The modern young men shifted their feet miserably; it was unbearable that an American should be witnessing such shameful revelations, and that they should be coming from one in their midst.

But these youths who found it so necessary to ridicule poor Subramaniam failed to understand why I laughed when, the conversation changing to the subject of cows, I watched their collective expression swiftly change to one of respect bordering on beatitude. For cow-worship is one facet of popular Hinduism which has not yet been totally superseded by twentieth-century faithlessness. True, it has taken on new forms of ritual. Mass cow worship is often practiced now in vast modern concrete stadiums, with prizes being distributed to the owners of the finest bovine specimens, but the religious aspect of the celebration is still evident. The cows are decorated with garlands and jewelry, fed bananas and sugarcane by people who have waited in line for hours to be granted that rare privilege, and when the satiated animals can eat no more they simply lie down or wander about, while hundreds of young girls perform sacred dances in their honor.

In India, where the cow wishes to go, she goes. She may be lying in the temple, where she may decide to get up, to go and lie instead in the middle of the street. If she is annoyed by the proximity of the traffic streaming past her, she may lumber to her feet again and continue down the street to the railway station, where, should she feel like reclining in front of the ticket window, no one will disturb her. On the highways she seems to know that the drivers of trucks and buses will spot her a mile away and slow down almost to a stop before they get to her, and that therefore she need not move out from under the shade of the particular banyan tree she has chosen for her rest. Her superior position in the world is agreed upon by common consent.

The most satisfying exposition I have seen of the average Hindu's feeling about this exalted beast is a little essay composed by a candidate for a post in one of the public services, entitled simply: "The Cow." The fact that it was submitted in order to show the aspirant's mastery of the English language, while touching, is of secondary importance.

THE COW

The cow is one wonderful animal, also he is quadruped and because he is female he gives milk—but he will do so only when he has got child. He is same like God, sacred to Hindu and useful to man. But he has got four legs together. Two are foreward and two are afterwards.

His whole body can be utilized for use. More so the milk. What it cannot do? Various ghee, butter, cream, curds, whey, kova and the condensed milk and so forth. Also, he is useful to cobbler, watermans and mankind generally.

His motion is slow only. That is because he is of amplitudinous species, and also his other motion is much useful to trees, plants as well as making fires. This is done by making flat cakes in hand and drying in the sun.

He is the only animal that extricates his feedings after eating. Then afterwards he eats by his teeth whom are situated in the inside of his mouth. He is incessantly grazing in the meadows.

His only attacking and defending weapons are his horns, especially when he has got child. This is done by bowing his head whereby he causes the weapons to be parallel to ground of earth and instantly proceeds with great velocity forwards.

He has got tail also, but not like other similar animals. It has hairs on the end of the other side. This is done to frighten away

the flies which alight on his whole body and chastises him unceasingly, whereupon he gives hit with it.

The palms of his feet are so soft unto the touch, so that the
grasses he eats would not get crushed. At night he reposes by
going down on the ground and then he shuts his eyes like his relative the horse which does not do so. This is the cow.

The moths and night insects flutter about my single oil lamp.
Occasionally, at the top of its chimney, one of them goes up in a
swift, bright flame. On the concrete floor in a fairly well-defined
ring around the bottom of my chair are the drops of sweat that
have rolled off my body during the past two hours. The doors
into both the bedroom and the bathroom are shut; I work each
night in the dressing room between them, because fewer insects
are attracted here. But the air is nearly unbreathable with the
stale smoke of cigarettes and bathi sticks burned to discourage
the entry of winged creatures. Today's paper announced an out-
break of bubonic plague in Bellary. I keep thinking about it, and
I wonder if the almost certain eventual victory over such dis-
eases will prove to have been worth its price: the extinction of
the beliefs and rituals which gave a satisfactory meaning to the
period of consciousness that goes between birth and death. I
doubt it. Security is a false god; begin making sacrifices to it and
you are lost.

BRUCE CHATWIN

(1940–89)

Bruce Chatwin was born in Sheffield, Yorkshire, in 1940. After a brief career as an archaeologist, he turned to writing, and in his short career—he died of AIDS in 1989—showed his skill at several genres. In his travel book *In Patagonia* he followed in a British tradition of adventurous travel that Evelyn Waugh and Peter Fleming had created during the high noon of empire. Readers in postimperial Britain quickly warmed to his accounts of meetings with strange people in marvelous lands. He went on to publish three much-acclaimed novels, *On the Black Hill*, *Utz*, and *The Viceroy of Ouidah*. In *The Songlines,* he consummated a lifelong interest in nomads. He also excelled in the short magazine piece: the kind of slick, clever writing that the weekend supplements of British newspapers used to specialize in. He traveled often to India, clearly excited by the country's treasure trove of exotic stories. The piece excerpted here on the Indian wolf-boy is characteristic of his writing; it lies on the borderlines of fact and fiction where Chatwin was often to be found, in both his life and work.

SHAMDEV: THE WOLF-BOY

Last Easter Saturday, Father Joseph de Souza put on a freshly laundered soutane and took the bus from Sultanpur to Lucknow, to celebrate Mass in the Cathedral. With him went an eight- or nine-year-old boy whom he was taking to Mother Teresa's

Mission of Charity. The boy was unable to speak. Instead, he would clench his fists against his neck, depressing his vocal chords to make a low muted noise halfway between a growl and a howl.

Along the road the bus passed through the forest of Musafirkhana, where, about four years earlier, the boy had been found at play with his foster-brothers—who, it was said, were wolf-cubs.

From Romulus and Remus to Mowgli in Kipling's *Jungle Book*, there have been stories of man-cubs being saved and suckled by wolves: as well as by pigs, sheep, leopards, bears, and, recently in the Sahara, by gazelles. No single case has been proved beyond doubt. It is conceivable that Pascal—the name bestowed on the new arrival by the mission Sisters—will turn out to be the exception.

Pascal immediately befriended the orphanage dog—although, one day, he took its ear in his mouth and bit hard. During the first week, he would rip off his clothes, chuck away his food, and when he got hold of a pair of glasses, he clashed them together like cymbals. During the second week, be began to settle down. He learned to greet people with the Hindu salutation *"Namaste!"* He liked to travel round the garden sitting upright in the back of a bicycle rickshaw. The Sisters did have to watch him with other children: for sometimes, without warning, he would flick his fingers into their eyes.

One morning, a troupe of Rajasthani entertainers came down the street with monkeys jingling their bells, and a bear on a chain. Someone held up Pascal so he could get a better look— and he, as if suddenly seized with a fit, struggled and tried to throw himself into the bear's arms. A mission worker, having watched this behavior, decided to rename Pascal "Baloo"—like Baloo the Bear in *The Jungle Book*—and wrote a short article about him for one of the Lucknow papers.

The article was syndicated in the foreign press. I was in Benares when I heard of it: I took the train to Sultanpur and looked up Father Joseph, who teaches at a school run by the Sisters of the Little Flowers of Bethlehem. He is a small, wrinkled, optimistic south Indian who has spent forty of his sixty-nine years in the Hindi north. In the hot weather he sleeps alone on the roof of a barracklike building, at the far end of the compound from the nuns. In the yard below there grew some leggy papayas. A kennel housed a ferocious Alsatian that yanked at its chain, howled, and bared its teeth as I passed. Father Joseph's colleague, Sister Clarice, then gave a tea party in my honor at which she and two other nuns told their version of Pascal's story:

Early in Easter week a Muslim woman came to the school with news that an "animal-child" was roaming the western part of the town, scavenging for scraps. The Sisters found him on Good Friday, filthy and abandoned, crouching in a niche in the wall of a mudbrick house. The owners of the house said that a laundrywoman had come to claim him a few days earlier.

"But she didn't want him back," Father Joseph interrupted, "seeing he's come from the jungle and all. That's what it is. Once a baby's been touched by an animal, they abandon him and all."

Father Joseph said that, in the course of his ministry, he had often heard stories of "wolf-children," but had never set eyes on one. He knew of one case where a mother had lost her child at nightfall, and returned to find a female wolf guarding it.

The Sisters succeeded in tying up the boy and taking him back to the school. When they bathed him, he bit them. He spat out some Cadbury's chocolate. They gave him dal and chapatis, but "he threw the plate and all"; and when he heard the Alsatian barking, he rushed toward the kennel and tried to get inside. The Alsatian suddenly went quiet. They then put the boy to bed and locked the room.

"I heard him growling in the night and all," said the old priest—and the morning had found him hunched against the door.

My train got to Sultanpur in the late afternoon. By a lucky coincidence, only a few hours earlier the Sisters had received a visit from the man who originally "rescued" the boy in the forest. His name was Narsing Bahadur Singh and he was the *thakur*, or headman, of the village of Narangpur, about three miles outside the town.

The thakur owned a food stall near the railway repair yards and would often take along his wolf-boy, whom he called Shamdev. He said that Shamdev was always getting lost, or running after pariah dogs, but usually had the knack of finding his way home. When Sister Clarice taxed him with a rumor she had heard: that he used to exhibit the boy in a booth, for money—he was extremely indignant and went away.

In the evening she and I took a rickshaw to Narangpur. The thakur was still at market, so we sat in his courtyard while a crowd of villagers entertained us with imitations of Shamdev's antics, growling and baring their teeth. Narsing Bahadur Singh, when he did appear, was an erect, mild-mannered man in his fifties, dressed in white handwoven khaki cloth, and with a striped towel draped over his shoulders. He owned six acres of land, planted corn, dal, and rice, and was accounted rich. He had, it turned out, a history of adopting stray children. Besides his own two sons, he had brought up four other boys found abandoned in the wild. One of these, a gawky adolescent called Ramdev, was bundling straw into a loft. The thakur was insistent on one point: Ramdev was a mad boy; Shamdev was *not* mad, he was a "wolf-boy."

With the help of Sister Clarice's translation, I pieced together an outline of the story: It had happened early one morning about five years ago. It was the dry season but he couldn't be sure what month. He had bicycled to see his cousin, who lived in a village on the far side of Musafirkhana forest, about twenty miles from Sultanpur. On his way back to the main trunk road, the track cut through thickets of bamboo and thornbushes and, behind one of these, he heard the noise of squealing. He crept up and saw the boy at play with four or five wolf-cubs. He was most emphatic that they were not dogs or jackals, but wolves.

The boy had very dark skin, fingernails grown into claws, a tangle of matted hair and calluses on his palms, his elbows, and knees. Some of his teeth were broken to sharp points. He ran rapidly on all fours, yet couldn't keep up with the cubs as they bolted for cover. The mother wolf was not in sight. The thakur caught up with the boy, and was bitten on the hand. He did, however, succeed in trussing him up in his towel, lashed him to the pillion of his bicycle, and rode home.

At first Shamdev cowered from people and would only play with dogs. He hated the sun and liked to curl up in shadowy places. After dark, he grew restless and they had to tie him up to stop him following the jackals that howled around the village at night. If anyone cut themselves, he immediately smelled the

scent of blood, and would scamper toward it. He caught chickens and ate them alive, including the entrails. Later, when he had
evolved a sign language of his own, he would cross his thumbs
and flap his hands: this meant "chicken" or "food."

Eventually the thakur decided to wean him off red meat. He
force-fed him with rice, dal, and chapatis, but these made him
sick. He took to eating earth, his chest swelled up, and they began
to fear for his life. Only gradually did he get used to the new diet.
After five months he began to stand: two years later he was
doing odd jobs, like taking straw to the cows.

"He's mine," said Narsing Bahadur Singh, angrily. "I want him
back. I will go to Lucknow to fetch him."

"I'll take you," I said.

At six the next morning he was waiting for the taxi, all dressed
up in spotless whites. As the taxi passed through the forest at
Musafirkhana he pointed to the track, but we couldn't go and
see the place because the driver was in a hurry and threatened to
dump us and return to Sultanpur.

There were at least a hundred mentally defective children at
the Mother Teresa Mission. We were greeted there by an elderly
man, Ananda Ralla Ram, who had been a barrister before devot-
ing himself to charity. He turned his legal mind onto the subject
of Shamdev and gave the thakur quite a grilling. We tried to
explore the story from every angle, in an effort to find a flaw or
contradiction. The thakur's answers were always consistent.

When the Sisters brought in the boy, he stood tottering in the
doorway, screwing up his eyes to see who it was. Then, recogniz-
ing his old friend, he jumped into the air, flung himself around
his neck, and grinned.

I watched him for about two hours. Nothing much happened. He cuffed a child; he made his growling noises; he made the sign for "chicken"; sometimes he would point to the sky, circling his index finger as if describing the sun or moon. The calluses had gone, but you could see the scar tissue on his knees. He also had scars on the sides of his head: these, according to the thakur, had been made by the wolf-mother when she picked him up with her teeth.

The thakur left the Mission with me. He had been gearing himself for a scene; but the firm smiles of the Sisters unnerved him. He asked, meekly, if he could come again. He seemed very upset when it was time to say good-bye. So was Shamdev, and they hugged one another.

The discovery of an authentic wolf-child would be of immense importance to students of human and animal behavior. But though I felt that Narsing Bahadur Singh was speaking the truth, it was a very different matter to prove it.

The best-documented account of Indian wolf-children is that of Kamala and Amala, who, in 1920, were dug out of a wolf lair in Orissa by the Reverend J. A. L. Singh. The younger girl, Amala, died—although her "sister" lived on for nine years at the orphanage of Midnapore, during which time Singh kept a diary of her adjustment to human life.

Extracts from the diary have recently been republished in a book called *The Wolf Children* by Charles Maclean. On reading through it, I kept being struck by parallels between the girls and Shamdev: their sharpened teeth, their calluses, the craving for blood, the earth-eating, chicken-killing, the love of darkness, and their friendship with dogs and jackals. Maclean, however, concluded that the Reverend Singh's story is shot with inconsistencies—and that it does not hang together.

Another investigator, Professor Robert Zingg, collected in his *Wolf Children and Feral Man* all the known texts relating to children reared by animals, as well as stories of The Wild Boy of Aveyron and the legendary Kaspar Hauser. As for Shamdev, by far the most interesting comparisons are to be made with the reports in Major-General Sir W. H. Skinner's *A Journey through the Kingdom of Oudh (1849–50)*: five of his six cases of wolf-children come from the region of Sultanpur. He writes:

> Zoolfikur Khan, a respectable landowner from Bankepoor in the estate of Hassanpoor, 10 miles from the Sultanpoor cantonments, mentions that about eight or nine years ago a trooper came to town with a lad of about 9 or 10 years of age whom he had rescued from wolves among the ravines of the road ... that he walked on his legs like other people when he saw him, though there were evident signs on his knees and elbows of having gone very long on all fours ... He could not talk or utter any very articulate sound ... he understood signs and understood exceedingly well and would assist the cultivators in turning trespassing cattle out of their fields ...

His story could be that of Shamdev.

During the nineteenth century, when such tales were commoner, the most famous "wolf-man" in India was Dina Sanichar, who lived at the Sicandra Orphanage in Agra from 1867 till his death in 1895. He probably gave Kipling the model for Mowgli. He, too, had a craving for raw meat and, when forced to give it up, would sharpen his teeth on stones.

In zoological terms, there are almost insuperable difficulties in the way of a female Indian wolf actually being able to rear a human baby. First, she would have to lose her own brood: to keep her milk, and to be on the lookout for a substitute cub. She would have to scent the baby but, instead of making a meal of it, allow its cries to stifle her hunger drives and signal to her maternal instincts. Finally, since a wolf-cub's period of dependence is so much shorter than a human infant's, she might have three litters of her own before her adopted child could fend for itself. She would also have to protect it and post "Keep off!" signals to other wolves whose hunger might get the better of them.

One alternative explanation is that the wolf-boys or girls are autistic children, abandoned by their parents once they realize their condition; who somehow survive in the forest and, when rescued, seem to *behave* like wolves. Or could it be that the wolves around Sultanpur have a natural affiliation with man? There are no absolute conclusions to be drawn. But I came away convinced that Shamdev's story was as convincing as any other. Someone should get to the bottom of it.

1978

ROBYN DAVIDSON

(1 9 5 0 –)

Born in Queensland, Australia, Robyn Davidson has spent much of her life in London and India. In the late 1970s she traveled 1,700 miles across Australia with camels—a journey that became the subject of her bestselling book, *Tracks* (1979). It was not long afterwards that she went to India and acquired the romantic desire of traveling with the Rabari nomads of western India on their migratory journey across the Thar Desert. The wish was not fulfilled until a decade later, and then with unexpected results. The book she published about her travels, *Desert Places* (1996), from which the following excerpt is taken, describes the threatened marginal ways of nomads in a world that seeks its redemption in embracing modernity. It also records unflinchingly the destruction of her own illusions about the old superseded world. The possibility of escape is no longer there: "One carries the self," she writes, "like a heavy old suitcase wherever one goes." But there are moments of intimacy and solitude, and Davidson often found herself discovering a strange, compelling beauty even amid the squalor of modernizing India.

from DESERT PLACES

Americans waved flags in their streets, Iraqis mopped up blood in theirs. The Kuwaiti ruling family came home to initiate the torture of anyone they didn't like. Arms dealers counted their winnings. In India those children who had decided not to immolate themselves as their chums had done in protest against the Mandal Commission went back to school. Religious fanatics cooled down temporarily, the better to incite hatred another day. Politicians threw chairs at each other in parliament. Petrol dribbled back into bowsers. All was right with the world again.

But was it really useful, I asked myself, to travel with a bunch of nomads no one has ever heard of? So what if the Rabari will be extinct within fifty years? Who in the world will give a damn? And what good would it do them even if a thousand people, even if a million people, *did* give a damn? And so what if nomadism was about to go out, phut, like a candle, the whole world over? The culture of the millennium had bigger things to worry about.

But I'd committed myself and there was no turning back. The Chaitri festival—an annual livestock fair—was to start in a few weeks. There, I could buy myself some camels and Dilip could fly in from Delhi or Canada or wherever he was to take his pictures. Along the way I would call in at Rabari dhanis (hamlets) until I found just that group . . .

Meanwhile I visited several villages with Koju but, as I had not been able to find an interpreter, the nets I pulled up were empty. Often I would drive for ten hellish hours for a prearranged meeting, only to find that my informant had disappeared to a wedding or a death or had just disappeared. And when I did find someone who purported to be "the representative of the Rabari," my obsession with the specific was usually met with vagueness or with promises of assistance which vanished when delivery time came. Others, lured by the smell of "phoren" wealth, offered their doubtful services for fabulous sums.

Eventually I found one young man—Purnendu Kaavori—who worked at the Institute for Development Studies in Jaipur. He had traveled with a group of Rajput graziers into Haryana, later writing a thesis about them. He was pleased to offer advice and help but warned me that he, a local who spoke the language, had had great difficulty in persuading any group to take him on migration. They would be doubly uncertain about taking a woman.

Narendra as usual came to the rescue. In the middle of a schedule that would kill a person of lesser vitality, he had managed to find Bhairon Singh Raika—an ex-nomad, now constable in the Rajasthan police force—whom I could employ to liaise with the Rabari.

For our first interview Bhairon Singh wore Dacron stovepipes and a white nylon shirt which clung, sweatily, to his concave chest. When he boasted of the level of fitness required to enter the police force and how many other applicants less physically endowed than himself had fallen by the wayside, it was difficult not to smile. He was one of the half-dozen Raika in service, he could speak a little Hindi, knew all the Raika from Jodhpur to Jupiter and plenty of others as well, and would, he assured me, be able to explain the situation to less cosmopolitan members of his caste. He would accompany me to Chaitri livestock festival to assist in the purchase of the camels; he would most certainly find me a dang (migrating herd) to travel with. In the meantime would I like to attend a Raika wedding in his own village, Baabara?

The next day we all took our spoonful of the proffered jaggery and yogurt, Koju brought his hands together in prayer before starting the engine and, thus fortified against bad luck,

Bhairon, Koju, and I quit the farm gates. This time, I felt sure, the logjam was going to move.

A cool desert wind wrapped us in dust as we sped along the bitumen. There was no horizon. Trees emerged by the side of the road, to be swallowed up again by the dun pastel of our cocoon. "Yesssss!" shouted Bhairon, ejecting me out of reverie with a bang on the shoulder. "Raika!" The jeep flashed past a smudge of red and glitter, and camels concealed among the trees. The deeper we penetrated Bhairon's country the happier and more garrulous he became. Every Raika we spotted precipitated another bellowing "yesss" and a lot of hysterical bouncing around in the backseat. Koju drove implacably on until we reached our destination—Baabara, a cluster of old stone bungalows.

Bhairon's people had previously been camel breeders from the northern deserts. They had arrived in this more fertile area a couple of generations ago, taken over an almost abandoned village, switched to sheep, and were now better off and better organized than many others of their caste. Important resources were located nearby in Jaipur: merchants, wool depots, veterinary hospitals, and various government agencies to control migration. Their flocks numbered in the thousands, earning them the nickname of "migrating millionaires." I had been told that some politicians and wealthy landowners were in the habit of giving their own sheep to these people to take on migration and that through these men the graziers could gain illegal access to protected (and rapidly disappearing) forests. When I asked Bhairon about this he pretended not to understand the question.

I was ushered into Bhairon's home. Up six front steps to a courtyard bordered by an L-shaped house consisting of a room for the buffalo, a kitchen, and two bedrooms. Mrs. Bhairon brought her only chair out into the courtyard. I was made to sit on it like a reigning monarch while Koju was given the charpoi. Crowds gathered, introductions were made. Bhairon bustled about and gave commands to his pregnant wife who, I imagined, wore a long-suffering look under her pink orni. All I had to do was smile a great deal and accept, graciously, his orgy of generosity. We were plied with the best food he could offer, drenched in expensive ghee. I wasn't hungry but not wishing to insult our host I watched Koju for clues. A rondo of etiquette ensued: Koju raising his hands politely to refuse the hovering ladle, Bhairon cajoling, Koju acquiescing to a tiny morsel, only to have a quarter pound of hot ghee dumped on his plate. Later he explained, "For Marwari man, guest is most important."

Our stomachs swollen, our belches politely thunderous, it was time to socialize. I was shown each of the rooms, all of the treasures. In the kitchen where Mrs. Bhairon had been thumping dough over a tiny fire, smoke and chili filled the air. Bhairon indicated his spouse and said, "She is not a good cook. No, a very bad cook, I think."

"She is a very good cook."

"But she is very ugly." He lifted the orni.

"Not at all. She is beautiful."

"Then she is your servant."

"No, she is my saheli (female friend)."

All this went down well and I had obviously passed the manners test. Even so, no one would let me help her with the work. I must sit and receive. Finally Bhairon brought out his *pièce de résistance*—a framed piece of paper on which it was stated that one Constable Bhairon Singh Raika had received twenty-five rupees and a commendation for bravery for helping to capture an infamous dacoit . . . One dollar did not seem a huge incentive for risking one's life in the badlands until I was told that the house next to his, a derelict but still beautiful building, had been bought for the price of a carton of my English cigarettes.

It was time to bathe and dress for the wedding. A partially closed-off corner of the courtyard was indicated and a bucket of well water brought to me. What to do? I was visible for a sweep of sixty degrees and anyone entering the courtyard would get a full view. I squatted down and hastily rinsed the bits I could get at, ending up with saturated clothes but mostly dry skin. Going behind the village wall for a shit was something of a test of ingenuity also. One had to step among the clustering turds, find a couple of square inches of spare dust and hope like hell no one came past. I now understood the logic of the village women's full skirts. As for using the jar of water to clean one's rear end, I never did learn the correct technique and it's not a subject about which one feels comfortable inquiring. I tried but never quite managed to conquer squeamishness. The world is divided between those cultures which touch their own feces and those which don't. And it seems to me that those which do have a greater understanding of humankind's relationship to earth, our alpha and omega.

Ablutions completed, a quite spectacular gold necklace was placed around my neck. Next came Mrs. Bhairon's second-best skirt. An orni was tucked into it and wrapped around my head. There followed bangles, anklets, and bells and everyone agreed that no one would ever guess I was a European. We all took photos of each other: me with two brass pots stacked on my head, my legs cut off at the knee, standing at a thirty-degree

angle to the horizontal plane of the photograph and looking
every inch a European, albeit of the deranged kind. Koju never
did learn to use that camera.

We squeezed our way up an alley to where the groom's party
buzzed around a red tractor like Fabergé wasps, all ruby and
marcasite. Every surface, saturated with the light absorbed during the day, was now giving it back to the night as a molten glow.
Pigs ran about and squealed. Dogs fought each other. A man
whose head and shoulders protruded a couple of feet above the
crowd placed himself in front of me and grabbed the gold necklace. "Giga," he said, which might have been a threat to strangle
me but which was, I found out later, his name. He roared with
laughter and went about his business. Some women festooned
in red and silver came out of a house singing. They were carrying a glittering bundle which, on closer inspection, proved to be
a four-year-old child. Battery-powered lights danced around his
gold brocade turban and his feet were pressed into gold-trimmed
shoes with backward curling points. Every other part of him
was covered in satins and tinsel. He was given to me to hold as if
he were the most precious thing they possessed, as if all the
pride of that vastly extended family were embodied in this exquisite, grave little boy—the bind rajah—the bridegroom.

Child marriages are illegal in India and one can see why this
should be so. Among the Rajputs, for example, it is a matter of
shame if a daughter reaches menarche in her parents' home.
Consequently, girls begin producing children while they are still
children themselves. But to the Rabari, who cling fiercely to the
tradition, it is a sensible practice. First of all it is difficult for
nomads to gather at one place so important events are made to
coincide. Often deaths will be mourned a week before the

marriages are celebrated ("mausar" feasts), to cut down costs but also, perhaps, to stress the cyclic nature of life. Tonight eight children would be married, thus forming important alliances and mutual support between families which would last lifetimes. After the marriage the girl would go to spend one night in her susural (in-laws' home), surrounded by affection, made to feel important and special, and then be brought home. There would be no consummation until well after maturity and, even then, she would go back and forth from susural to parents' home many times until she felt comfortable in her new role and until the communities decided the couple was ready to live together. Usually when the woman had her children she would take the newborn back to her parents' home, sometimes for months. Divorce in many communities was allowed, though frowned upon and usually had less to do with incompatibility than with infertility. Once again this would be a decision taken by the elders. If a husband died, then it was possible for a woman to marry again, though most often widows, particularly if they had children, preferred to remain single. All in all marriage was a pragmatic affair and individual desires came a poor second to the harmony of the group.

We were to take the bind rajah to his wedding in style. Fifteen people packed themselves into my jeep and we set off into the moonlight and dust, the women singing through their noses. When we passed a small shrine by the side of the track everyone let out an almighty whoop of greeting. The tiny boy smiled and blinked like a pampered cat.

The bindani's (bride's) village was a maze of small rooms and courtyards, a domestic logic that was difficult at first to understand. On a platform about thirty women were ablaze in primary colors and precious metals. I was taken to sit with them. When the woman next to me found out I had been married, she pulled the orni down over my face and pushed me to the ground. Shrieks of delight at this game which everyone joined in. I was instructed in the four or five methods a married woman must use to peep through her orni when there are in-laws or strange men present, using fingers deftly to form the little hole which allows just one eye to show, a most disconcerting gesture and, paradoxically, provocative. Once again there was much poking of my breasts, not as discreet this time, after which it was announced that I was indeed female. I was rescued by Bhairon and made to lie on a string bed covered with quilts in the courtyard. The groom was brought to me and although he occasionally nodded off in my lap, he never once whined or fidgeted. I'd shake him gently awake, as was my duty, and he'd stare at me for a second before breaking into a smile—dignified as a grandfather.

Into this courtyard forgotten in the depth of time came a skinny young man in Terylene flares and a message T-shirt. Pressed to his ear was a radio blaring out Hindi movie songs in competition with the women's voices. He knew a great deal about "phoren" and announced to all present that western women had wicked morals and that they did not breastfeed their children. He was one of the educated elite and his only ambition was to land a government job so that he would never have to work again. He talked about money and disco music and was scornful of grazing as a profession. Was the future of the Rabari incarnate in this young man?

At the bride's compound (the bindanis were even tinier than the binds) some hired musicians were singing devotional songs to men stoned on opium. The Rabari, so sensible and shrewd with their money, do not practice the economically crippling—and spreading—system of dowry. Customs surrounding bride price (the opposite of dowry) vary from place to place but are usually more symbolic than financial. A family will try to marry all its daughters in one go, so although the celebrations may be lavish they only empty the coffers once. On this occasion the bridegroom's family displayed the gifts presented to the bride—a set of clothes, some silver anklets, foodstuffs, and a little money. These were inspected carefully for any trace of meanness by various mothers, aunties, and grannies, and pronounced satisfactory.

The night passed in a blur. People coming and going, bursts of singing, snoring from various charpois, hawking, coughing and spitting, the arrival of plates of food, rats nesting in hair or nibbling feet. At some point I went to sleep under the spacious sky but was woken shortly afterwards by visitors coming by for a "dekho" at the chief guest. At dawn there was corn gruel and yogurt, after which I was led to another section of the village where a thousand Rabari had gathered from far and wide for the party, dressed up in their very best. This was a death–wedding feast and it was a huge and expensive occasion. Along the flat rooftops, lined up like geranium pots, were rows of bejeweled heads. The joke about my married status had swept through the whole gathering. Banks of women pulled my orni over my face or tried to teach me the peephole trick. Dust rose into a sky as white as paper.

When I returned to the courtyard the groom greeted me by putting out his arms to be picked up, and with a heart-melting smile. No western child would have stood this stress for an hour.

But this little creature, perhaps because he had never been separated from community life, did not once lose his composure during the whole four days. But then, grace under pressure is a valued trait among the pastoralists. In a few years this baby would be out with the herds, battling the world for his bread.

By mid-afternoon I found myself sitting in a small room at the front of a carpet of tightly packed men's faces. I had contracted some kind of stomach bug and was anxious about an undignified dash for the door using fifty turbans as stepping-stones. There were millions of flies, too many bodies, heat. I thought that a little food in my stomach might combat the waves of nausea, so in my exhaustion reached out to take a sticky sweet with my left hand. A common breath was held, an old man said "aahhhh," and just in time I checked myself. I took it with my right hand, everyone laughed, the shyness eased, and we began to talk.

There was trouble out on the dang. An old man had come back by bus with the news. The shepherds had had to bribe a forest officer with five thousand rupees to graze the flock—the equivalent of five months' income. Each owner would contribute a percentage of the money proportionate to the size of his flock but it was still a big financial loss to the village. That wasn't all. A few shepherds had been arrested for falsifying the number of sheep they had, so as to pay less tax to the state government. Now one of them had skipped jail, and the police were looking for him. This, too, would require money for bribes. The top numberdar (leader of migration), who had returned for the wedding only two days before, would have to journey back to the dang immediately to sort out the mess.

I asked what they thought of politics and how they might vote. They replied that their only concern was survival and whatever politician might help them with that would receive their vote. On the other hand most of them didn't bother to vote, either because they had no belief in the efficacy of a democracy wormy with corruption or because they were out on the dang, hundreds of miles from home. So large a collection of shepherds was a rare occasion, most of them having little opportunity to leave the herds and come home. Their chief concern was with grazing rights, government control on the sale of wool, the loss of land to farmers, and the dangers of migration. They made clear that these problems were common to all the pashupalak (animal herders) irrespective of caste.

But one man announced that he belonged to the BJP. He was fat and buttery, gold rings adorned his fingers, and, although he was dressed in traditional Raika clothes, he looked like a badly cast actor next to his lean, sun-shriveled relatives. He owned a shop in a nearby town. He could speak a little English and informed me that his fellow Raika were illiterate and ignorant, so there was no point in asking them about anything. He added that the reason the Muslims caused so much trouble was that they ate beef and therefore their "brain temperature was very high."

I wondered how much he influenced the others. He was, after all, wealthy and literate. He knew about the bureaucratic world. Did they rely on his judgment? From the way they listened to him respectfully but distantly, I suspected not. The nomads are the most tolerant of people and I saw virtually no communalist tendencies among them. They sell their meat to Muslims. It is

Muslims who shear their sheep. There are Muslim graziers and so far the sense of comradeship with them, because of their common occupations, common problems, is strong. Besides, how can one find the time to stick to the finer points of Hinduism when one is out on the dang unable to wash or perform rituals? And how can one sneer at the cow-eaters when one sometimes indulges in a bit of mutton on the quiet? But when the nomads stopped wandering as one day they must . . . ?

There were Muslim Rabari present at the wedding. Centuries ago when the Mughals invaded, they caused many problems for the Rabari, who often acted as spies for the Rajput rulers. One particular group was captured by the invaders and taken to Delhi. It was here that they were forced to eat beef, thereby becoming instantly de-Hinduized. Their descendants were followers of Islam but they still performed ceremonies at various caste functions and their affinity with their original caste seemed as strong as their identity as Mohammedans.

I could discipline my raging stomach no longer. Blocking the door stood all seven feet of Giga. He grabbed me by the gold necklace like a New York mugger. (Rabari humor is sometimes opaque.) Hastily I took it off and made a dash for the nearest wall, to be followed and laughed at by children who were curious about a "phoren's" body functions. Giga had lent the necklace and was no doubt worried that I was about to head for the hills with it. And yet it was he who, two days later, after I'd spent another sleepless, opium-filled night at his house, and was now saying good-bye to a hundred friends, took both my hands gently in his, pressed them together in front of his heart, and said, "We are your children."

E. M. FORSTER

(1879–1970)

The author of *Howard's End* (1910) and *A Passage to India* (1924) was born among the prim and snobbish Victorian middle classes. He did not know about sex until he was thirty, and he lived with his mother until the age of sixty-five. Much of his long life, however, was a discreet attempt to escape and overturn the prejudices of his class and age. The attempt began at Cambridge and Bloomsbury, and then Egypt, where he had his first sexual encounter with a poor Muslim bus conductor. India, which he first saw in 1912–13, made him an even more determined critic of imperialism and strengthened his ethic of "personal relationships," which he hoped would overcome the bitterness between the ruler and the ruled. But, as is evident in the following report of a Muslim wedding, an English irony remained even in his most sympathetic portraits of India and Indians. On a second visit to India in 1921, he worked for a few weeks as secretary to the Maharajah of a small state in central India. The Maharajah was witty and incompetent; his kingdom was falling apart. In this atmosphere of intrigue and decrepitude—well-described in *The Hill of Devi* (1953)—Forster confided his sexual tastes to the Maharajah who promptly arranged for the court barber to have an affair with his timid-seeming English secretary. Shortly after his second visit, Forster published *A Passage to India*.

from ABINGER HARVEST

ADRIFT IN INDIA

1. THE NINE GEMS OF UJJAIN

"There is the old building," said he, and pointed to a new building.

"But I want the ruins of which the stationmaster spoke; the palace that King Vikramaditya built, and adorned with Kalidas, and the other eight. Where is it? Where are they?"

"Old building," he repeated more doubtfully, and checked the horse. Far out to the left, behind a grove of trees, a white and fantastic mass cut into the dusty horizon. Otherwise India prevailed. Presently I said, "I think you are driving me wrong," and, since now nothing happened at all, added, "Very well, drive me in that direction." The horse then left the road and proceeded with a hesitating step across the fields.

Ujjain is famous in legend and fact, and as sacred as Benares, and surely there should have been steps, and temples, and the holy river Sipra. Where were they? Since leaving the station we had seen nothing but crops and people, and birds, and horses as feeble as our own. The track we were following wavered and blurred, and offered alternatives; it had no earnestness of purpose like the tracks of England. And the crops were haphazard too—flung this way and that on the enormous earth, with patches of brown between them. There was no place for anything, and nothing was in its place. There was no time either. All the small change of the north rang false, and nothing remained certain but the dome of the sky and the disk of the sun.

Where the track frayed out into chaos the horse stopped, but the driver repeated "Old, very old," and pointed to the new building. We left the horse to dream. I ordered him to rejoin it. He said that he would, but looking back I found that he, too, was dreaming, sitting upon his heels, in the shadow of the castor-oil plants. I ordered him again, and this time he moved, but not in the direction of the horse. "Take care; we shall all lose one another," I shouted. But disintegration had begun, and my expedition was fraying out, like the track, like the fields.

Uncharioted, unattended, I reached the trees, and found under them, as everywhere, a few men. The plain lacks the romance of solitude. Desolate at the first glance, it conceals numberless groups of a few men. The grasses and the high crops sway, the distant path undulates, and is barred with brown bodies or heightened with saffron and crimson. In the evening the villages stand out and call to one another across emptiness with drums and fires. This clump of trees was apparently a village, for near the few men was a sort of enclosure surrounding a kind of street, and gods multiplied. The ground was littered with huts and rubbish for a few yards, and then the plain resumed; to continue in its gentle confusion as far as the eye could see.

But all unobserved, the plain was producing a hill, from the summit of which were visible ruins—the ruins. The scene amazed. They lay on the other side of a swift river, which had cut a deep channel in the soil, and flowed with a violence incredible in that drowsy land. There were waterfalls, chattering shallows, pools, and to the right a deep crack, where the whole stream gathered together and forced itself between jaws of stone. The river gave nothing to the land; no meadows or water weeds edged it. It flowed, like the Ganges of legend, precipitate out of heaven across earth on its way to plunge under the sea and purify hell.

On the opposite bank rose the big modern building, which now quaintly resembled some castle on the Loire. The ruins lay close to the stream—a keep of grey stone with a water-gate and steps. Some of the stones had fallen, some were carved, and, crossing the shallows, I climbed them. Beyond them appeared more ruins and another river.

This second river had been civilized. It came from the first and returned to it through murmurous curtains and weirs, and in its brief course had been built a water palace. It flowed through tanks of carved stone, and mirrored pavilions and broken cause-ways, whence a few men were bathing, and lovingly caressed their bodies and whispered that holiness may be gracious and life not all an illusion, and no plain interminable. It sang of cer-tainties nearer than the sky, and having sung was reabsorbed into the first. As I gazed at it I realized that it was no river, but part of the ruined palace, and that men had carved it, as they had carved the stones.

Going back, I missed the shallows and had to wade. The pools, too shallow for alligators, suggested leeches, but all was well, and in the plain beyond a tonga wandered aimlessly. It was mine, and my driver was not surprised that we had all met again. Safe on the high road, I realized that I had not given one thought to the past. Was that really Vikramaditya's palace? Had Kalidas and the other eight ever prayed in those radiant waters? Kalidas describes Ujjain. In his poem of *The Cloud Messenger*—a poem as ill-planned and charming as my own expedition—he praises the beloved city. He feigns that a demigod, exiled from his lady, employs a cloud to take her a message from him. An English cloud would go, but this is Hindu. The poem is occupied by an account of the places it might pass if it went far enough out of its course, and of those places the most out-of-the-way is Ujjain. Were the cloud to stray thither, it would enter the city with Sipra, the sacred stream, and would hear the old country people singing songs of mirth in the streets. While maidens clapped their hands, and peacocks their wings, it might enter perfumed balconies as a shower, or as a sunset radiance might cling round the arm of Shiva. In the evening, when women steal to their lovers "through darkness that a needle might divide," the cloud might show them the way by noiseless lightning flash, and weary of their happiness and its own might repose itself among sleeping doves till dawn. Such was Kalidas' account of his home, and the other eight—was not one of them a lexicographer?—may have sported there with him. The groves near must have suggested to him the magic grove in *Sakuntala*, where the wood nymphs pushed wedding garments through the leaves. "Whence came these ornaments?" one of the characters inquires, "Has the holy hermit created them by an effort of his mind?" The conclusion, though natural, is wrong. "Not quite," answers another. "The sweet trees bore them unaided. While we gathered blossoms, fairy hands were stretched out." Cries a third, "We are only poor girls. How shall we know how such ornaments are put on? Still, we have seen pictures. We can imitate them." They adorn the bride . . .

But it is only in books that the past can glow, and Kalidas faded as soon as I felt the waters of the Sipra round my ankle. I thought not of Sakuntala's ornaments, but of my own, now spread on the splashboard, and I wondered whether they would dry before we reached the railway station. One confusion enveloped Ujjain and all things. Why differentiate? I asked the driver what kind of trees those were, and he answered "Trees"; what was the name of that bird, and he said "Bird"; and the plain, interminable, murmured, "Old buildings are buildings, ruins are ruins."

[1914]

2. ADVANCE, INDIA!

The house of the rationalistic family (Mohammedans) lay close below that of my friends (English). We could see its red walls and corrugated iron roof through the deodars, and its mass cut into the middle distances though without disturbing the line of the snows. It was a large house, but they were not, I believe, prominent in their community, and only flashed into notoriety on the occasion of this marriage, which was the first of its kind that the province had seen. We did not know them, but had received an invitation, together with the rest of the station, and as the sun was declining we clambered down and joined the crowd in their garden.

A public wedding! It would actually take place here. In the center of the lawn was a dais on which stood a sofa, an armchair, and a table, edged with torn fringe, and round this dais a couple of hundred guests were grouped. The richer sat on chairs, the poorer on a long carpet against the wall. They were of various religions and races—Mohammedans, Hindus, Sikhs, Eurasians, English—and of various social standings, though mainly subordinate Government clerks; and they had come from various motives, friendship, curiosity, hostility—the ceremony nearly ended in a tumult, but we did not know this until the next day. The snows were seventy miles off in front, the house behind; the less rationalistic part of the family remained in purdah there and watched the marriage through the blinds. Such was the setting.

After long delay the personages mounted. The Moulvi took the armchair—a handsome, elderly man robed in black velvet and gold. He was joined by the bridegroom, who looked self-possessed, and by the unveiled bride. They sat side by side on the sofa, while guests murmured: "This is totally contrary to the Islamic law," and a child placed vasefuls of congested flowers. Then the bridegroom's brother arrived, and had a long conversation with the Moulvi. They grew more and more excited—gesticulated, struck their breasts, whispered and sighed at one another vehemently. There was some difficulty, but what it was no one could say. At last an agreement was reached, for the brother turned to the audience and announced in English that the marriage ceremony would begin with verses from the Koran. These were read, and "the next item," said the brother, "is a poem upon Conscience. An eminent poet will recite on Conscience in Urdu, but his words will be translated." The poet and his interpreter then joined the group on the dais, and spoke alternately, but not very clearly, for the poet himself knew English, and would correct the interpreter, and snatch at the manuscript. Arid verities rose into the evening air, the more depressing for the rags of Orientalism that clothed them. Conscience was this and that, and whatsoever the simile, there was no escaping her. "The sun illumines the world with light. Blessed be the sun and moon and stars, without which our eyes, that seem like stars, could not see. But there is another light, that of conscience—" and then conscience became a garden where the bulbul of eloquence ever sang and the dews of oratory dropped, and those who ignored her would "roll among thorns." When she had had her fling the pair were made man and wife. Guests murmured, "Moulvi is omitting such-and-such an exhortation: most improper." Turning to the company, and more particularly to those upon the carpet, he said that it was not important how one was married, but how one behaved after marriage. This was his main point, and while he was making it we were handed refreshments, and the ceremony was more or less over.

It was depressing, almost heartrending, and opened the problem of India's future. How could this jumble end? Before the Moulvi finished a gramophone began, and before that was silent a memorable act took place. The sun was setting, and the orthodox withdrew from us to perform their evening prayer. They gathered on the terrace behind, to the number of twenty, and prostrated themselves toward Mecca. Here was dignity and unity; here was a great tradition untainted by private judgment; they had not retained so much and rejected so much; they had accepted Islam unquestioningly, and the reward of such an acceptance is beauty. There was once a wedding in England where a talented lady, advanced, but not too advanced, rewrote her daughter's marriage service. Bad there, the effect was worse in India, where the opportunities for disaster are larger. Crash into the devotions of the orthodox birred the gramophone—

I'd sooner be busy with my little Lizzie,

and by a diabolic chance reached the end of its song as they ended the prayer. They rejoined us without self-consciousness, but the sun and the snows were theirs, not ours; they had obeyed; we had entered the unlovely chaos that lies between obedience and freedom—and that seems, alas! the immediate future of India. Guests discussed in nagging tones whether the rationalistic family had gone too far or might not have gone further. The bride might, at all events, have been veiled; she might, at all events, have worn English clothes. Eurasian children flew twittering through the twilight like bats, cups clinked, the gramophone was restarted, this time with an Indian record, and during the opening notes of a nautch we fled.

Next morning a friend (Sikh) came to breakfast, and told us that some of the guests had meant to protest against the innovations, and that the Moulvi had insisted in justifying himself to them; that was why he had argued on the dais and spoken afterwards. There was now great trouble among the Mohammedans in the station, and many said there had been no marriage at all. Our friend was followed by the bridegroom's brother, who thanked us for coming, said there had been no trouble in the community, and showed us the marriage lines. He said—"Some old-fashioned gentlemen did not understand at first—the idea was new. Then we explained, and they understood at once. The lady is advanced, very advanced. . . ." It appeared that she had advanced further than her husband, and the brother seemed thankful all was over without a scandal. "It was difficult," he cried. "We Moslems are not as advanced as the Hindus, and up here it is not like Bombay side, where such marriages are commoner. But we have done what we ought, and are consequently content." High sentiments fell from his lips, conscience shone and flowered and sang and banged, yet somehow he became a more dignified person. It hadn't at all events been an easy thing for two bourgeois families to jerk out of their rut, and it is actions like theirs, rather than the thoughts of a philosopher or the examples of kings, that advance a society. India had started— one had that feeling while this rather servile little clerk was speaking. For good or evil she had left the changeless snows and was descending into a valley whose farther side is still invisible.

"Please write about this" were his parting words. "Please publish some account of it in English newspaper. It is a great step forward against superstition, and we want all to know."

[1914]

ALLEN GINSBERG

(1926–97)

Allen Ginsberg, born in New Jersey to a mentally unstable mother, studied at Columbia University, New York, where he met the other leaders—Jack Kerouac, William Burroughs, Neal Cassady—of what came to be known later as the "Beat Generation." While still at Columbia, Ginsberg began experimenting with psychedelic drugs and writing visionary poetry. In the midst of the unprecedented prosperity of postwar America, he spoke of spiritual exhaustion and anomie. In the early 1950s, he traveled to the Yucatan valley in Mexico and experimented with more drugs there. In 1956, the year Ginsberg's mother died in a mental hospital, the publishing house City Lights in San Francisco published his great poem, *Howl*, and found itself accused of peddling obscenity by the police. Ginsberg's sense of alienation from the mainstream of American life, which took him to Buddhism in his later life, and established him, by the time he died in 1997, in the distinguished tradition of American dissenters, was what set him on his journeys. In 1962, Ginsberg traveled with his lover Peter Orlovsky to South America, Europe, Morocco, and India. It was a difficult time for India, then involved in a disastrous war with China. But Ginsberg was deep in his own world, as is evident in these excerpts from the journals he kept in Benares, where the city, itself phantasmagoric with its burning ghats and widows and pilgrims, seemed to match Ginsberg's longing for self-forgetting and oblivion.

from INDIAN JOURNALS

17 Dec '62

Long walk this morn to Manikarnika ghat—sat inside red stone porch with Saddhus & smoked ganja pipe & inquired about guru of good looking saddhu from Nimtallah—reminiscent red haired Naga saddhu knew him. Cow laid its head on my lap to be scratched. American tourists floating by in rowboats.

Dream: I meet Buddy Isenberg & Burroughs—turns out Isenberg is a nice girl—we sit at cafe table & talk, I apologize for writing so late. Nice dinky soft mannish looking girl. My demeanor is excessively self assured, is demeanor. Strange I should dream twice of girls in one day. "At my age" I said to Peter.

This morning while my back was turned from the table I heard a great thump—turned around to see a monkey jump on the table loaded with oranges & bananas, snatch one banana & leap out to the balcony, disappearing thru the lavatory window—next sitting on high branch of adjoining tree peeling the banana & staring at me thru the big leaves.

Incense in the room tonite, bought straw mats to cover half the slate-black tile floor.

What Vanity? What possible divine
blessing on all this Politics.
What invocation beyond Millions
of Votes for 1960 Hopes

What rat Curse or Dove vow slipt from my hands
                    to help this multitude
Smirking at the ballot box, deceived,
                    sensible, rich, full of onions,
voting for W. C. Williams with one
                    Foot in the grave and an eye
in a daisy out the window

18 Dec '62—

Sitting on rock at Harischandra Ghat—down below a sand slope at the water's edge blackened with ashes, a high pile of firewood ablaze and a man's head bent back blackened nose & mouth unburnt, black fuzzy hair, the rest of the chest belly outlined along down thighs at top of the pyre, feet sticking out the other end—now turned toes down—cry of geese & rabble of white longnecked good goose swan boids pecking in the water's edge a few feet from fire.

  Nearby scows filled with sand from the other side of the river, laborers carrying baskets of grey sand up the brick stairway from the river—"Oh—the head's going to fall off—" The pile darkening, white ash floating up—a few watchers squatted on bricks facing the pyre—Pole man comes & tucks a foot into fire—then circles around & pushes length of pole against the black head (lain back with open black throat & adam's apple silhouetted against the small flames against the green river) til the body's balanced on the center of the collapsing charred logs. Donkeys led along the sand path, children running with kites, a black baby with no pants & pigtails, balancing a stick of bamboo—A saddhu in orange robes sitting up on a stone porch on the embankment under turrets of an old small castle—rather

Venetian the scene—Rectangular-sailed boats going down
stream—the air above the pyre curling in the heat, like a transparent water veil between my eyes & the greenfields & trees
along the horizon on the other side of the Ganges—and the
embankments, red temples spires, toy mosques, trees and squat
white shrines walling in the bend of the river upstream to the
long red train bridge at Raj Ghat an inch high.

18 Dec and a torn burlap bag to cover the squat pantsdropd lavatory window that opens on the staircase of the house, so
ascending passersby can see the diarrheic mud bubble down
from the asshole of P. Orlovsky & Company, Inc.

This morning down to the burning ghats & sat with same
group of sadhus in their eyrie in the sandy basement porch of a
pilgrim's rest house—fire with a pot of boiling lentils, embers
from the burning ghat down below at 10 AM—a trident and
bamboo lance & brass water-pot begging stoup scattered around,
one friendly Sadhu named "Shambhu Bharti Baba" with whom
I've sat and smoked before—today seeing my difficulty handling
the red clay pipe he made & accompanied me smoking a cigarette mixed with ganja—I also partook of two pipes tho I
coughed & the cold snot bubbled out my nostril from the strain-
wheeze—brought some bananas & green seed fruits to distrib-
ute, gifts—and camera so made photos—the Naga Sadhu (S b
b) wanted his very confusingly, as he don't talk but makes finger
gestures—he got to his feet, stripped off his g-string & pulled
down his cock under between his legs—one yogic ball bumping
out—like cunt—for a photo—I took a dozen, all the group
smoking round the pot & ashes—one standing of the Naga

sadhu with his pots & brass tridents etc. then high put on my shoes & walked back along the ghats home, & slept in dark closed room a half an hour—read Mayakovsky

  elegy to Lenin—"and
              child-like,
                       wept the grey-bearded old"
  and Brooklyn Bridge poem—I didn't remember it was so lovely
  —"in the grisly mirage of evening
      . . . the naked soul
              of a building
      will show
              in a window's translucent light"

Jodrell Bank's deposit of heavenly radio waves

  Shot some M, last nite, up on mattress reading The Statesman (Calcutta), Time, Mayakovsky, writing postcards, washing socks handkerchiefs undershirt, Peters cock, necking with him,
  While below the balcony under the streetlight one milk shop clattered pails
  in the darkness, the Desasumedh Ghat beggars kept thin fingers moving under dried burlap, counting beads Jai Ram Jai Citaram, & the woman on the opposite corner with
  long wild hair crouched against a bidi shop steps rocking back & forth—I gave her 25 NP when I went out before dawn to buy milk & cigarettes—
  now the square begins working—I feel like An American in Paris in 1920—The naiveté of neighborhoods awakening, radios turned on too loud to the Hindi news in the milk shop,

First lights turned on across the street, in the Cigarette and fried noodle peppers stall at the gate of the market,

three rickshaws circling to take off up street and look for cold dark business

Householders wrapped in shawls carrying brass waterpots trudging into the Ganges steps, passing & observing the beggar man in the mid-street shrouded in his own burlap shawl—he'd moved all night praying—

and carrying flowers to adorn the Lingams in the temples overlooking the starlit, planet-lit river—

arguments between Ram & Cita in Hindi voices tinnily rickochetting all the way up to my balcony from the radio—

Walkers coughing & trudging river street in Paterson too at this hour—

Him crouched under street lite on the corner counting a basketful of small potatos

Such a basket as I bought last night to contain my bananas & oranges, from white glued paperbags written in ledger sheets Hindi another day in a dark office—

Martial music to accompany the morning's broadcast, and the sound of a claxon with a throat inflammation in the background—

Peter lying dressed up in pants on mattress picking his red mustache, with long hollywood Christlike hair & Christ's small beard stubble—

I found out Octavio Paz is in Delhi the Ambassador of Mexico, arranging train rides for his tennis team—a headache—

Blake's photo on the wall, waiting waiting waiting—with his life mask eyes closed—thinking—or receiving radio messages from the cosmos source—

The rickshaw wallahs had slept all night crouched covered with their shawls on the red leather slope plastic of lowered rickshaws—

at night their bells rang in tune back & forth, speeding down the hill to Godolia from Chowk, up & down answering alarm clock tingalings in the dead streets—an iceman's tingaling, a knife sharpener's charged bellsound—

A huge black tree looming over my window obliterating half the square, all nite lights shining thru its leaves from milk shop where a vat of white cow buffalo lact bubbles over a charcoal trench.

Coughs answering back & forth across the square, and the splash of the streetcorner waterpipe faucet, clearing the throat near dawn—

a big white cow with horns had walked slowly up the street alone, looking for something to do—cows all last night in repulsive play, chasing each other in the traffic to lick the red asshole pads they drop streams of urine thru on the puddled street—black bulls horning the girls in front of Sardau's Hindu Hotel, separated by silver giant wire trees, knobby with ceramic eyes—

Wet charcoal & first white smoke impregnating the air to the tops of the trees—the monkeys asleep—the weasles aware— few rare ants—cigarette ashes cleaned from the trays in paper bag on the porch with banana & orange peels (the cows' lot) waiting the sweeper

Morning not yet come, Dec 19, 1962 must be 4 or 5 AM in Benares, writing & fingering my cock & remembering Shostakovitche's dead March as the radio bounces & crashes across India with brass violins—

The smell of frying meat cakes and potatos, Jai Citaram in a toneless voice, & gentle gossip near the rickshaws, the clanging of a temple bell at worship time early a few blocks away.

A lady already arrived with small baskets of parsley & radishes sits in the road where it turns down to the river steps, coughs & spits on the ground & bides in the gloom as the first blue light breaks open clouds in the East sky over the river, seen from balcony thru trees and a few balconied chickenwired houses leaning over the steps.

The present is sufficient subject like Cezanne "I turn my head this way or that an inch, & the composition changes."

and a high voiced automatic chant from one man emerges up from the street amidst the voices of first male gossip & the lighting of matches as the morning walkers glide back & forth & accumulate—but not a hatchet, I didn't accumulate a hatchet, only straw brooms & mats & baskets & no more.

19 Dec 1962—

Well, where now me, what next,
lying here in the church gloom naked mattress
like a Corpse under Covers, just come into Peter's mouth
with his cock in my mouth and pubic hair spread on my beard
cupping his soft ass halves with my palms—
now alone with all the french doors closed & darkened
in late afternoon against the skull drum & girl cry of streets of
     Market below my balcony—
What next soul task, in all this morphined ease
drowsing to wake at midnight in the oldest city in the world—
no need to rush out and carry burlap bags full of dung to
     make money

my checks arrive from around the world,

enough to lay here Oblomov all my fourth decade on the planet

with the stars rising and falling and half moon

disappearing as I peep out the blinds some nights weeks hence

reappeared hanging over the wrinkled old river—

rush out by airplane Vancouver New York Moscow

and shout & weep before mind gangs of new kids born
    between wars

with the tan red stain on my index finger dying deeper,
    cigarettes & tea

in too many Cafes from Santiago to Kyoto—

What possible poem to imagine any more, who can't
    even read Blake or Kabir with two hours rat minded light-
    hunger—

Now seem the thrills of scanning the scaly dragon dream
    universe

equal in endlessness boredom to passing my moons playing
    Cards

in third class trains circling the equator, thinking letters to
    write

or creating a network of poetry slaves drugged by the lunacy
    of electronic brain meat—

or simply going home & sitting in the backyard watching the
    cherry blossoms fatten on my tree—

having to pay no taxes to anyone, mumbling in my bedsheets
    while

the same car lights of childhood prison the decade on my
    ceiling—

perhaps even dream up a monster God in the spotted whorls
    of vast eyeball—

My cup runneth over, my speed spilled into one familiar soft
    mouth
month after month, as if another birth won't connect life
together after death, all be black beforgotten from before—
Not even doom, not even Hell except what this is already
my mouth dry and having to get up & go out in the chill
    twilight to take a pee
trying to write a poem—whatever that could·be,
scribbling in a vast book of blank pages, hoping my death will
    make sense of chaos notations—
dashes which lead only to the next consciousness trying to
    shake itself and be free
like a vulture circling over a green donkey field, like Lenin
    wagging his beard
and raising his index finger into the air to signal the rag-
    booted masses
a new Futurity! Archaic Eden and electric Serpent and my soul
    Eve
Curious over the fruit before her face, noisily humming with
    radio messages inside.
Poetry's the old apple tastes of death's tasteless eternity,
Morphine worm that eats itself—Peter goes to fetch chicken
    Tanduri
from the rickshaw thoroughfare a mile away—he's got his
    body out on the streets
in alleys with bright bulbs and cloth patterns, and plaster
    Vishnus lying on a painted snakey bed—the same
    endlessness
that wandering leads me mornings to the stone porch and the
    trident and fire & pipe

and naked saddhus who don't talk, crosslegged smoking dope
    to overlook the corpse meat-dolls
people bodies bursting and black-charred falling apart on log
    woodpiles by Ganges green fields
morning down below long bridges in the distance filling
    empty space half thousand miles
to familiar Calcutta filled with newspapers and war and
    burning trams
by railroad stations where soldiers wave from trains at
    homeless lepers sleeping months on huge concrete floors.
India's hopeless existence, repeating the name of the Lord in
    the Kali Yuga, begging workless disconnected from rocket
    dams bursting over the torrential mudpie oceans—
We'll be on the moon before I die, & maybe eat bread on
    Saturn—
receive some heavenly message radio waves at Jodrell Bank—
    escape in the mind
to rearrange the molecules of existence to a new Kaleido-
    scope China—
See perhaps beautiful yellow cheeks and brows, new bellies to
    dominate the four
directions of space & fill up time with their fried Pork Chow
    Mein—
even if everybody eats Peking Duck with orange sauce, and
    has two children
won't life be as useless as ever? But I wouldn't know
    anymore—what others should do
with the vital breath, and the lungs and testacles we have all
    been given—
Once I thought to rebuild the world to supreme Reality

Emulsive consciousness developing in national brains and
    factories incandescent with human toys—
What, robots with light bulbs to do our dying for us—eat our
    steak, and let us fuck them too—
Once I thought the cracked walls of the moral house peeled
    back, beneath the spectral plaster
saw the vast Bauhaus built in God by God for God in Man—
Once I thought that by laugher & patience, by not scheming,
    by no ascetic sneer,
the giant radiostation of eternity would tune us in to an
    endless program
that broadcast only ourselves forever—now I hear the ringing
    of gongs and skull drums in Hindu temples,
cries on the streets, peasant women waving sticks at hungry
    cows, the light bulb burning white
only so I can transcribe the wierd suffering details
for whom to read, myself & my fond dying indifferent
    trapped fellows—
Ah—in comes Peter with two big dead stuffed chickens to eat.

II

So we ate cold chicken squatting on a mattress, 25 rupees 5 dol-
lars worth while the old lady beggar I been watching on the corner steps downstairs rocked back & forth on her heels for the
4th successive day. Sleepless as last night no sleep, & all morn
feeding bananas to monkeys on the roof at sunrise & then to
Police to give papers registration address—the policeman a jolly
type baffled by our presence: "Why do you want to say here in
India so long?"

Baffled myself out on the balcony staring down at the evening crowds and lights, a gang of cows & bulls burping angrily—gathered together munching the dried refuse of leaf-plates piled near the corner water pump. I stared in wonder—are they all walking corpses? At the burning ground the bodies are just the same, only they're not moving, they're dead corpses, here—all these gongs being rung & cigaretts sold across the road—and along came mincing an Indian devotee with the step of Quepie Doll Hugh Herbert, & he was covered with flowers round his neck, carrying a brass tray of little white sugarballs (god food. Prasad)—approached by a beggar he stoped gaily & dug up a palmful of candy, gave it to outstretched hand, & went mincing his way on the concrete path to the river, to temple probably to mind his evening before sleepdeath tonite. "They're all mad" I said to Peter, "Chinese invasions indeed!" They'll see some kinda Chinese invasion aint been seen any old thousand years ever.

III

In bed all day recovering awake from sleepless nite 3/4 grain M—going on & off balcony to stare down at street—Bulls grunting, they eat offal & garbage—some sleep in the concrete garbage dump tanks on Godowlia Corner—

Processions of rat-a-tat drums marching down the street—straggling behind big drum, four coolies beating posters advertising a hot romantic movie—fat hero with big tits & double chin & Indian movie queen with round cheeks—"Kum Kum"—and a whisp of hair arranged over the eyebrow—a child ahead banging cymbals.

Or a marriage procession in yellow & orange silk the groom, his long shirt tied to bride's veiled sari figure followed by a dozen ratty relatives & a couple of wheezing old beggars banging on drums rhythmically.

or several times a day on the street a small group carrying a shoulder-high bamboo litter with a corpse swathed in orange or white shroud—saying aloud the gang Jai Citaram or Ram Nam Ram Nam—threading their way thru slow moving cows, rickshaws abycicle, hand carts with huge wheels, oxcarts dragged along by wood yoke to the ox-hump—the procession to the burning ghats passing down a main street or into little streets & thin alleyways crowded with potato chop stalls & teashops & portable salt-snacks, bearers carrying wicker baskets of brown dry hot noodles & roast peas.

Went down for milk & cigarettes—at the tobacco stall always greeted by Jai Guru or Jai Hind—I reply Jai Tarama or Jai Krishna or Jai Citaram & namaste clasped hands to brow or breast, clutching cigarettes & matches in one fist.

The dood (milk) shop, mixer salesman squatting barefoot on a wet stone board, pouring tea & milk from aluminum cup to glass or clay pot—the local dogs "fried in ghee"—mangy Breughel curs with gentle manners, three dogs living together in the milk stall alley each has an injured foot & pink flesh showing thru scarred, ribbed dogbitten flea buzzed hairskin. One dog walks on 3 legs, the left back leg retracted up above the level of his balls, as if a spasm came & left it tied up there—barks with hideous gargle at rival dogs invading his milk shop pavement territory—licks up the charcoal-milk-cow-piss-dish-water running in pools in the broken concrete. I gave him some milk several days ago.

I had chicken bones to dispose of in a Quality Restaurant box—sneaked him a handful and as I left heard the snarling & yipes of a 4 dog fight—I sneaked guiltily around the Ganges side street market looking for a trash barrow to leave my cannibal bones hid from Hindu Paranoiac gazers.

Sat & drank nice warm milk & watched the big white cow (always stealing vegetables in broad daylight from the gang of peasant women with baskets of herbs) lick the mangy three legged dog's neck with his big wise tongue.

Dec 22, 8 PM—

Walking (in dhoti & lumberjack shirt) thru Benares alleyways, turning corners past toy stands, thru red gates up Vishwanath alley past the temple—thru a grate seeing crowd round the lingam chanting slow-beat of drum vary-voiced tuneless mass—beautiful harmonies, ending as I passed out the back courtyard past the huge stone cow, with acceleration of drums—past the square where in daytime sell red and blue & yellow bright colored powders displayed in cones of dust—

down to Manikarnika ghat (with small photos of Howrah & Naga saddhu naked in pocket—to show him—arrived on street thru woodpile up alley down steps to take a crap by riverside, pushing aside open rear of my dhoti, sick diarrhea, washing my skin on the steps of river (with left hand?) No, right—

then up to Dharmashala sand-floored base level & sat in circles with Sadhus & a university bursar & the Naga I knew & silver haird fellow with boxer's or alcoholic's face but he cold sober smoking ganja by firelight—logs from burning pits brought up in clay dishes or iron tongs, still red & shining in square ash bed banked with sand—Shiva trident in ground—Sadhu came over,

saw pix asked me to send him—to some difficult address in a Calcutta ghat—I promised—Sat smoking pipe (coughing firesmoke
blown & my eyes watering & nose running) then moved over
against wall on straw mat, touched Sadhu Naga's foot & con-
versed w/ English speaking Bursar—

then after long hour by fire, started home, blue sky specked
with stars, there was Orion's belt near in the sky—I squatted to
pee over a high stone path right down into the river, with bub-
bing noise falling down the 15 feet—

as squatting to pee

on the night Ganges—

Back there the firelit ghats.

Looking back I saw the several log fires burning orange, noticed
& remembered it to record, as Haiku.

By home—an argument between a Hindu w/ club & a blue
turbaned Sikh—crowd circled—up the street the prone body,
rag covered, can flat on ground a few feet away—one lit a match
to her head, new shaven a few weeks ago—blood trickling down
skull—a "motor" accident.

HERMANN HESSE

(1 8 7 7 – 1 9 6 2)

The German writer Hermann Hesse, who won the Nobel Prize for Literature in 1946 and became fashionable in the 1960s with his novels *Siddhartha* (1927) and *The Glass-Bead Game* (1943), was born in 1877 in a family of Indophiles. Both his grandfather and father had worked for long years as missionaries in south India; many languages and cultures passed through their house in a town near the Black Forest. Hesse himself traveled to India as late as 1911, after he had already established his reputation as a novelist. But as the following excerpt from his essay "Childhood of the Magician" (1923) shows, Hesse's great preoccupations—the soulless mechanization of modern life, the rise of western militarism, the need for self-knowledge and stillness—seem to have been created by a childhood steeped in India, enriched by what were then only the intimations of a "wider world, a greater homeland, a more ancient descent, a broader context."

from CHILDHOOD OF THE MAGICIAN
(1923)

Again and yet again, lovely and ancient saga,
I descend into your fountain,
Hear your golden lieder,
How you laugh, how you dream, how softly you weep.

As a warning from your depths
Comes the whispered word of magic;
Drunken and asleep, so I seem,
And you call me forth and away . . .

Not by parents and teachers alone was I educated, but by higher, more arcane and mysterious powers as well, among them the god Pan, who stood in my grandfather's glass cabinet in the guise of a little dancing Hindu idol. This deity, and others too, took an interest in me during my childhood years, and long before I could read and write they so filled me with age-old Eastern images and ideas that later, whenever I met a Hindu or Chinese sage, it was like a reunion, a homecoming. And yet I am a European, was, in fact, born with the sign of the Archer on the ascendant, and all my life have zealously practiced the Western virtues of impetuosity, greed, and unquenchable curiosity. Fortunately, like most children, I had learned what is most valuable, most indispensable for life before my school years began, taught by apple trees, by rain and sun, river and woods, bees and beetles, taught by the god Pan, taught by the dancing idol in my grandfather's treasure room. I knew my way around in the world, I associated fearlessly with animals and stars. I was at home in orchards and with fishes in the water, and I could already sing a good number of songs. I could do magic too, a skill that I unfortunately soon forgot and had to relearn at a very advanced age—and I possessed all the legendary wisdom of childhood.

To this, formal schooling was now added, and it came easy to me, was amusing. The school prudently did not concern itself with those important accomplishments that are indispensable for life, but chiefly with frivolous and attractive entertainments, in which I often took pleasure, and with bits of information, many that have remained loyally with me all my life; for instance, today I still know beautiful, witty Latin sayings, verses, and maxims and the number of inhabitants in many cities in all quarters of the globe, not as they are today, of course, but as they were in the 1880s.

Up to my thirteenth year I never seriously considered what I should one day become or what profession I should choose. Like all boys, I loved and envied many callings: the hunter, the raftsman, the railroad conductor, the high-wire performer, the Arctic explorer. My greatest preference by far, however, would have been to be a magician. This was the deepest, most profoundly felt direction of my impulses, springing from a certain dissatisfaction with what people call "reality" and what seemed to me at times simply a silly conspiracy of the grownups; very early I felt a definite rejection of this reality, at times timorous, at times scornful, and the burning wish to change it by magic, to transform it, to heighten it. In my childhood this magic wish was directed toward childish external goals: I should have liked to make apples grow in winter and through magic to fill my purse with gold and silver. I dreamed of crippling my enemies by magic and then shaming them through my magnanimity, and of being called forth as champion and king; I wanted to be able to find buried treasures, to raise the dead, and to make myself invisible. It was this art of making oneself invisible that I considered most important and coveted most deeply. This desire, as for all the magic powers, has accompanied me all my life in many forms, which often I did not immediately recognize. Thus it happened later on, long after I had grown up and was practicing the calling of writer, that I frequently tried to disappear behind my creations, to rechristen myself and hide behind playfully contrived names—attempts which oddly enough were frequently misunderstood by my fellow writers and were held against me. When I look back, it seems to me that my whole life has been influenced by this desire for magic powers; how the objects of these magical wishes changed with the times, how I gradually withdrew my efforts from the outer world and concentrated them upon myself, how I came to aspire to replace the crude invisibility of the magic cloak with the invisibility of the wise man who, perceiving all, remains always unperceived—this would be the real content of my life's story.

I was an active and happy boy, playing with the beautiful, many-colored world, at home everywhere, not less with animals and plants than in the primeval forest of my own fantasies and dreams, happy in my powers and abilities, more delighted than consumed by my burning desires. I exercised many magic powers at that time without knowing it, much more completely than I was ever able to do later on. It was easy for me to win love, easy to exercise influence over others, I had no trouble playing the role of ringleader or of the admired one or the man of mystery. For years at a time I kept my younger friends and relations respectfully convinced of my literally magic power, of my mastery over demons, of my title to crowns and buried treasures. For a long time I lived in paradise, although my parents early made me acquainted with the serpent. Long enduring was my childish dream that the world belonged to me, that only the present existed, that everything was disposed about me to be a beautiful game. If on occasion discomfort or yearning arose in me, if now and then the happy world seemed shadowed and ambiguous, then for the most part it was easy for me to find my way into that other freer, more malleable world of fantasy, and when I returned from it, I found the outer world once more charming and worthy of my love. For a long time I lived in paradise.

There was a wooden shed in my father's small garden where I kept rabbits and a tame raven. There I spent endless hours, long as geological ages, in warmth and blissful ownership; the rabbits smelled of life, of grass and milk, of blood and procreation; and in the raven's hard, black eye shone the lamp of eternal life. In the same place I spent other endless epochs in the evenings, beside a guttering candle with the warm, sleeping animals, alone or in the company of a friend, and sketched out plans for discovering immense treasures, finding the mandrake root and launching victorious crusades throughout the world, which was so much in need of deliverance, crusades on which I would execute robbers, free miserable captives, raze thieves' strongholds, have traitors crucified, forgive runaway vassals, win kings' daughters, and understand the language of animals.

There was an enormously big heavy book in my grandfather's large library; I often looked through it and read here and there. This inexhaustible book contained marvelous old pictures— sometimes you could find them when you first opened the book and leafed about, there they were bright and inviting; sometimes you could search for a long time and not find them at all, they were gone, magicked away as though they had never existed. There was a story in this book, exceedingly beautiful and incomprehensible, that I read again and again. It too was not always to be found, the hour had to be favorable, often it had completely disappeared and would keep itself hidden, often it seemed as though it had changed its residence and address; sometimes when you read it, it was strangely friendly and almost understandable, at other times it was all dark and forbidding like the door in the attic behind which at times in the twilight you could hear ghosts chattering or groaning. Everything was full of reality and everything was full of magic, the two grew confidently side by side, both of them belonged to me.

Then too the dancing idol from India which stood in my grandfather's fabulous glass cabinet was not always the same idol, did not always have the same face, did not dance the same dance at all hours. Sometimes he was an idol, a strange and rather droll figure such as are made and worshipped in strange, incomprehensible countries by strange and incomprehensible people. At other times he was a magical object, full of meaning, infinitely sinister, avid for sacrifices, malevolent, harsh, unreliable, sardonic—he seemed to be tempting me to laugh at him in order afterward to take vengeance on me. He could change his expression although he was made of yellow metal; sometimes he leered. Again at other times he was all symbol, was neither ugly nor beautiful, neither evil nor good, laughable nor frightful, but simply old and inscrutable as a rune, as a lichen on a rock, as the lines on a pebble, and behind his form, behind his face and image, lived God, the Infinite lurked there, which at that time as a boy, without knowing its name, I recognized and revered not less than in later days when I called it Shiva, Vishnu, named it God, Life, Brahman, Atman, Tao, or Eternal Mother. It was father, was mother, it was woman and man, sun and moon.

And around the idol in the glass cabinet and in other of Grandfather's cabinets stood and hung and lay many other beings and objects, strings of wooden beads like rosaries, rolls of palm leaves inscribed with ancient Hindu writing, turtles carved out of green soapstone, little images of God made of wood, of glass, of quartz, of clay, embroidered silk and linen covers, brass cups and bowls, and all this came from India and from Ceylon, from Paradise Island with its fern trees and palm-lined shores and gentle doe-eyed Singhalese, it came from Siam and from Burma, and everything smelled of the sea, of spice and far places, of cinnamon and sandalwood, all had passed through brown and yellow hands, been drenched by tropic rains and Ganges water, dried by the equatorial sun, shaded by primeval forests. All these things belonged to my grandfather, and he, the ancient, venerable, and powerful one with the white beard, omniscient, mightier than any father and mother, he possessed other things and powers as well, his were not only the Hindu idols and toys, all the carved, painted, magically endowed objects, the coconut-shell cups and sandalwood chests, the hall and the library, he was a magician too, a wise man, a sage. He understood all the languages of mankind, more than thirty, perhaps the language of the gods as well, perhaps that of the stars, he could write and speak Pali and Sanskrit, he could sing the songs of the Kanarese, of Bengal, Hindustan, Senegal, he knew the religious exercises of the Mohammedans and the Buddhists though he was a Christian and believed in the triune God; for many years and decades he had lived in hot, dangerous, Oriental countries, had traveled in boats and in oxcarts, on horses and donkeys, no one knew as well as he that our city and our country were only a very small part of the earth, that a thousand million people had other beliefs than ours, other customs, languages, skin colors, other gods, virtues, and vices. I loved him, honored him, and feared him, from him I expected everything, to him I attributed everything, from him and his god Pan disguised in the likeness of an idol I learned unceasingly. This man, my mother's father, was hidden in a forest of mysteries, just as his face was hidden in the white forest of his beard; from his eyes there flowed sorrow for the world and there also flowed blithe wisdom, as the case might be, lonely wisdom and divine roguishness; people from many lands knew him, visited and honored him, talked to him in English, French, Indian, Italian, Malayan and went off after long conversations leaving no clue to their identity, perhaps his friends, perhaps his emissaries, perhaps his servants, his agents. From him, from this unfathomable one, I knew, came the secret that surrounded my mother, the secret, age-old mystery, and she too had been in India for a long time, she too could speak and sing in Malayan and Kanarese, she exchanged phrases and maxims with her aged father in strange, magical tongues. And at times she possessed, like him, the stranger's smile, the veiled smile of wisdom.

My father was different. He stood alone, belonging neither to the world of the idols and of my grandfather nor to the workaday world of the city. He stood to one side, lonely, a sufferer and a seeker, learned and kindly, without falseness and full of zeal in the service of truth, but far removed from that noble and tender but unmistakable smile—he had no trace of mystery. The kindliness never forsook him, nor his cleverness, but he never disappeared in the magic cloud that surrounded my grandfather, his face never dissolved in that childlikeness and godlikeness whose interplay at times looked like sadness, at times like delicate mockery, at times like the silent, inward-looking mask of God. My father did not talk to my mother in Hindu languages, but spoke English and a pure, clear, beautiful German faintly col-

ored with a Baltic accent. It was this German he used to attract
and win me and instruct me; at times I strove to emulate him,
full of admiration and zeal, all too much zeal, although I knew
that my roots reached deeper into my mother's soil, into the
dark-eyed and mysterious. My mother was full of music, my
father was not, he could not sing.

Along with me, sisters were growing up, and two older brothers, envied and admired. Around us was the little city, old and
hunchbacked, and around it the forest-covered mountains, severe
and somewhat dark, and through its midst flowed a beautiful
river, curving and hesitant, and all this I loved and called home,
and in the woods and river, I was well acquainted with the growing things and the soil, stones and caves, birds and squirrels,
foxes and fishes. All this belonged to me, was mine, was home—
but in addition there were the glass cabinet and the library and
the kindly mockery in the omniscient face of my grandfather,
and the dark, warm glance of my mother, and the turtles and
idols, the Hindu songs and sayings, and these things spoke to me
of a wider world, a greater homeland, a more ancient descent, a
broader context. And high up in his wire cage sat our grave par-
rot, old and wise, with a scholar's face and a sharp beak, singing
and talking, and he too came from afar, from the unknown, flut-
ing the language of the jungles and smelling of the equator.
Many worlds, many quarters of the earth, extended arms, sent
forth rays which met and intersected in our house. And the
house was big and old, with many partly empty rooms, with cel-
lars and great resounding corridors that smelled of stone and
coolness, and endless attics full of lumber and fruit and drafts
and dark emptiness. Rays of light from many worlds intersected
in this house. Here people prayed and read the Bible, here they

studied and practiced Hindu philology, here much good music was played, here there was knowledge of Buddha and Lao-tse, guests came from many countries with the breath of strangeness and of foreignness on their clothes, with odd trunks of leather and of woven bark and the sound of strange tongues, the poor were fed here and holidays were celebrated, science and myth lived side by side. There was a grandmother, too, whom we rather feared and did not know very well because she spoke no German and read a French Bible. Complex and not understood by everyone was the life of this house, the play of light here was many-colored, rich and multitudinous were the sounds of life. It was beautiful and it pleased me, but more beautiful still was the world of my wishful thinking, richer still the play of my waking dreams. Reality was never enough, there was need of magic.

Magic was native to our house and to my life. Besides the cabinets of my grandfather there were my mother's cabinets as well, full of Asiatic textiles, cloths, and veils. There was magic too in the leering glance of the idol, and mystery in the smell of many ancient rooms and winding stairways. And there was much inside me that corresponded to these externals. There were objects and connections that existed only within me and for me alone. Nothing was so mysterious, so incommunicable, so far removed from commonplace actuality as were these, and yet there was nothing more real. This was true even of the capricious comings and goings of the pictures and stories in that big book, and the transformations in the aspect of things which I saw occurring from hour to hour. How different was the look of our front door, the garden shed, and the street on a Sunday evening from on a Monday morning! What a completely different face the wall clock and the image of Christ in the living room wore on a day when Grandfather's spirit dominated than when my father's spirit did, and how very completely all this changed again in those hours when no one else's spirit but my own gave things their signature, when my soul played with things and bestowed on them new names and meanings! At such times a familiar chair or stool, a shadow beside the oven, the headline in a newspaper, could be beautiful or ugly and evil, significant or banal, could cause yearning or fear, laughter or sadness. How little there was that was fixed, stable, enduring! How alive everything was, undergoing transformation and longing for change, on the watch for dissolution and rebirth!

PICO IYER

(1957–)

Pico Iyer was born to Indian parents in England and subsequently moved to America. He was educated in England and now lives in California and Japan. His first book, *Video Nights in Kathmandu* (1988), caught skillfully the opening moments of the vast and multifaceted process we have come to know as cultural globalization. In subsequent years, Iyer continued to report on the different ways in which Asian societies confronted and assimilated American pop culture. In *The Lady and the Monk* (1993) Iyer wrote about his own ambiguous journey to the East. In recent years, Iyer has attempted to describe the workings of what he calls "the global soul": the rootless cosmopolitan who is denied the certainties and self-righteousness of exile by cheap air travel, and who is restlessly at home wherever he is. Iyer has written several travel essays on India. But few of them can match the subtle power of the following excerpt from his novel *Abandon* (2003). Iyer describes here a jaded English academic's journey to Delhi, Jaipur, and Agra, and invests these over-familiar sites of tourism with a sense of the uncanny and the mysterious.

from ABANDON

British Airways flies through the night to London, and then through another night to Delhi. When he arrived, in the dark of 1 a.m., there were figures coming toward him out of the mist,

98

shrouded in blankets, only their eyes staring out through the phantasmal chill: "Sir, please, sir, come with me." "Sir, best price for you." It was always like a graveyard outside the international airport—he remembered even from his trip in college—and the number of figures had increased, moving without direction in the brown light, wrapped in turbans, their dark eyes sharp.

He got into a broken-down Ambassador, some of the shawled figures getting in on all sides, turning around from the front to smile or gawk at him, scrambling into the backseat to sit beside him and guard his carry-on. As they drove into the spectral capital in the night—it was 2 a.m. now, local time—he felt as if he were moving through a battlefield at the end of some medieval war. Here and there, figures were sitting by small fires along the side of the road, their eyes wild as the headlights caught them, while others plodded along with bullocks in the middle of the half-deserted street. The air was brown, over everything a kind of filthy mist, and the buildings that came occasionally looming out of the dark, illuminated, looked more unreal than ever, like painted models. India had the one thing that California lacked, he realized—the theme of all his research coming back to him—native ghosts. Everywhere the sense of unseen and unburied spirits taking over the imperial city while the people slept.

He took an early breakfast—one thing they still did well here—at a hotel Martine had told him about once, scribbled off a card to her, and then returned through the fog, less mysterious now the sun had risen, to catch the early flight to Jaipur. At the other end, pushing his way through the confusion of the small terminal, all the mystery and menace of the thronging crowds gone in the morning light, he found a man, impeccably got up in dark suit and tie, holding up a sign on which "Mr. MacMillane" had been written.

The man led him farther out into the clamor, and opened the door to a grey Mercedes. Hussein was putting him up in a hotel near his house—his way of showing that he knew foreign tastes—and so they drove out into the town: huge billboards with large women spilling out of saris and men dancing around miniskirts, little stalls that looked like they'd been swept forty years ago toward a wastepaper basket they'd never quite reached, the commotion of cows and bicycles and ringing bells made many times worse by the sudden profusion of cars. In such a world, he thought, who wouldn't want to gather in secret at dead of night and take himself out of all this? The human impulse to escape would never go away: God has to be understood in the context of everything that is not Him.

As they drew away from the town—the clangor and the big streets quickly fading—the driver put on a tape (another sign of Hussein's wish to be seen as sophisticated, or else just his habit of directing everything), and the blowing winds and uprising sands of desert music came up as they passed, almost instantly, into open spaces. Already the villages around them were nothing but mud-baked houses, children crowding over fires, the wind outside sending red and orange and green and blue scarves fleeting against their faces in the dust. Dark eyes watched the carriage from their fairy tales move past, beseeching, angry, startled, and soon even they were gone, and there was nothing but brown earth, brown walls, dry stone—an ancient space of almost atavistic emptiness.

At last they came to a large driveway—he could have been in California, he thought, in Palm Springs or some other garish attempt to fill the empty space—and pulled up to a huge house, crumbling but clearly elegant. Hussein was waiting for him at the door (the driver having called ahead when they were two minutes away), and came out to greet him as if they were oldest friends. Talk, he recalled, was never difficult in India, especially for an Englishman people were eager to impress.

He was led into an old-fashioned reception room—the stuff of Indian fantasy, he thought—and Hussein circled around the topic at hand, asking him about the flight, offering him a drink, so perfectly slipping into the part he had chosen to play that it became quite impossible to see him. He, too, had become archetypal—the employer's prerogative—and every last urbanity seemed like another veil thrown up, or a kind of fog. He could no more be identified than the men looming up in the mist the evening before.

"You must be exhausted," he said in that Indian way that was more warning than commiseration. "And absolutely famished. Let me get you something to take the edge off your hunger before we have a look at the manuscript." He was daring him, he realized, to see him as cliché; in India, a man in a house like this would do everything possible to insist on his distance from the role, so as to lure his visitor into an assumption and then leave him at a disadvantage. The first prerogative of power is to do as it chooses and not even look at the rules it is breaking.

"Of course I don't expect you to come to any decision right away. In fact, I wouldn't want you to; haste would be a kind of waste, don't you think? Besides, this is India." Every sentence reminding him of where he stood and whom he was seeing. "But I'd like you to take just a peek at it. Before you return to your hotel. So you can think about what you have to work with."

They walked into a library—again, it looked like a Sherlock Holmes movie, with a huge spherical globe at the center and nineteenth-century editions covering all the shelves, a scattering of dust—and the man extracted a key and pulled something out from a desk. "Here, don't be shy," his host offered, and he came around and found himself looking at a book like none he'd ever seen. A few Arabic characters were printed on the cover, framed by curlicues, and inside were pages upon pages of small script, written as tightly as a Quran. As in an illuminated manuscript from England, some characters were written in red, and gold had been used unsparingly.

"It's beautiful."

"Isn't it? One of the few things that didn't get carted off to the British Museum. In any case, I don't, as I say, want you to say anything now. Mum's the word. Just take the image back to the hotel, join me for dinner, and you can look at it properly in the morning."

The whole thing was a charade, of course: he recalled Sefadhi's advice to authenticate nothing, however impressive it looked. His job was only to give the man a little time. "It doesn't really matter what he has"—the professor's final words. "These old palaces in India are full of everything. The important thing is that the awareness that he has something does not get out. That we keep it to ourselves."

Bearing this in mind, he checked into his hotel and lay out in the sun. Outside the walls, the desert wind blew, and at dusk the lights came on as in a miniature. For all the otherworldliness of the setting, he ran a long bath in his cabana, and thought of her; he called, once it was late enough, but all he could hear—this was still India—was her tentative "Hello? Hello?" and then a startled putting down of the receiver: she must have deemed it an intruder, or someone from her past.

He dined with his generous host, heard about Mountbatten and the Travellers' Club, pulled out such pieces of his past—Oxford, Wodehouse—as were part of the local currency, and, in the morning, returned early to spend all day with the text. Whatever it was, it was beautiful—he thought of the dome of the mosque in Damascus, of Persian carpets he had seen, and the Qurans so small they fit inside an earlobe. Not all the script was intelligible to him, but it didn't matter: he was walking through another world, of cool courtyards and the sound of water, and above everything there was a patterning of gold and peacock blue.

The book might have been drawn up by some loyal retainer a generation ago; that would take nothing away from its radiance. The centuries collapsed in India, so no one really seemed to care what was new and what was millennia-old, any more than they would worry about whether this copy of *Reader's Digest* came from last week or a century before.

On his last night in the place, after dinner, Hussein asked him if he wanted to see something "absolutely unexpected," and he followed him up some small, narrow, winding stairs to a rooftop, where his host (ever-surprising) kept a telescope. Lights were intermittent from this vantage point, but the older man fumbled and cursed at the lenses till they could see the planets as clearly as he had seen her, a few days before.

"You've come to some conclusion about my manuscript," said the man, screwing up a lens.

"Not at all. All I can tell you is it's beautiful, which you know already. As you also know, the likelihood of its being original, or worth anything, is next to nothing, I'm afraid."

The man held on to his demeanor as if he was remembering what the English said about sangfroid.

"What I'd recommend is keeping it here, with all your other treasures"—a nice touch—"and enjoying it whenever possible. Whatever you might get for it would not be worthy of it in any way."

This had been Sefadhi's suggestion, and again it seemed to work: the Englishman from across the seas had somehow converted disappointment into something to be cherished.

"You wouldn't recommend other appraisers?"

"Obviously, it wouldn't be in my interests to do so. But even to be disinterested for the moment"—"Be an Englishman with him," Sefadhi had said, "that's all he wants"—"I think too many hands would only injure what is, whatever its provenance, a gesture of love."

These were the right words to use, and the man smiled again, flattered at the quality of the messenger, if not his message. "Jolly good," he said, in that engagingly antiquated way the foreigner remembered from his other visit. "Shall we go down and celebrate with a cigar?" The "celebrate" a gesture of thanks to him.

On the way back to Delhi, he stopped off in Agra, as he'd promised her. "I know it made me almost fall asleep with disappointment when I was a teenager," he'd said, "but our eyes change.

Grow up. Before, I didn't know that the gardens were a diagram of Paradise, and I couldn't read the inscription on the dome. I knew nothing about Shah Jahan's connection with the Sufis— the way his son had had the Upanishads translated into Persian, and his daughter had been so ardent a mystic she would have been a sheikh if she had been a he. I was like a nonbeliever staring at a sacred manuscript. I think I'll have grown into it, in a way."

When he walked through the main gateway this time, he thought of the court chronicler of Akbar, centuries before: "Through order, the world becomes a medium of truth and reality; and that which is but external receives through it a spiritual meaning." Amidst the dust and the noise and the crowds of the city around, the cab drivers with their whispers, the boys with their carpet shops "close close," the squiggled commotion of nonlinear India—surely no clearer when Shah Jahan was on the throne—the building made a different kind of sense. In its way, in fact, it seemed a kind of Sufi parable: while the visitors thronged into the main chamber, bright with lapis and carnelian and jade, letting their voices echo around its great dome, the real meaning of the place, Martine had told him, was all underground. "You've got to go there at dusk," she'd said, "after the heat's gone down, and the crowds have begun to thin out. Just before the gates are closed. If you're lucky, the small gate will be open. The whole point of the Taj is what you can't see."

He went back to a hotel for lunch, having taken in the details and oriented himself, as meticulous as any spy circling around his prey—every Sufi poem has a face it shows the world, and a secret life that is its own: a Sufi building is a model of the soul.

Then, in late afternoon, he went back through the great gates, paying again, just as lights were beginning to come on across the Yamuna, and water buffalo were gathering along the far shore to drink. The crowds of villagers in flaming orange and scarlet and golden saris—antidotes to the deserts where they lived—were just about gone now, subdued into murmurings, and as the sun declined into mist across the polluted river, guards were walking about the benches with torches, making sure no one was hiding in the dark.

As he hovered around the great entrance, trying to make himself unobtrusive, suddenly, amazed, he saw a faint light—a naked bulb only—shining from the bottom of a flight of stairs plunging down. He descended quickly, so quickly he almost slipped on the recently washed steps, and at the bottom he came out into a strange inner chamber, hushed and small, where two men were pouring water on the floor.

One of the men—both dark, and dressed in the clothes of the poor, dirty white shirts and grey trousers—shuffled over to one of the great caskets in the room, and placed a lighted stick of incense on it. Then a rose. A few moments later, he took another stick of incense and a rose and put them on the other casket, built like an afterthought on the side, housing the man who dreamed up the palace, now beside his wife. The decorations on his tomb were flowers, on hers verses from the Quran.

Above them, just faintly coming down the steps, were the last voices of sightseers trying out the echo, amazed to have the great dome talk back to them and no one else. Their voices climbing up toward the rafters, and then reverberating around and around them in circles. But the caskets they were so busily serenading were empty ones, ruses to distract the world from the real spirits buried in this underground place.

The men said nothing, just went quietly, devotedly, about their task. He was the only other one in the company of the tombs. His feet on the marble floor—Damascus again—were cold. He felt in some way that he didn't try to explain to himself, or even to make clear, that being here was a large part of what reading his poems, seeing her was about. Under the public exterior, there was always an unvisited deep vault.

RUTH PRAWER JHABVALA

(1 9 2 7 –)

Ruth Prawer Jhabvala was born in Germany, in a family of Polish Jews, and was educated in London. In 1951, she married an Indian architect and began a long and productive stay in India. In 1975, she moved to New York. She is primarily known now for her screen adaptations of novels by E. M. Forster and Henry James, and for her long collaboration with the producer-director team Merchant-Ivory. But Jhabvala's corpus of novels and short stories, which include the Booker Prize–winning *Heat and Dust* (1975), established her as one of the most insightful chroniclers of both middle-class Indians and the western Indophiles. Her fastidious irony seems to hide an exasperation with the double-talk of modernizing Indians, and with the well-off westerners who claim to find a special spiritual wisdom in India. But her Chekhovian sensitivity to mood and setting manages to override the frequently stereotypical depiction of Indians and westerners. The short story excerpted here has all her stock characters: the old British memsahib, her Indian guru, the western-educated Indian, and his weak and confused English wife. Their profound dependence upon each other gives the story its pathos, but its real power lies in its evocative sense of place and the moments of solitude in which Jhabvala catches her characters.

TWO MORE UNDER
THE INDIAN SUN

Elizabeth had gone to spend the afternoon with Margaret. They were both English, but Margaret was a much older woman and they were also very different in character. But they were both in love with India, and it was this fact that drew them together. They sat on the veranda, and Margaret wrote letters and Elizabeth addressed the envelopes. Margaret always had letters to write; she led a busy life and was involved with several organizations of a charitable or spiritual nature. Her interests were centered in such matters, and Elizabeth was glad to be allowed to help her.

There were usually guests staying in Margaret's house. Sometimes they were complete strangers to her when they first arrived, but they tended to stay weeks, even months, at a time—holy men from the Himalayas, village welfare workers, organizers of conferences on spiritual welfare. She had one constant visitor throughout the winter, an elderly government officer who, on his retirement from service, had taken to a spiritual life and gone to live in the mountains at Almora. He did not, however, very much care for the winter cold up there, so at that season he came down to Delhi to stay with Margaret, who was always pleased to have him. He had a soothing effect on her—indeed, on anyone with whom he came into contact, for he had cast anger and all other bitter passions out of his heart and was consequently always smiling and serene. Everyone affectionately called him Babaji.

He sat now with the two ladies on the veranda, gently rocking himself to and fro in a rocking chair, enjoying the winter sunshine and the flowers in the garden and everything about him. His companions, however, were less serene. Margaret, in fact, was beginning to get angry with Elizabeth. This happened quite frequently, for Margaret tended to be quickly irritated, and especially with a meek and conciliatory person like Elizabeth.

"It's very selfish of you," Margaret said now.

Elizabeth flinched. Like many very unselfish people, she was always accusing herself of undue selfishness, so that whenever this accusation was made by someone else it touched her closely. But because it was not in her power to do what Margaret wanted, she compressed her lips and kept silent. She was pale with this effort at obstinacy.

"It's your duty to go," Margaret said. "I don't have much time for people who shirk their duty."

"I'm sorry, Margaret," Elizabeth said, utterly miserable, utterly ashamed. The worst of it, almost, was that she really wanted to go; there was nothing she would have enjoyed more. What she was required to do was take a party of little Tibetan orphans on a holiday treat to Agra and show them the Taj Mahal. Elizabeth loved children, she loved little trips and treats, and she loved the Taj Mahal. But she couldn't go, nor could she say why.

Of course Margaret very easily guessed why, and it irritated her more than ever. To challenge her friend, she said bluntly, "Your Raju can do without you for those few days. Good heavens, you're not a honeymoon couple, are you? You've been married long enough. Five years."

"Four," Elizabeth said in a humble voice.

"Four, then. I can hardly be expected to keep count of each wonderful day. Do you want me to speak to him?"

"Oh no."

"I will, you know. It's nothing to me. I won't mince my words." She gave a short, harsh laugh, challenging anyone to stop her from speaking out when occasion demanded. Indeed, at the thought of anyone doing so, her face grew red under her crop of gray hair, and a pulse throbbed in visible anger in her tough, tanned neck.

Elizabeth glanced imploringly toward Babaji. But he was rocking and smiling and looking with tender love at two birds pecking at something on the lawn.

"There are times when I can't help feeling you're afraid of him," Margaret said. She ignored Elizabeth's little disclaiming cry of horror. "There's no trust between you, no understanding. And married life is nothing if it's not based on the twin rocks of trust and understanding."

Babaji liked this phrase so much that he repeated it to himself several times, his lips moving soundlessly and his head nodding with approval.

"In everything I did," Margaret said, "Arthur was with me. He had complete faith in me. And in those days—Well." She chuckled. "A wife like me wasn't altogether a joke."

Her late husband had been a high-up British official, and in those British days he and Margaret had been expected to conform to some very strict social rules. But the idea of Margaret conforming to any rules, let alone those! Her friends nowadays often had a good laugh at it with her, and she had many stories to tell of how she had shocked and defied her fellow countrymen.

"It was people like you," Babaji said, "who first extended the hand of friendship to us."

"It wasn't a question of friendship, Babaji. It was a question of love."

"Ah!" he exclaimed.

"As soon as I came here—and I was only a chit of a girl, Arthur and I had been married just two months—yes, as soon as I set foot on Indian soil, I knew this was the place I belonged. It's funny isn't it? I don't suppose there's any rational explanation for it. But then, when was India ever the place for rational explanations."

Babaji said with gentle certainty, "In your last birth, you were one of us. You were an Indian."

"Yes, lots of people have told me that. Mind you, in the beginning it was quite a job to make them see it. Naturally, they were suspicious—can you blame them? It wasn't like today. I envy you girls married to Indians. You have a very easy time of it."

Elizabeth thought of the first time she had been taken to stay with Raju's family. She had met and married Raju in England, where he had gone for a year on a Commonwealth scholarship, and then had returned with him to Delhi; so it was some time before she met his family, who lived about two hundred miles out of Delhi, on the outskirts of a small town called Ankhpur. They all lived together in an ugly brick house, which was divided into two parts—one for the men of the family, the other for the women. Elizabeth, of course, had stayed in the women's quarters. She couldn't speak any Hindi and they spoke very little English, but they had not had much trouble communicating with her. They managed to make it clear at once that they thought her too ugly and too old for Raju (who was indeed some five years her junior), but also that they did not hold this against her and were ready to accept her, with all her shortcomings, as the will of God. They got a lot of amusement out of her, and she enjoyed being with them. They dressed and undressed her in new saris, and she smiled good-naturedly while they stood around her clapping their hands in wonder and doubling up with laughter. Various fertility ceremonies had been performed over her, and before she left she had been given her share of the family jewelry.

"Elizabeth," Margaret said, "if you're going to be so slow, I'd rather do them myself."

"Just these two left," Elizabeth said, bending more eagerly over the envelopes she was addressing.

"For all your marriage," Margaret said, "sometimes I wonder how much you do understand about this country. You live such a closed-in life."

"I'll just take these inside," Elizabeth said, picking up the envelopes and letters. She wanted to get away, not because she minded being told about her own wrong way of life but because she was afraid Margaret might start talking about Raju again.

It was cold inside, away from the sun. Margaret's house was old and massive, with thick stone walls, skylights instead of windows, and immensely high ceilings. It was designed to keep out the heat in summer, but it also sealed in the cold in winter and became like some cavernous underground fortress frozen through with the cold of earth and stone. A stale smell of rice, curry, and mango chutney was chilled into the air.

Elizabeth put the letters on Margaret's work table, which was in the drawing room. Besides the drawing room, there was a dining room, but every other room was a bedroom, each with its dressing room and bathroom attached. Sometimes Margaret had to put as many as three or four visitors into each bedroom, and on one occasion—this was when she had helped to organize a conference on Meditation as the Modern Curative—the drawing and dining rooms too had been converted into dormitories, with string cots and bedrolls laid out end to end. Margaret was not only an energetic and active person involved in many causes but she was also the soul of generosity, ever ready to throw open her house to any friend or acquaintance in need of shelter. She had thrown it open to Elizabeth and Raju three years ago, when they had had to vacate their rooms almost overnight because the landlord said he needed the accommodation for his relatives. Margaret had given them a whole suite—a bedroom and dressing room and bathroom—to themselves and they had had all their meals with her in the big dining room, where the table was always ready laid with white crockery plates, face down so as not to catch the dust, and a thick white tablecloth that got rather stained toward the end of the week. At first, Raju had been very grateful and had praised their hostess to the skies for her kind and generous character. But as the weeks wore on, and every day, day after day, two or three times a day, they sat with Margaret and whatever other guests she had around the table, eating alternately lentils and rice or string beans with boiled potatoes and beetroot salad, with Margaret always in her chair at the head of the table talking inexhaustibly about her activities and ideas—about Indian spirituality and the Mutiny and village uplift and the industrial revolution—Raju, who had a lot of ideas of his own and rather liked to talk, began to get restive. "But Madam, Madam," he would frequently say, half rising in his chair in his impatience to interrupt her, only to have to sit down again, unsatisfied, and continue with his dinner, because Margaret was too busy with her own ideas to have time to take in his.

Once he could not restrain himself. Margaret was talking about—Elizabeth had even forgotten what it was—was it the first Indian National Congress? At any rate, she said something that stirred Raju to such disagreement that this time he did not restrict himself to the hesitant appeal of "Madam" but said out loud for everyone to hear, "Nonsense, she is only talking nonsense." There was a moment's silence; then Margaret, sensible woman that she was, shut her eyes as a sign that she would not hear and would not see, and, repeating the sentence he had interrupted more firmly than before, continued her discourse on an even keel. It was the other two or three people sitting with them around the table—a Buddhist monk with a large shaved skull, a welfare worker, and a disciple of the Gandhian way of life wearing nothing but the homespun loincloth in which the Mahatma himself had always been so simply clad—it was they who had looked at Raju, and very, very gently one of them had clicked his tongue.

Raju had felt angry and humiliated, and afterward, when they were alone in their bedroom, he had quarreled about it with Elizabeth. In his excitement, he raised his voice higher than he would have if he had remembered that they were in someone else's house, and the noise of this must have disturbed Margaret, who suddenly stood in the doorway, looking at them. Unfortunately, it was just at the moment when Raju, in his anger and frustration, was pulling his wife's hair, and they both stood frozen in this attitude and stared back at Margaret. The next instant, of course, they had collected themselves, and Raju let go of Elizabeth's hair, and she pretended as best she could that all that was happening was that he was helping her comb it. But such a feeble subterfuge would not do before Margaret's penetrating eye, which she kept fixed on Raju, in total silence, for two disconcerting minutes; then she said, "We don't treat English girls that way," and withdrew, leaving the door open behind her as a warning that they were under observation. Raju shut it with a vicious kick. If they had had anywhere else to go, he would have moved out that instant.

Raju never came to see Margaret now. He was a proud person, who would never forget anything he considered a slight to his honor. Elizabeth always came on her own, as she had done today, to visit her friend. She sighed now as she arranged the letters on Margaret's work table; she was sad that this difference had arisen between her husband and her only friend, but she knew that there was nothing she could do about it. Raju was very obstinate. She shivered and rubbed the tops of her arms, goose-pimpled with the cold in that high, bleak room, and returned quickly to the veranda, which was flooded and warm with afternoon sun.

Babaji and Margaret were having a discussion on the relative merits of the three ways toward realization. They spoke of the way of knowledge, the way of action, and that of love. Margaret maintained that it was a matter of temperament, and that while she could appreciate the beauty of the other two ways, for herself there was no path nor could there ever be but that of action. It was her nature.

"Of course it is," Babaji said. "And God bless you for it."

"Arthur used to tease me. He'd say, 'Margaret was born to right all the wrongs of the world in one go.' But I can't help it. It's not in me to sit still when I see things to be done."

"Babaji," said Elizabeth, laughing, "once I saw her—it was during the monsoon, and the river had flooded and the people on the bank were being evacuated. But it wasn't being done quickly enough for Margaret! She waded into the water and came back with someone's tin trunk on her head. All the people shouted, 'Memsahib, Memsahib! What are you doing?' but she didn't take a bit of notice. She waded right back in again and came out with two rolls of bedding, one under each arm."

Elizabeth went pink with laughter, and with pleasure and pride, at recalling this incident. Margaret pretended to be angry and gave her a playful slap, but she could not help smiling, while Babaji clasped his hands in joy and opened his mouth wide in silent, ecstatic laughter.

Margaret shook her head with a last fond smile. "Yes, but I've got into the most dreadful scrapes with this nature of mine. If I'd been born with an ounce more patience, I'd have been a pleasanter person to deal with and life could have been a lot smoother all round. Don't you think so?"

She looked at Elizabeth, who said, "I love you just the way you are."

But a moment later, Elizabeth wished she had not said this. "Yes," Margaret took her up, "that's the trouble with you. You

love everybody just the way they are." Of course she was refer-
ring to Raju. Elizabeth twisted her hands in her lap. These hands
were large and bony and usually red, although she was otherwise
a pale and rather frail person.

The more anyone twisted and squirmed, the less inclined was
Margaret to let them off the hook. Not because this afforded
her any pleasure but because she felt that facts of character must
be faced just as resolutely as any other kinds of fact. "Don't
think you're doing anyone a favor," she said, "by being so indul-
gent toward their faults. Quite on the contrary. And especially in
marriage," she went on unwaveringly. "It's not mutual pamper-
ing that makes a marriage but mutual trust."

"Trust and understanding," Babaji said.

Elizabeth knew that there was not much of these in her marriage. She wasn't even sure how much Raju earned in his job at
the municipality (he was an engineer in the sanitation department), and there was one drawer in their bedroom whose contents she didn't know, for he always kept it locked and the key
with him.

"I'll lend you a wonderful book," Margaret said. "It's called
Truth in the Mind, and it's full of the most astounding insight. It's
by this marvelous man who founded an ashram in Shropshire.
Shafi!" she called suddenly for the servant, but of course he
couldn't hear, because the servants' quarters were right at the
back, and the old man now spent most of his time there, sitting
on a bed and having his legs massaged by a granddaughter.

"I'll call him," Elizabeth said, and got up eagerly.

She went back into the stone-cold house and out again at the
other end. Here were the kitchen and the crowded servant quar-

ters. Margaret could never bear to dismiss anyone, and even the servants who were no longer in her employ continued to enjoy her hospitality. Each servant had a great number of dependents, so this part of the house was a little colony of its own, with a throng of people outside the rows of peeling hutments, chatting or sleeping or quarreling or squatting on the ground to cook their meals and wash their children. Margaret enjoyed coming out there, mostly to advise and scold—but Elizabeth felt shy, and she kept her eyes lowered.

"Shafi," she said, "Memsahib is calling you."

The old man mumbled furiously. He did not like to have his rest disturbed and he did not like Elizabeth. In fact, he did not like any of the visitors. He was the oldest servant in the house— so old that he had been Arthur's bearer when Arthur was still a bachelor and serving in the districts, almost forty years ago.

Still grumbling, he followed Elizabeth back to the veranda.

"Tea, Shafi!" Margaret called out cheerfully when she saw them coming.

"Not time for tea yet," he said.

She laughed. She loved it when her servants answered her back; she felt it showed a sense of ease and equality and family irritability, which was only another side of family devotion. "What a cross old man you are," she said. "And just look at you—how dirty."

He looked down at himself. He was indeed very dirty. He was unshaven and unwashed, and from beneath the rusty remains of what had once been a uniform coat there peeped out a ragged assortment of gray vests and torn pullovers into which he had bundled himself for the winter.

"It's hard to believe," Margaret said, "that this old scarecrow is a terrible, terrible snob. You know why he doesn't like you, Elizabeth? Because you're married to an Indian."

Elizabeth smiled and blushed. She admired Margaret's forthrightness.

"He thinks you've let down the side. He's got very firm principles. As a matter of fact, he thinks I've let down the side too. All his life he's longed to work for a real memsahib, the sort that entertains other memsahibs to tea. Never forgave Arthur for bringing home little Margaret."

The old man's face began working strangely. His mouth and stubbled cheeks twitched, and then sounds started coming that rose and fell—now distinct, now only a mutter and a drone—like waves of the sea. He spoke partly in English and partly in Hindi, and it was some time before it could be made out that he was telling some story of the old days—a party at the Gymkhana Club for which he had been hired as an additional waiter. The sahib who had given the party, a Major Waterford, had paid him not only his wages but also a tip of two rupees. He elaborated on this for some time, dwelling on the virtues of Major Waterford and also of Mrs. Waterford, a very fine lady who had made her servants wear white gloves when they served at table.

"Very grand," said Margaret with an easy laugh. "You run along now and get our tea."

"There was a little Missie sahib too. She had two ayahs, and every year they were given four saris and one shawl for the winter."

"Tea, Shafi," Margaret said more firmly, so that the old man, who knew every inflection in his mistress's voice, saw it was time to be off.

"Arthur and I've spoiled him outrageously," Margaret said. "We spoiled all our servants."

"God will reward you," said Babaji.

"We could never think of them as servants, really. They were more our friends. I've learned such a lot from Indian servants. They're usually rogues, but underneath all that they have beautiful characters. They're very religious, and they have a lot of philosophy—you'd be surprised. We've had some fascinating conversations. You ought to keep a servant, Elizabeth—I've told you so often." When she saw Elizabeth was about to answer something, she said, "And don't say you can't afford it. Your Raju earns enough, I'm sure, and they're very cheap."

"We don't need one," Elizabeth said apologetically. There were just the two of them, and they lived in two small rooms. Sometimes Raju also took it into his head that they needed a servant, and once he had even gone to the extent of hiring an undernourished little boy from the hills. On the second day, however, the boy was discovered rifling the pockets of Raju's trousers while their owner was having his bath, so he was dismissed on the spot. To Elizabeth's relief, no attempt at replacing him was ever made.

"If you had one you could get around a bit more," Margaret said. "Instead of always having to dance attendance on your husband's mealtimes. I suppose that's why you don't want to take those poor little children to Agra?"

"It's not that I don't want to," Elizabeth said hopelessly.

"Quite apart from anything else, you ought to be longing to get around and see the country. What do you know, what will you ever know, if you stay in one place all the time?"

"One day you will come and visit me in Almora," Babaji said.

"Oh Babaji, I'd love to!" Elizabeth exclaimed.

"Beautiful," he said, spreading his hands to describe it all. "The mountains, trees, clouds . . ." Words failed him, and he could only spread his hands farther and smile into the distance, as if he saw a beautiful vision there.

Elizabeth smiled with him. She saw it too, although she had never been there: the mighty mountains, the grandeur and the peace, the abode of Shiva where he sat with the rivers flowing from his hair. She longed to go, and to so many other places she had heard and read about. But the only place away from Delhi where she had ever been was Ankhpur, to stay with Raju's family.

Margaret began to tell about all the places she had been to. She and Arthur had been posted from district to district, in many different parts of the country, but even that hadn't been enough for her. She had to see everything. She had no fears about traveling on her own, and had spent weeks tramping around in the mountains, with a shawl thrown over her shoulders and a stick held firmly in her hand. She had traveled many miles by any mode of transport available—train, bus, cycle, rickshaw, or even bullock cart—in order to see some little-known and almost inaccessible temple or cave or tomb. Once she had sprained her ankle and lain all alone for a week in a derelict rest house, deserted except for one decrepit old watchman, who had shared his meals with her.

"That's the way to get to know the country," she declared. Her cheeks were flushed with the pleasure of remembering everything she had done.

Elizabeth agreed with her. Yet although she herself had done none of these things, she did not feel that she was on that account cut off from all knowledge. There was much to be learned from living with Raju's family in Ankhpur, much to be learned from Raju himself. Yes, he was her India! She felt like laughing when this thought came to her. But it was true.

"Your trouble is," Margaret suddenly said, "you let Raju bully you. He's got something of that in his character—don't contradict. I've studied him. If you were to stand up to him more firmly, you'd both be happier."

Again Elizabeth wanted to laugh. She thought of the nice times she and Raju often had together. He had invented a game of cricket that they could play in their bedroom between the steel almirah and the opposite wall. They played it with a rubber ball and a hairbrush, and three steps made a run. Raju's favorite trick was to hit the ball under the bed, and while she lay flat on the floor groping for it he made run after run, exhorting her with mocking cries of "Hurry up! Where is it? Can't you find it?" His eyes glittered with the pleasure of winning; his shirt was off, and drops of perspiration trickled down his smooth, dark chest.

"You should want to do something for those poor children!" Margaret shouted.

"I do want to. You know I do."

"I don't know anything of the sort. All I see is you leading an utterly useless, selfish life. I'm disappointed in you, Elizabeth. When I first met you, I had such high hopes of you. I thought, Ah, here at last is a serious person. But you're not serious at all. You're as frivolous as any of those girls that come here and spend their days playing mah-jongg."

Elizabeth was ashamed. The worst of it was she really had once been a serious person. She had been a schoolteacher in

England, and devoted to her work and her children, on whom she had spent far more time and care than was necessary in the line of duty. And, over and above that, she had put in several evenings a week visiting old people who had no one to look after them. But all that had come to an end once she met Raju.

"It's criminal to be in India and not be committed," Margaret went on. "There isn't much any single person can do, of course, but to do nothing at all—no, I wouldn't be able to sleep at nights."

And Elizabeth slept not only well but happily, blissfully! Sometimes she turned on the light just for the pleasure of looking at Raju lying beside her. He slept like a child, with the pillow bundled under his cheek and his mouth slightly open, as if he were smiling.

"But what are you laughing at!" Margaret shouted.

"I'm not, Margaret." She hastily composed her face. She hadn't been aware of it, but probably she had been smiling at the image of Raju asleep.

Margaret abruptly pushed back her chair. Her face was red and her hair disheveled, as if she had been in a fight. Elizabeth half rose in her chair, aghast at whatever it was she had done and eager to undo it.

"Don't follow me," Margaret said. "If you do, I know I'm going to behave badly and I'll feel terrible afterward. You can stay here or you can go home, but *don't follow me*."

She went inside the house, and the screen door banged after her. Elizabeth sank down into her chair and looked helplessly at Babaji.

He had remained as serene as ever. Gently he rocked himself in his chair. The winter afternoon was drawing to its close, and the sun, caught between two trees, was beginning to contract into one concentrated area of gold. Though the light was failing, the garden remained bright and gay with all its marigolds, its phlox, its pansies, and its sweet peas. Babaji enjoyed it all. He sat wrapped in his woolen shawl, with his feet warm in thick knitted socks and sandals.

"She is a hot-tempered lady," he said, smiling and forgiving. "But good, good."

"Oh, I know," Elizabeth said. "She's an angel. I feel so bad that I should have upset her. Do you think I ought to go after her?"

"A heart of gold," said Babaji.

"I know it." Elizabeth bit her lip in vexation at herself.

Shafi came out with the tea tray. Elizabeth removed some books to clear the little table for him, and Babaji said, "Ah," in pleasurable anticipation. But Shafi did not put the tray down.

"Where is she?" he said.

"It's all right, Shafi. She's just coming. Put it down, please."

The old man nodded and smiled in a cunning, superior way. He clutched his tray more tightly and turned back into the house. He had difficulty in walking, not only because he was old and infirm but also because the shoes he wore were too big for him and had no laces.

"Shafi!" Elizabeth called after him. "Babaji wants his tea!" But he did not even turn around. He walked straight up to

Margaret's bedroom and kicked the door and shouted, "I've brought it!"

Elizabeth hurried after him. She felt nervous about going into Margaret's bedroom after having been so explicitly forbidden to follow her. But Margaret only looked up briefly from where she was sitting on her bed, reading a letter, and said, "Oh, it's you," and "Shut the door." When he had put down the tea, Shafi went out again and the two of them were left alone.

Margaret's bedroom was quite different from the rest of the house. The other rooms were all bare and cold, with a minimum of furniture standing around on the stone floors; there were a few isolated pictures hung up here and there on the whitewashed walls, but nothing more intimate than portraits of Mahatma Gandhi and Sri Ramakrishna and a photograph of the inmates of Mother Teresa's Home. But Margaret's room was crammed with a lot of comfortable, solid old furniture, dominated by the big double bed in the center, which was covered with a white bedcover and a mosquito curtain on the top like a canopy. A log fire burned in the grate, and there were photographs everywhere—family photos of Arthur and Margaret, of Margaret as a little girl, and of her parents and her sister and her school and her friends. The stale smell of food pervading the rest of the house stopped short of this room, which was scented very pleasantly by woodsmoke and lavender water. There was an umbrella stand that held several alpenstocks, a tennis racquet, and a hockey stick.

"It's from my sister," Margaret said, indicating the letter she was reading. "She lives out in the country and they've been snowed under again. She's got a pub."

"How lovely."

"Yes, it's a lovely place. She's always wanted me to come and run it with her. But I couldn't live in England anymore, I couldn't bear it."

"Yes, I know what you mean."

"What do you know? You've only been here a few years. Pour the tea, there's a dear."

"Babaji was wanting a cup."

"To hell with Babaji."

She took off her sandals and lay down on the bed, leaning against some fat pillows that she had propped against the head-board. Elizabeth had noticed before that Margaret was always more relaxed in her own room than anywhere else. Not all her visitors were allowed into this room—in fact, only a chosen few. Strangely enough, Raju had been one of these when he and Elizabeth had stayed in the house. But he had never properly appreciated the privilege; either he sat on the edge of a chair and made signs to Elizabeth to go or he wandered restlessly around the room looking at all the photographs or taking out the tennis racquet and executing imaginary services with it; till Margaret told him to sit down and not make them all nervous, and then he looked sulky and made even more overt signs to Elizabeth.

"I brought my sister out here once," Margaret said. "But she couldn't stand it. Couldn't stand anything—the climate, the water, the food. Everything made her ill. There are people like that. Of course, I'm just the opposite. You like it here too, don't you?"

"Very, very much."

"Yes, I can see you're happy."

Margaret looked at her so keenly that Elizabeth tried to turn away her face slightly. She did not want anyone to see too much of her tremendous happiness. She felt somewhat ashamed of herself for having it—not only because she knew she didn't deserve it but also because she did not consider herself quite the right person to have it. She had been over thirty when she met Raju and had not expected much more out of life than had up till then been given to her.

Margaret lit a cigarette. She never smoked except in her own room. She puffed slowly, luxuriously. Suddenly she said, "He doesn't like me, does he?"

"Who?"

"'Who?'" she repeated impatiently. "Your Raju, of course."

Elizabeth flushed with embarrassment. "How you talk, Margaret," she murmured deprecatingly, not knowing what else to say.

"I know he doesn't," Margaret said. "I can always tell."

She sounded so sad that Elizabeth wished she could lie to her and say that no, Raju loved her just as everyone else did. But she could not bring herself to it. She thought of the way he usually spoke of Margaret. He called her by rude names and made coarse jokes about her, at which he laughed like a schoolboy and tried to make Elizabeth laugh with him; and the terrible thing was sometimes she did laugh, not because she wanted to or because what he said amused her but because it was he who urged her to, and she always found it difficult to refuse him anything. Now when she thought of this compliant laughter of hers she was filled with anguish, and she began unconsciously to wring her hands, the way she always did at such secretly appalling moments.

But Margaret was having thoughts of her own, and was smiling to herself. She said, "You know what was my happiest time of all in India? About ten years ago, when I went to stay in Swami Vishwananda's ashram."

Elizabeth was intensely relieved at the change of subject, though somewhat puzzled by its abruptness.

"We bathed in the river and we walked in the mountains. It was a time of such freedom, such joy. I've never felt like that before or since. I didn't have a care in the world and I felt so—light. I can't describe it—as if my feet didn't touch the ground."

"Yes, yes!" Elizabeth said eagerly, for she thought she recognized the feeling.

"In the evening we all sat with Swamiji. We talked about everything under the sun. He laughed and joked with us, and sometimes he sang. I don't know what happened to me when he sang. The tears came pouring down my face, but I was so happy I thought my heart would melt away."

"Yes," Elizabeth said again.

"That's him over there." She nodded toward a small framed photograph on the dressing table. Elizabeth picked it up. He did not look different from the rest of India's holy men—naked to the waist, with long hair and burning eyes.

"Not that you can tell much from a photo," Margaret said. She held out her hand for it, and then she looked at it herself, with a very young expression on her face. "He was such fun to be with, always full of jokes and games. When I was with him, I used to feel—I don't know—like a flower or a bird." She laughed gaily, and Elizabeth with her.

"Does Raju make you feel like that?"

Elizabeth stopped laughing and looked down into her lap. She tried to make her face very serious so as not to give herself away.

"Indian men have such marvelous eyes," Margaret said. "When they look at you, you can't help feeling all young and nice. But of course your Raju thinks I'm just a fat, ugly old memsahib."

"Margaret, Margaret!"

Margaret stubbed out her cigarette and, propelling herself with her heavy legs, swung down from the bed. "And there's poor old Babaji waiting for his tea."

She poured it for him and went out with the cup. Elizabeth went after her. Babaji was just as they had left him, except that now the sun, melting away between the trees behind him, was even more intensely gold and provided a heavenly background, as if to a saint in a picture, as he sat there at peace in his rocking chair.

Margaret fussed over him. She stirred his tea and she arranged his shawl more securely over his shoulders. Then she said, "I've got an idea, Babaji." She hooked her foot around a stool and drew it close to his chair and sank down on it, one hand laid on his knee. "You and I'll take those children up to Agra. Would you like that? A little trip?" She looked up into his face and was eager and bright. "We'll have a grand time. We'll hire a bus and we'll have singing and games all the way. You'll love it." She squeezed his knee in anticipatory joy, and he smiled at her and his thin old hand came down on the top of her head in a gesture of affection or blessing.

RUDYARD KIPLING

(1865–1936)

Rudyard Kipling spent the first five years of his life in India. It was an idyllic childhood, enclosed by servants and sensuous sights. Its memory was sharpened by a traumatic uprooting to England, described most poignantly in his short story "Baa Baa Black Sheep," and worked its way into almost everything he wrote about India. It even survived his later strident allegiances to the British Empire. Or, perhaps his sincerely felt awareness of the white man's burden made for another kind of intimacy with the brown man. Certainly, the stories Kipling wrote on his return to India as a young journalist in the 1880s and the later novel *Kim* (1901) show a feeling for Indian landscapes and peoples that writers much more politically correct have seemed to lack. In the following excerpt from *Kim*, where the half-Irish boy Kim travels with a Tibetan lama on the Grand Trunk Road, Kipling's eye takes in the labor gangs on the railway tracks as well as the bridegroom's pony turning "aside to snatch a mouthful from a passing fodder cart." Both knowledge and admiration rest behind the vision of the hillmen of Kulu and Kangra and the "Ooryas from down country" and the "wayside shrines—sometimes Hindu, sometimes Mussalman—which the lowcaste of both creeds share with beautiful impartiality."

from KIM

"Now let us walk," muttered the lama, and to the click of his rosary they walked in silence mile upon mile. The lama, as usual, was deep in meditation, but Kim's bright eyes were open wide. This broad, smiling river of life, he considered, was a vast improvement on the cramped and crowded Lahore streets. There were new people and new sights at every stride—castes he knew and castes that were altogether out of his experience.

They met a troop of long-haired, strong-scented Sansis with baskets of lizards and other unclean food on their backs, their lean dogs sniffing at their heels. These people kept their own side of the road, moving at a quick, furtive jog-trot, and all other castes gave them ample room; for the Sansi is deep pollution. Behind them, walking wide and stiffly across the strong shadows, the memory of his leg-irons still on him, strode one newly released from the jail; his full stomach and shiny skin to prove that the Government fed its prisoners better than most honest men could feed themselves. Kim knew that walk well, and made broad jest of it as they passed. Then an Akali, a wild-eyed, wild-haired Sikh devotee in the blue-checked clothes of his faith, with polished-steel quoits glistening on the cone of his tall blue turban, stalked past, returning from a visit to one of the independent Sikh States, where he had been singing the ancient glories of the Khalsa to College-trained princelings in top-boots and white-cord breeches. Kim was careful not to irritate that man; for the Akali's temper is short and his arm quick. Here and there they met or were overtaken by the gaily dressed crowds of whole villages turning out to some local fair; the women, with their babes on their hips, walking behind the men, the older boys prancing on sticks of sugarcane, dragging rude brass models of locomotives such as they sell for a half-penny, or flashing the sun into the eyes of their betters from cheap toy mirrors. One could see at a glance what each had bought; and if there were any doubt it needed only to watch the wives comparing, brown arm against brown arm, the newly purchased dull glass bracelets that come from the North-West. These merrymakers stepped slowly, calling one to the other and stopping to haggle with sweet-meat sellers, or to make a prayer before one of the wayside shrines—sometimes Hindu, sometimes Mussalman—which the low-caste of both creeds share with beautiful impartiality. A solid line of blue, rising and falling like the back of a caterpillar in haste, would swing up through the quivering dust and trot past to a chorus of quick cackling. That was a gang of *changars*— the women who have taken all the embankments of all the North-ern railways under their charge—a flat-footed, big-bosomed, strong-limbed, blue-petticoated clan of earth carriers, hurrying north on news of a job, and wasting no time by the road. They belong to the caste whose men do not count, and they walked with squared elbows, swinging hips, and heads on high, as suits women who carry heavy weights. A little later a marriage proces-sion would strike into the Grand Trunk with music and shout-ings, and a smell of marigold and jasmine stronger even than the reek of the dust. One could see the bride's litter, a blur of red and tinsel, staggering through the haze, while the bridegroom's bewreathed pony turned aside to snatch a mouthful from a pass-ing fodder cart. Then Kim would join the Kentish-fire of good wishes and bad jokes, wishing the couple a hundred sons and no daughters, as the saying is. Still more interesting and more to be shouted over it was when a strolling juggler with some half-trained monkeys, or a panting, feeble bear, or a woman who tied goats' horns to her feet, and with these danced on a slack-rope, set the horses to shying and the women to shrill, long-drawn quavers of amazement.

The lama never raised his eyes. He did not note the money-lender on his goose-rumped pony, hastening along to collect the cruel interest; or the long-shouting, deep-voiced little mob—still in military formation—of native soldiers on leave, rejoicing to be rid of their breeches and puttees, and saying the most outrageous things to the most respectable women in sight. Even the seller of Ganges water he did not see, and Kim expected that he would at least buy a bottle of that precious stuff. He looked steadily at the ground, and strode as steadily hour after hour, his soul busied elsewhere. But Kim was in the seventh heaven of joy. The Grand Trunk at this point was built on an embankment to guard against winter floods from the foothills, so that one walked, as it were, a little above the country, along a stately corridor, seeing all India spread out to left and right. It was beautiful to behold the many-yoked grain and cotton wagons crawling over the country roads: one could hear their axles, complaining a mile away, coming nearer, till with shouts and yells and bad words they climbed up the steep incline and plunged on to the hard main road, carter reviling carter. It was equally beautiful to watch the people, little clumps of red and blue and pink and white and saffron, turning aside to go to their own villages, dispersing and growing small by twos and threes across the level plain. Kim felt these things, though he could not give tongue to his feelings, and so contented himself with buying peeled sugarcane and spitting the pith generously about his path. From time to time the lama took snuff, and at last Kim could endure the silence no longer.

"This is a good land—the land of the South!" said he. "The air is good; the water is good. Eh?"

"And they are all bound upon the Wheel," said the lama. "Bound from life after life. To none of these has the Way been shown." He shook himself back to this world.

"And now we have walked a weary way," said Kim. "Surely we shall soon come to a *parao* [a resting place]. Shall we stay there? Look, the sun is sloping."

"Who will receive us this evening?"

"That is all one. This country is full of good folk. Besides"— he sunk his voice beneath a whisper—"we have money."

The crowd thickened as they neared the resting place which marked the end of their day's journey. A line of stalls selling very simple food and tobacco, a stack of firewood, a police station, a well, a horse trough, a few trees, and, under them, some trampled ground dotted with the black ashes of old fires, are all that mark a *parao* on the Grand Trunk; if you except the beggars and the crows—both hungry.

By this time the sun was driving broad golden spokes through the lower branches of the mango trees; the parakeets and doves were coming home in their hundreds; the chattering, grey-backed Seven Sisters, talking over the day's adventures, walked back and forth in twos and threes almost under the feet of the travellers; and shufflings and scufflings in the branches showed that the bats were ready to go out on the night picket. Swiftly the light gathered itself together, painted for an instant the faces and the cart-wheels and the bullocks' horns as red as blood. Then the night fell, changing the touch of the air, drawing a low, even haze, like a gossamer veil of blue, across the face of the country, and bringing out, keen and distinct, the smell of wood smoke and cattle and the good scent of wheaten cakes cooked on ashes. The evening patrol hurried out of the police station with important coughings and reiterated orders; and a live charcoal ball in the cup of a wayside carter's hookah glowed red while Kim's eye mechanically watched the last flicker of the sun on the brass tweezers.

The life of the *parao* was very like that of the Kashmir Serai on a small scale. Kim dived into the happy Asiatic disorder which, if you only allow time, will bring you everything that a simple man needs.

His wants were few, because, since the lama had no caste scruples, cooked food from the nearest stall would serve; but, for luxury's sake, Kim bought a handful of dung cakes to build a fire. All about, coming and going round the little flames, men cried for oil, or grain, or sweetmeats, or tobacco, jostling one another while they waited their turn at the well; and under the men's voices you heard from halted, shuttered carts the high squeals and giggles of women whose faces should not be seen in public.

Nowadays, well-educated natives are of opinion that when their womenfolk travel—and they visit a good deal—it is better to take them quickly by rail in a properly screened compartment; and that custom is spreading. But there are always those of the old rock who hold by the use of their forefathers; and, above all, there are always the old women—more conservative than the men—who toward the end of their days go on a pilgrimage. They, being withered and undesirable, do not, under certain circumstances, object to unveiling. After their long seclusion, during which they have always been in business touch with a thousand outside interests, they love the bustle and stir of the open road, the gatherings at the shrines, and the infinite possibilities of gossip with like-minded dowagers. Very often it suits a long-suffering family that a strong-tongued, iron-willed old lady should disport herself about India in this fashion; for certainly pilgrimage is grateful to the Gods. So all about India, in the most remote places, as in the most public, you find some knot of grizzled servitors in nominal charge of an old lady who is more or less curtained and hid away in a bullock cart. Such men are staid and discreet, and when a European or a high-caste native is near will net their charge with most elaborate precautions; but in the ordinary haphazard chances of pilgrimage the precautions are not taken. The old lady is, after all, intensely human, and lives to look upon life.

Kim marked down a gaily ornamented *ruth* or family bullock cart, with a broidered canopy of two domes, like a double-humped camel, which had just been drawn into the *parao*. Eight men made its retinue, and two of the eight were armed with rusty sabers—sure signs that they followed a person of distinction, for the common folk do not bear arms. An increasing cackle of complaints, orders, and jests, and what to a European would have been bad language, came from behind the curtains. Here was evidently a woman used to command.

Kim looked over the retinue critically. Half of them were thin-legged, grey-bearded Ooryas from down country. The other half were duffle-clad, felt-hatted hillmen of the North; and that mixture told its own tale, even if he had not overheard the incessant sparring between the two divisions. The old lady was going south on a visit—probably to a rich relative, most probably to a son-in-law, who had sent up an escort as a mark of respect. The hillmen would be of her own people—Kulu or Kangra folk. It was quite clear that she was not taking her daughter down to be wedded, or the curtains would have been laced home and the guard would have allowed no one near the car. A merry and a high-spirited dame, thought Kim, balancing the dung cake in one hand, the cooked food in the other, and piloting the lama with a nudging shoulder. Something might be made out of the meeting. The lama would give him no help, but, as a conscientious *chela*, Kim was delighted to beg for two.

He built his fire as close to the cart as he dared, waiting for one of the escort to order him away. The lama dropped wearily to the ground, much as a heavy fruit-eating bat cowers, and returned to his rosary.

"Stand farther off, beggar!" The order was shouted in broken Hindustani by one of the hillmen.

"Huh! It is only a *pahari* [a hillman]," said Kim over his shoulder. "Since when have the hill-asses owned all Hindustan?"

The retort was a swift and brilliant sketch of Kim's pedigree for three generations.

"Ah!" Kim's voice was sweeter than ever, as he broke the dung cake into fit pieces. "In *my* country we call that the beginning of love-talk."

A harsh, thin cackle behind the curtains put the hillman on his mettle for a second shot.

"Not so bad—not so bad," said Kim with calm. "But have a care, my brother, lest we—*we*, I say—be minded to give a curse or so in return. And our curses have the knack of biting home."

The Ooryas laughed; the hillman sprang forward threateningly. The lama suddenly raised his head, bringing his huge tam-o'-shanter hat into the full light of Kim's new-started fire.

"What is it?" said he.

The man halted as though struck to stone. "I—I—am saved from a great sin," he stammered.

"The foreigner has found him a priest at last," whispered one of the Ooryas.

"*Hai!* Why is that beggar brat not well beaten?" the old woman cried.

The hillman drew back to the cart and whispered something to the curtain. There was dead silence, then a muttering.

"This goes well," thought Kim, pretending neither to see nor hear.

"When—when—he has eaten"—the hillman fawned on Kim—"it—it is requested that the Holy One will do the honor to talk to one who would speak to him."

"After he has eaten he will sleep," Kim returned loftily. He could not quite see what new turn the game had taken, but stood resolute to profit by it. "Now I will get him his food." The last sentence, spoken loudly, ended with a sigh as of faintness.

"I—I myself and the others of my people will look to that—if it is permitted."

"It is permitted," said Kim, more loftily than ever. "Holy One, these people will bring us food."

"The land is good. All the country of the South is good—a great and terrible world," mumbled the lama drowsily.

"Let him sleep," said Kim, "but look to it that we are well fed when he wakes. He is a very holy man."

Again one of the Ooryas said something contemptuously.

"He is not a *fakir*. He is not a down-country beggar," Kim went on severely, addressing the stars. "He is the most holy of holy men. He is above all castes. I am his *chela*."

"Come here!" said the flat thin voice behind the curtain; and Kim came, conscious that eyes he could not see were staring at him. One skinny brown finger heavy with rings lay on the edge of the cart, and the talk went this way:

"Who is that one?"

"An exceedingly holy one. He comes from far off. He comes from Tibet."

"Where in Tibet?"

"From behind the snows—from a very far place. He knows the stars; he makes horoscopes; he reads nativities. But he does not do this for money. He does it for kindness and great charity. I am his disciple. I am called also the Friend of the Stars."

"Thou art no hillman."

"Ask him. He will tell thee I was sent to him from the Stars to show him an end to his pilgrimage."

"Humph! Consider, brat, that I am an old woman and not altogether a fool. Lamas I know, and to these I give reverence, but thou art no more a lawful *chela* than this my finger is the pole of this wagon. Thou art a casteless Hindu—a bold and unblushing beggar, attached, belike, to the Holy One for the sake of gain."

"Do we not all work for gain?" Kim changed his tone promptly to match that altered voice. "I have heard"—this was a bow drawn at a venture—"I have heard—"

"What hast thou heard?" she snapped, rapping with the finger.

"Nothing that I well remember, but some talk in the bazaars, which is doubtless a lie, that even Rajahs—small Hill Rajahs—"

"But nonetheless of good Rajput blood."

"Assuredly of good blood. That these even sell the more comely of their womenfolk for gain. Down south they sell them—to zemindars and such-all of Oudh."

If there be one thing in the world that the small Hill Rajahs deny it is just this charge; but it happens to be one thing that the bazaars believe, when they discuss the mysterious slave-traffics of India. The old lady explained to Kim, in a tense, indignant whisper, precisely what manner and fashion of malignant liar he was. Had Kim hinted this when she was a girl, he would have been pommeled to death that same evening by an elephant. This was perfectly true.

"*Ahai!* I am only a beggar's brat, as the Eye of Beauty has said," he wailed in extravagant terror.

"Eye of Beauty, forsooth! Who am I that thou shouldst fling beggar endearments at me?" And yet she laughed at the long-forgotten word. "Forty years ago that might have been said, and not without truth. Ay, thirty years ago. But it is the fault of this gadding up and down Hind that a king's widow must jostle all the scum of the land, and be made a mock by beggars."

"Great Queen," said Kim promptly, for he heard her shaking with indignation, "I am even what the Great Queen says I am;

but nonetheless is my master holy. He has not yet heard the Great Queen's order that—"

"Order? I order a Holy One—a Teacher of the Law—to come and speak to a woman? Never!"

"Pity my stupidity. I thought it was given as an order—"

"It was not. It was a petition. Does this make all clear?"

A silver coin clicked on the edge of the cart. Kim took it and salaamed profoundly. The old lady recognized that, as the eyes and the ears of the lama, he was to be propitiated.

"I am but the Holy One's disciple. When he has eaten perhaps he will come."

"Oh, villain and shameless rogue!" The jeweled forefinger shook itself at him reprovingly; but he could hear the old lady's chuckle.

"Nay, what is it?" he said, dropping into his most caressing and confidential tone—the one, he well knew, that few could resist. "Is—is there any need of a son in thy family? Speak freely, for we priests—" That last was a direct plagiarism from a *fakir* by the Taksali Gate.

"We priests! Thou art not yet old enough to—" She checked the joke with another laugh. "Believe me, now and again, we women, O priest, think of other matters than sons. Moreover, my daughter has borne her man-child."

"Two arrows in the quiver are better than one; and three are better still." Kim quoted the proverb with a meditative cough, looking discreetly earthward.

"True—oh, true. But perhaps that will come. Certainly those down-country Brahmins are utterly useless. I sent gifts and monies and gifts again to them, and they prophesied."

"Ah," drawled Kim, with infinite contempt, "they prophesied!" A professional could have done no better.

"And it was not till I remembered my own Gods that my prayers were heard. I chose an auspicious hour, and—perhaps the Holy One has heard of the Abbot of the Lung-Cho lamasery. It was to him I put the matter, and behold in the due time all came about as I desired. The Brahmin in the house of the father of my daughter's son has since said that it was through his prayers—which is a little error that I will explain to him when we reach our journey's end. And so afterwards I go to Buddh Gaya, to make *shraddha* for the father of my children."

"Thither go we."

"Doubly auspicious," chirruped the old lady. "A second son at least!"

"O Friend of all the World!" The lama had waked, and, simply as a child bewildered in a strange bed, called for Kim.

"I come! I come, Holy One!" He dashed to the fire, where he found the lama already surrounded by dishes of food, the hillmen visibly adoring him and the Southerners looking sourly.

"Go back! Withdraw!" Kim cried. "Do we eat publicly like dogs?" They finished the meal in silence, each turned a little from the other, and Kim topped it with a native-made cigarette.

"Have I not said an hundred times that the South is a good land? Here is a virtuous and high-born widow of a Hill Rajah on pilgrimage, she says, to Buddh Gaya. She it is sends us those dishes; and when thou art well rested she would speak to thee."

"Is this also thy work?" The lama dipped deep into his snuff-gourd.

"Who else watched over thee since our wonderful journey began?" Kim's eyes danced in his head as he blew the rank smoke through his nostrils and stretched him on the dusty ground. "Have I failed to oversee thy comforts, Holy One?"

"A blessing on thee." The lama inclined his solemn head. "I have known many men in my so long life, and disciples not a few. But to none among men, if so be thou art woman-born, has my heart gone out as it has to thee—thoughtful, wise, and courteous; but something of a small imp."

"And I have never seen such a priest as thou." Kim considered the benevolent yellow face wrinkle by wrinkle. "It is less than three days since we took the road together, and it is as though it were a hundred years."

"Perhaps in a former life it was permitted that I should have rendered thee some service. Maybe"—he smiled—"I freed thee from a trap; or, having caught thee on a hook in the days when I was not enlightened, cast thee back into the river."

"Maybe," said Kim quietly. He had heard this sort of speculation again and again, from the mouths of many whom the English would not consider imaginative. "Now, as regards that woman in the bullock cart, *I* think she needs a second son for her daughter."

"That is no part of the Way," sighed the lama. "But at least she is from the Hills. Ah, the Hills, and the snow of the Hills!"

He rose and stalked to the cart. Kim would have given his ears to come too, but the lama did not invite him; and the few words he caught were in an unknown tongue, for they spoke some common speech of the mountains. The woman seemed to ask questions which the lama turned over in his mind before answering. Now and again he heard the sing-song cadence of a Chinese quotation. It was a strange picture that Kim watched between drooped eyelids. The lama, very straight and erect, the deep folds of his yellow clothing slashed with black in the light of the *parao* fires precisely as a knotted tree-trunk is slashed with the shadows of the low sun, addressed a tinsel and lacquered *ruth* which burned like a many-colored jewel in the same uncertain light. The patterns on the gold-worked curtains ran up and down, melting and re-forming as the folds shook and quivered to the night wind; and when the talk grew more earnest the jeweled forefinger snapped out little sparks of light between the embroideries. Behind the cart was a wall of uncertain darkness speckled with little flames and alive with half-caught forms and faces and shadows. The voices of early evening had settled down to one soothing hum whose deepest note was the steady chumping of the bullocks above their chopped straw, and whose highest was the tinkle of a Bengali dancing girl's *sitar*. Most men had eaten and pulled deep at their gurgling, grunting hookahs, which in full blast sound like bull-frogs.

At last the lama returned. A hillman walked behind him with a wadded cotton quilt and spread it carefully by the fire.

"She deserves ten thousand grandchildren," thought Kim. "Nonetheless, but for me, those gifts would not have come."

"A virtuous woman—and a wise one." The lama slackened off, joint by joint, like a slow camel. "The world is full of charity to those who follow the Way." He flung a fair half of the quilt over Kim.

"And what said she?" Kim rolled up in his share of it.

"She asked me many questions and propounded many problems—the most of which were idle tales which she had heard from devil-serving priests who pretend to follow the Way. Some

I answered, and some I said were foolish. Many wear the Robe, but few keep the Way."

"True. That is true." Kim used the thoughtful, conciliatory tone of those who wish to draw confidences.

"But by her lights she is most right-minded. She desires greatly that we should go with her to Buddh Gaya; her road being ours, as I understand, for many days' journey to the southward."

"And?"

"Patience a little. To this I said that my Search came before all things. She had heard many foolish legends, but this great truth of my River she had never heard. Such are the priests of the lower hills! She knew the Abbot of Lung-Cho, but she did not know of my River—nor the tale of the Arrow."

"And?"

"I spoke therefore of the Search, and of the Way, and of matters that were profitable; she desiring only that I should accompany her and make prayer for a second son."

"Aha! 'We women' do *not* think of anything save children," said Kim sleepily.

"Now, since our roads run together for a while, I do not see that we in any way depart from our Search if so be we accompany her—at least as far as—I have forgotten the name of the city."

"*Ohé!*" said Kim, turning and speaking in a sharp whisper to one of the Ooryas a few yards away. "Where is your master's house?"

"A little behind Saharunpore, among the fruit gardens." He named the village.

"That was the place," said the lama. "So far, at least, we can go with her."

"Flies go to carrion," said the Oorya, in an abstracted voice.

"For the sick cow a crow; for the sick man a Brahmin." Kim breathed the proverb impersonally to the shadow tops of the trees overhead.

The Oorya grunted and held his peace.

"So then we go with her, Holy One?"

"Is there any reason against? I can still step aside and try all the rivers that the road overpasses. She desires that I should come. She very greatly desires it."

Kim stifled a laugh in the quilt. When once that imperious old lady had recovered from her natural awe of a lama he thought it probable that she would be worth listening to.

He was nearly asleep when the lama suddenly quoted a proverb: "The husbands of the talkative have a great reward hereafter." Then Kim heard him snuff thrice, and dozed off, still laughing.

The diamond-bright dawn woke men and crows and bullocks together. Kim sat up and yawned, shook himself, and thrilled with delight. This was seeing the world in real truth; this was life as he would have it—bustling and shouting, the buckling of belts, and beating of bullocks and creaking of wheels, lighting of fires and cooking of food, and new sights at every turn of the approving eye. The morning mist swept off in a whorl of silver, the parrots shot away to some distant river in shrieking green hosts: all the well wheels within earshot went to work. India was awake, and Kim was in the middle of it, more awake and more excited than anyone, chewing on a twig that he would presently use as a toothbrush; for he borrowed right- and left-handedly from all the customs of the country he knew and loved. There was no need to worry about food—no need to spend a cowrie at the crowded stalls. He was the disciple of a holy man annexed by a strong-willed old lady. All things would be prepared for them, and when they were respectfully invited so to do they would sit and eat. For the rest—Kim giggled here as he cleaned his teeth—his hostess would rather heighten the enjoyment of the road. He inspected her bullocks critically, as they came up grunting and blowing under the yokes. If they went too fast—it was not likely—there would be a pleasant seat for himself along the pole; the lama would sit beside the driver. The escort, of course, would walk. The old lady, equally of course, would talk a great deal, and by what he had heard that conversation would not lack salt. She was already ordering, haranguing, rebuking, and, it must be said, cursing her servants for delays.

"Get her her pipe. In the name of the Gods, get her her pipe and stop her ill-omened mouth," cried an Oorya, tying up his shapeless bundles of bedding. "She and the parrots are alike. They screech in the dawn."

"The lead bullocks! *Hai!* Look to the lead bullocks!" They were backing and wheeling as a grain cart's axle caught them by the horns. "Son of an owl, where dost thou go?" This to the grinning carter.

"*Ai! Yai! Yai!* That within there is the Queen of Delhi going to pray for a son," the man called back over his high load. "Room for the Queen of Delhi and her Prime Minister the grey monkey climbing up his own sword!" Another cart loaded with bark for a down-country tannery followed close behind, and its driver added a few compliments as the *ruth* bullocks backed and backed again.

From behind the shaking curtains came one volley of invective. It did not last long, but in kind and quality, in blistering, biting appropriateness, it was beyond anything that even Kim had heard. He could see the carter's bare chest collapse with amazement, as the man salaamed reverently to the voice, leaped from the pole, and helped the escort haul their volcano on to the main road. Here the voice told him truthfully what sort of wife he had wedded, and what she was doing in his absence.

"Oh, *shabash*!" murmured Kim, unable to contain himself, as the man slunk away.

"Well done, indeed? It is a shame and a scandal that a poor woman may not go to make prayer to her Gods except she be jostled and insulted by all the refuse of Hindustan—that she must eat *gâli* [abuse] as men eat *ghi*. But I have yet a wag left to my tongue—a word or two well spoken that serves the occasion. And *still* am I without my tobacco! Who is the one-eyed and luckless son of shame that has not yet prepared my pipe?"

It was hastily thrust in by a hillman, and a trickle of thick smoke from each corner of the curtains showed that peace was restored.

If Kim had walked proudly the day before, disciple of a holy man, today he paced with tenfold pride in the train of a semi-royal procession, with a recognized place under the patronage of an old lady of charming manners and infinite resource. The escort, their heads tied up native fashion, fell in on either side the cart, shuffling enormous clouds of dust.

The lama and Kim walked a little to one side; Kim chewing his stick of sugarcane, and making way for no one under the status of a priest. They could hear the old lady's tongue clack as steadily as a rice husker. She bade the escort tell her what was going on on the road; and so soon as they were clear of the *parao* she flung back the curtains and peered out, her veil a third across her face. Her men did not eye her directly when she addressed them, and thus the proprieties were more or less observed.

A dark, sallowish District Superintendent of Police, faultlessly uniformed, an Englishman, trotted by on a tired horse, and, seeing from her retinue what manner of person she was, chaffed her.

"O mother," he cried, "do they do this in the zenanas? Suppose an Englishman came by and saw that thou hadst no nose?"

"What?" she shrilled back. "Thine own mother has no nose? Why say so, then, on the open road?"

It was a fair counter. The Englishman threw up his hand with the gesture of a man hit at sword-play. She laughed and nodded.

"Is this a face to tempt virtue aside?" She withdrew all her veil and stared at him.

It was by no means lovely, but as the man gathered up his reins he called it a Moon of Paradise, a Disturber of Integrity, and a few other fantastic epithets which doubled her up with mirth.

"That is a *nut-cut* [rogue]," she said. "All police constables are *nut-cuts*; but the police wallahs are the worst. *Hai*, my son, thou hast never learned all that since thou camest from *Belait* [Europe]. Who suckled thee?"

"A *pahareen*—a hillwoman of Dalhousie, my mother. Keep thy beauty under a shade—O Dispenser of Delights," and he was gone.

"These be the sort"—she took a fine judicial tone, and stuffed her mouth with *pan*—"These be the sort to oversee justice. They know the land and the customs of the land. The others, all new from Europe, suckled by white women and learning our tongues from books, are worse than the pestilence. They do harm to Kings." Then she told a long, long tale to the world at large, of an ignorant young policeman who had disturbed some small Hill Rajah, a ninth cousin of her own, in the matter of a trivial land case, winding up with a quotation from a work by no means devotional.

Then her mood changed, and she bade one of the escort ask whether the lama would walk alongside and discuss matters of religion. So Kim dropped back into the dust and returned to his sugarcane. For an hour or more the lama's tam-o'-shanter showed like a moon through the haze; and, from all he heard, Kim gathered that the old woman wept. One of the Ooryas half apologized for his rudeness overnight, saying that he had never known his mistress of so bland a temper, and he ascribed it to the presence of the strange priest. Personally, he believed in Brahmins, though, like all natives, he was acutely aware of their cunning and their greed. Still, when Brahmins but irritated with begging demands the mother of his master's wife, and when she sent them away so angry that they cursed the whole retinue (which was the real reason of the second off-side bullock going lame, and of the pole breaking the night before), he was prepared to accept any priest of any other denomination in or out of India. To this Kim assented with wise nods, and bade the Oorya observe that the lama took no money, and that the cost of his and Kim's food would be repaid a hundred times in the good luck that would attend the caravan henceforward. He also

told stories of Lahore city, and sang a song or two which made
the escort laugh. As a town-mouse well acquainted with the latest songs by the most fashionable composers—they are women
for the most part—Kim had a distinct advantage over men from
a little fruit-village behind Saharunpore, but he let that advantage be inferred.

At noon they turned aside to eat, and the meal was good,
plentiful, and well-served on plates of clean leaves, in decency,
out of drift of the dust. They gave the scraps to certain beggars,
that all requirements might be fulfilled, and sat down to a long,
luxurious smoke. The old lady had retreated behind her curtains,
but mixed most freely in the talk, her servants arguing with and
contradicting her as servants do throughout the East. She compared the cool and the pines of the Kangra and Kulu hills with
the dust and the mangoes of the South; she told a tale of some
old local Gods at the edge of her husband's territory; she roundly
abused the tobacco which she was then smoking, reviled all
Brahmins, and speculated without reserve on the coming of
many grandsons.

CLAUDE LÉVI-STRAUSS

(1908–)

Claude Lévi-Strauss, the French social anthropologist, was born in Brussels and studied at the Sorbonne. In the mid-1930s he did field research on the Indians of Brazil. He taught at the New School for Social Research during Hitler's occupation of France. He traveled to the Indian subcontinent in the late 1940s, before he became the pioneer of postwar anthropology with such books as *The Elementary Structures of Kinship* (1949) and *The Savage Mind* (1962). His intellectual autobiography, *Tristes Tropiques* (1955), presents a melancholy vision of old societies clumsily making themselves over in the image of Europe. "The first thing we see," he wrote, "as we travel around the world is our own filth, thrown into the face of mankind." He brought an ironic sense of history to India, which he saw as a "very old tapestry" with "exquisite and faded colors" which has been "worn threadbare by long use and tirelessly darned."

from TRISTES TROPIQUES

Originally a fishing village, then, as a result of the English colonial presence, a small port and trading center, Karachi had been promoted to the rank of capital in 1947. In the long avenues of the former compound, lined by collective or individual barracklike structures—the latter, private residences of officials or officers—each one standing separately in its patch of dusty veg-

etation, hordes of refugees slept out in the open and were leading a wretched existence on the pavement, bloody with the spittle of betel chewers, while the Parsee millionaires were busy
building Babylonian palaces for western businessmen. For months
on end, from dawn till dusk, a procession of men and women in
rags filed past (in Moslem countries, the segregation of women
is not so much a religious practice as a mark of bourgeois pres-
tige, and the poorest members of the community are not even
entitled to have a sex), each carrying a basket full of newly
mixed concrete, which he or she tipped into the shuttering,
before going back, without a pause, to the mixers to reload for
another round. Each wing was in use almost before it was finished, since a room with board could be let at more per day than
a woman worker earned in a month; in this way, the cost of
building a luxury hotel could be regained in nine months. So, the
work had to be done quickly, and the foremen were not much
concerned about whether the different blocks were all exactly in
line. There had probably been no change since the days when
the Satraps compelled slaves to pour mud and pile up bricks for
the building of their rickety palaces; the line of women basket
carriers, silhouetted against the sky on top of the scaffolding,
could indeed have served as a model for the friezes on one of
those palaces.

Cut off from native life (which in this desert was itself an artificial effect of colonization) by a few miles made impassable by
an intolerable monsoon-like, but never resolved, humidity, and
even more so by the fear of dysentery ("Karachi tummy"), a
community of businessmen, industrialists and diplomats lan-
guished in the heat and boredom of these bare cement cells
which served as bedrooms and which seemed to be designed in

this way not only for reasons of economy but still more to facili-
tate the process of disinfection that took place each time one of
them was vacated by the human specimen who had been immo-
bilized there for a few weeks or months. And my memory at
once leapfrogs over another three thousand kilometers to link
this picture with another, connected with the temple of the goddess Kali, the oldest and most revered sanctuary in Calcutta. On
the banks of a stagnant pond, and in an atmosphere redolent
with that mixture of physical deformity and fierce commercial
exploitation in which the popular religious life of India is conducted, not far from bazaars overflowing with pious color plates
and painted plaster divinities, stands the "Rest House," the modern shelter built by the religious organizers to house the pilgrims.
It is a long cement hall, divided into two parts, one for the men
and the other for the women, and each lined with platforms, also
made of bare cement, intended for use as beds. I was asked to
admire the gutters and the water-cocks. As soon as the human
cargo has got up and been dispatched to its devotions, during
which it begs for the healing of its ulcers, cankers, scabs and running sores, the whole building is washed out by means of hoses
so that the stalls are clean and fresh for the next batch of pilgrims. Nowhere, perhaps, except in concentration camps, have
human beings been so completely identified with butcher's meat.

However, this was not meant as anything more than a temporary lodging. A little further on, at Narrayanganj, the jute workers earn their living inside a gigantic spider's web formed by
whitish fibers hanging from the walls and floating in the air.
They then go home to the "coolie lines," brick troughs with neither light nor flooring, and each occupied by six or eight individ-
uals; they are arranged in rows of little streets with surface

drains running down the middle, which are flooded thrice daily to clear away the dirt. Social progress is now tending to replace this kind of dwelling by "workers' quarters," prisons in which two or three workers share a cell three meters by four. There are walls all around, and the entrance gates are guarded by armed policemen. The communal kitchens and eating quarters are bare cement rooms, which can be swilled out and where each individual lights his fire and squats on the ground to eat in the dark.

Once, during my first teaching post in the Landes area, I had visited poultry yards specially adapted for the cramming of geese: each bird was confined to a narrow box and reduced to the status of a mere digestive tube. In this Indian setting, the situation was the same, apart from two differences: instead of geese, it was men and women I was looking at, and instead of being fattened up, they were, if anything, being slimmed down. But in both instances, the breeder only allowed his charges one form of activity, which was desirable in the case of the geese, and inevitable in the case of the Indians. The dark and airless cubicles were suited neither for rest, leisure nor love. They were mere points of connection with the communal sewer, and they corresponded to a conception of human life as being reducible to the pure exercise of the excretory functions.

Alas, poor Orient! In Dacca, that secretive city, I visited various middle-class households. Some were as luxurious as the antique shops on Third Avenue in New York; others, belonging to comfortably off people, were as full of cane pedestal tables, fringed tea-cloths and china as a suburban villa in Bois Colombes. Some, in the old style, were like our poorest peasant cottages, and the cooking was done on a stove of beaten earth, at the far end of a muddy little courtyard. On the other hand, there were three-roomed flats for well-to-do young married couples in buildings indistinguishable from the low-priced blocks put up, as part of the postwar reconstruction, at Châtillon-sur-Seine or Givors, except that in Dacca the rooms were made of bare cement (as was the washroom, with its single tap), and as scantily furnished as a little girl's bedroom. Squatting on the concrete floor, in the dim light of a single bulb hanging by its flex from the ceiling, I once—oh, Arabian Nights!—ate a dinner full of succulent ancestral savors, picking up the food with my fingers: first, *Khichuri*, rice and the small lentils which are called pulses in English, and the multicolored varieties of which can be seen standing in sackfuls in the markets. Then *nimkorma*, broiled chicken; *chingri cari*, an oily fruity stew of giant shrimps, and another stew with hard-boiled eggs called *dimer tak*, accompanied by cucumber sauce, *shosha*; finally the dessert, *firni*, made of rice and milk.

I was the guest of a young teacher; also present were his brother-in-law, who acted as butler, a maid, a baby, and lastly my host's wife who was in process of being emancipated from purdah. She was like a silent, frightened doe, but, in order to underline her recent liberation, her husband showered sarcastic remarks on her, with a tactlessness which embarrassed me as much as it did her. Since I was an anthropologist, he made her bring out her personal underwear from a modest little chest of drawers, so that I could note the different items. With a little encouragement he would have made her undress in front of me, so anxious was he to prove his esteem for western ways, of which he knew nothing.

I could thus see, taking shape before my very eyes, an Asia characterized by workers' dwellings and cheap blocks of flats.

This Asia of the future, which rejects all forms of exoticism, may link up again, after an eclipse of five thousand years, with that dreary yet efficient style of life which the Asiatics perhaps invented in 3000 BC. It subsequently moved across the earth's surface, making a temporary halt in the New World, so that we tend to think of it as being specifically American; but then, as early as 1850, it resumed its advance westwards, reaching first Japan and now at last its place of origin, after going right round the world.

In the valley of the Indus, I wandered among the austere remains of the oldest Oriental culture, which have managed to withstand the passing of the centuries, sand, floods, saltpeter and Aryan invasions: Mohenjo-Daro and Harappa, hardened outcrops of bricks and shards. These ancient settlements present a disconcerting spectacle. The streets are all perfectly straight and intersect each other at right angles; there are workers' districts, in which all the dwellings are identical, industrial workshops for the grinding of grain, the casting and engraving of metals and the manufacture of clay goblets, fragments of which lie strewn on the ground; municipal granaries which occupy several blocks (as we might be tempted to say, making a transposition in time and space); public baths, water pipes and sewers; and solid but unattractive residential districts. No monuments or large pieces of sculpture, but, at a depth of between ten and twenty yards, flimsy trinkets and precious jewels, indicative of an art devoid of mystery and uninspired by any deep faith, and intended merely to satisfy the ostentatiousness and sensuality of the rich. The complex as a whole reminds the visitor of the advantages and defects of a large modern city; it foreshadows those more advanced forms of western civilization, of which the United States of America today provides a model, even for Europe.

It is tempting to imagine that, after four or five thousand years of history, the wheel has come full circle—that the urban, industrial, bourgeois civilization first begun in the towns of the Indus valley was not so very different, in its underlying inspiration, from that which was destined to reach its peak on the other side of the Atlantic, after a prolonged period of involution in the European chrysalis. When the Old World was still young, it was already anticipating the features of the New.

I therefore mistrust superficial contrasts and the apparently picturesque; they may not be lasting. What we call the exotic expresses an inequality of rhythm, which can be significant over a few centuries and temporarily obscure destinies which might well have remained united or parallel, like those of Alexander and the Greek kings on the banks of the Jumna, the Scythian and Parthian empires, the Roman naval expeditions to the coasts of Vietnam and the cosmopolitan courts of the Mogol emperors. When we cross the Mediterranean by plane in the direction of Egypt, we are surprised at first by the somber symphony of colors formed by the brownish-green of the palm groves, the green of the water—which we finally feel justified in describing as eau-de-Nil—the yellowish-grey sand and the purple mud; and even more than by the landscape, we are surprised by the plan of the villages as seen from the air: they sprawl beyond their boundaries and present that intricate and untidy arrangement of houses and little streets which is the sign of the Orient. Here we seem to have the opposite of the New World which, whether Spanish or Anglo-Saxon, and in the sixteenth century as well as the twentieth, shows a marked preference for geometrical layouts.

After Egypt, the flight over Arabia offers a series of variations on a single theme—the desert. First of all, rocks like ruined, red-brick castles emerge from the opalescent sand; elsewhere intricate designs, like the tracery of tree branches—or even more like seaweed or crystals—made by the paradoxical behavior of the wadis which, instead of bringing their waters together in a single stream, branch outwards into tiny rivulets. Further on, the ground seems to have been trampled by some monstrous beast, which has done its best to press it dry with furious stampings.

How delicately colored are the sands! The desert takes on flesh tints: peach-bloom, mother-of-pearl, the iridescence of raw fish. At Aqaba, the water, although beneficent, reflects the pitilessly hard blue of the sky, while the uninhabitable rocky ranges shade off into soft pearly greys.

Toward the end of the afternoon, the sand gradually merges into the mist, which is itself a kind of celestial sand that has joined forces with the earth against the limpid blue-green of the sky. The desert loses its undulations and eminences; it merges with the evening, in a vast, uniform rosy mass which, as yet, has hardly more substance than the sky. The desert has become a desert even in relationship to itself. Gradually the mist spreads everywhere until there is nothing left but night.

After the touchdown at Karachi, day dawns over the incomprehensible, lunar desert of Thar; then small groups of fields appear, still separated by long stretches of desert. As the light strengthens, the cultivated areas fuse together to form a continuous surface of pink and green tints, like the exquisite and faded

colors of some very old tapestry, which has been worn threadbare by long use and tirelessly darned. This is India.

The fields are irregular, yet there is nothing untidy about the
collocations of shapes and colors. However they are grouped,
they present a balanced pattern, as if a great deal of thought had
been given to the drawing of their individual outlines in relationship to the whole. They might be geographical musings by Paul
Klee. The whole scene has a rarefied quality, an extreme and
arbitrary preciosity, in spite of the recurrence of the triple theme:
village, network of fields, pond surrounded by trees.

As the plane lands at, and takes off from, Delhi, one gets a
brief glimpse of a romantic India, with ruined temples set in a
vivid green undergrowth. Then the floods begin. The water
seems so stagnant, so dense and so muddy that it is more like oil
floating in streaks across the surface of another form of water
constituted by the earth. The plane goes over Bihar with its
rocky hills and forests, and then comes the beginning of the
delta. The land is cultivated to the last inch, and each field looks
like a jewel of green gold, pale and shimmering because of the
water with which it is impregnated, and surrounded by the flaw-
less dark rim of its hedges. There are no sharp angles; all the
edges are rounded, yet fit against each other like the cells of a
living tissue. At the approaches to Calcutta, the small villages
increase in number, and their huts appear piled up like ants' eggs
in nests of greenery, the vividness of which is still further intensified by the dark red tiles of certain roofs. The plane lands in
torrential rain.

Beyond Calcutta lies the delta of the Brahmaputra, a monster
of a river, and such a meandering mass that it seems more like a
beast than a watercourse. All around, as far as the eye can see,

the countryside is obliterated by water, except for the jute fields which, when looked at from above, form mossy squares of a greenness all the sharper through being so cool and fresh. Villages surrounded by trees emerge from the water like bunches of flowers with, all around, a swarm of boats.

Caught as it is, between sand without men and men without earth, India offers a very ambiguous appearance. The impression I was able to form during the eight hours it took me to cross from Karachi to Calcutta disassociated India definitely from the New World. It has neither the rigid chessboard pattern of the Middle West or Canada made up of identical units, each with a precise spatter of farm buildings in the same place on the same side; nor, still less so, the deep velvety green of the tropical forest, which is only just being encroached upon here and there by the bold inroads made by the pioneer zones. When the European looks down on this land, divided into minute lots and cultivated to the last acre, he experiences an initial feeling of familiarity. But the way the colors shade into each other, the irregular outlines of the fields and rice swamps which are constantly rearranged in different patterns, the blurred edges which look as if they had been roughly stitched together, all this is part of the same tapestry, but—compared to the more clearly defined forms and colors of a European landscape—it is like a tapestry with the wrong side showing.

ANDRÉ MALRAUX

(1901–76)

André Malraux, who was born into a wealthy Parisian family, assumed almost as many poses as it was possible to assume in the twentieth century: He was, often simultaneously, archaeologist, aesthete, anticolonial revolutionary, novelist, Communist activist, and diplomat. He was also one of the last old-fashioned Orientalists, prone to making large generalizations about the worldviews of the East and the West. But his curiosity was prodigious, and his knowledge seems, in this time of narrow specialization, impressively wide-ranging. As the Minister of Culture of France, he traveled widely, meeting such international celebrities as Mao Tse-Tung and Pandit Nehru, with whom he held improbably long conversations about the state of the world. He went to India in the late 1950s. His primary response to the religious and artistic marvels of Benares, and the Ajanta and Elephanta caves, was, as recorded in his autobiography, *Anti-Memoirs* (1967), rhapsodical. But, as this excerpt shows, behind the exuberant flourishes and often arcane prose there lies a genuine sense of wonder, and the intelligent admiration provoked by an older, more mysterious culture in a cultivated sensibility from Europe.

from ANTI-MEMOIRS

The town from which one reaches Ellora is Aurangabad, a Muslim city dominated by the tomb of Aurangzeb's wife, a rugged

Taj Mahal amid rose bushes that have gone back to nature, which reminded me of the archaeological museum at Autun, a kitchen-garden with Celtic steles and Romanesque statues growing among the artichokes.

The town from which one reaches Elephanta is Bombay.

Like Calcutta, Bombay, which was born in the nineteenth century, is not at all a modernized Indian town: it is a town as Anglo-Indian as Agra, Lahore and Aurangabad are Indo-Muslim. The Red Fort, from whose gigantic gateway a woebegone camel emerged, the domes of marble and confectionery surrounded by woods full of squirrels, the Victorian Gothic buildings (inspired by what cathedrals?) bristling with outsize dentists' advertisements designed in the form of Sanskrit invocations, the dusty coconut palms overgrown with a jumble of old tires—all this blurred into a single derisory backdrop as soon as one entered the sacred caves. Their link with the bowels of the earth suggested an entire subterranean India, secretly watching over the India of the villages, the animals, the processions of urn-carrying women, the majestic trees, while the towns, chimerical and theatrical, made ready to return to dust. The caves of Ellora reign over the bare and unprepossessing plain which they overlook, while those of Elephanta seem hidden away in their island where the gulf shone with a Hellenic radiance beneath the gulls of the Arabian Sea. But they are all united in their sacred darkness. As soon as one entered Elephanta, the glittering ocean was borne away, like the towns, like the India of the British Raj, the India of the Moguls, the India of Nehru—all perishable offerings to the famous *Majesty*, the gigantic triple head of Shiva.

Photographs, and even the cinema, give no idea of the scale. These heads, fifteen to twenty feet high, are smaller than those of the Bayon at Angkor; but, colossal in comparison to the figures around them, they fill the cave as the Pantocrator fills the Byzantine cathedrals of Sicily. Like the Pantocrator, this Shiva stops below the shoulders without becoming a bust. Hence its disturbing aspect of severed head and divine apparition. It is not simply a question of its being "one of the most beautiful statues in India," whatever meaning one may assign to the word "beautiful."

Here, recognizable at first glance, is a masterpiece of sculpture. A full face and two monumental profiles, whose planes (notably those of the eyes) are worthy of the very highest works of art in spite of a seductiveness which is more to do with the jewelry than with the faces.

But then there is Shiva, the cavernous gloom, the sense of the Sacred. This figure belongs, like those of Moissac, to the domain of the great symbols, and what this symbol expresses, it alone can express. This face with its eyes closed on the flow of time as on a funeral chant is to the dancing Shiva of Ellora what the latter is to the *Dances of Death* of the South, and even to the fabulous figures of Madurai.

Finally, as with many of the works which make up the treasury of humanity's imaginary museum, there is the conjunction of the artistic effect of the work, its religious effect and another, unforeseeable, effect. The effect of the *Pharaoh Zoser* arises from the fact that the weathering of the stone has turned it into a death's-head, that of the *Winged Victory* from the fact that fate has devised the perfect mythical creature which men have looked for in vain in the angels: wings being the arms of birds, the *Victory* is perfect only without arms. The famous line that runs from the point of the breast to the tip of the wing was born of this amputation. The perfection (in this sense) of Shiva demanded the sacred gloom, the absence of a body, even a dancing one, the two profiles still embedded in the mountain, the mask with closed eyes—but above all the unique creation by which the Shiva of Elephanta is also *the symbol of India.*

In the neighboring cave, they were chanting verses from the *Bhagavad Gita.* It is familiar to all Hindus. It was recited during Gandhi's funeral wake, and during the fourteen hours of his cremation. Mysteriously in harmony with the subterranean temple, with the colossal Shiva, it seemed the very voice of this sanctuary to which it owed nothing.

Then, standing in their great chariot drawn by white horses,
Krishna and Arjuna sounded their sacred conches . . .
And Arjuna, filled with deep compassion, spoke despairingly . . .

The two legendary armies of India are face to face. The old king whom Arjuna is fighting against is blind. His charioteer has the magical power of knowing what is happening on the battlefield. He hears the dialogue begin, in the midst of the enemy army, in the chariot with the white horses, between Prince Arjuna and his charioteer, who is Krishna and will become the supreme Deity. The *Gita* is divine speech reported by magic to a blind Priam enclosed in his darkness.

Arjuna looks at those who are to die, and Krishna reminds him that if the greatness of man is to free himself from fate, it is

not for the warrior to free himself from courage. It is the fratri-
cidal combat of the epics, and for us the Trojan sadness of Arjuna
seems like the desolate echo of the voice of Antigone:

> Krishna, I see such omens of evil!
> What can we hope from this killing of kinsmen?
> What do I want with victory, empire,
> Or their enjoyment?
> How can I care for power or pleasure,
> My own life, even?

The chanting voice was answered by another, as Krishna
answers Arjuna in the poem.

Your words are wise, Arjuna, but your sorrow is for nothing.
The truly wise mourn neither for the living or the dead.
There never was a time when I did not exist, nor you, nor any of
    these kings.
Nor is there any future in which we shall cease to be . . .

This chant began the Revelation which my companions knew
by heart, accompanied in the darkness by the distant surge of
the ocean and streaked with the cries of gulls: the song of the
Deity who transcends, animates and destroys worlds, and of the
spirit which transmigrates through bodies and souls, the Atman:

> Know this Atman, unborn, undying,
> Never ceasing, never beginning,
> Deathless, birthless, unchanging for ever.

How can it die the death of the body?
Worn-out garments are shed by the body:
Worn-out bodies are shed by the dweller
Within the body . . .

I had heard this last stanza in Benares. Here it had shed its funereal overtones; and what followed took on among these unseeing gods an even greater solemnity than among the funeral pyres:

There is day, also, and night in the universe;
The wise know this, declaring the day of Brahma
A thousand ages in span
And the night a thousand ages.
Day dawns, and all those lives that lay hidden asleep
Come forth and show themselves, mortally manifest:
Night falls, and all are dissolved
Into the sleeping germ of life . . .
And all the creatures exist within me:
As the vast air, wandering world-wide,
Remains within the ether always,
So these, my wandering creatures,
Are always within me . . .
. . . I am Being and non-Being, immortality and death . . .

One of my companions answered the distant chant with one of the most celebrated verses of the poem, and his voice reached across the enormous pillars, muffled and yet carried by the low roof of the caves:

Who can kill immortality? ...

For the chanting priests, was this response rising out of the silence as mysteriously natural as my wish for the poor couple at Madurai had been? They had fallen silent. At Benares, I had re-read the *Gita*. From its subterranean depths, from all that it owes to an earlier Brahmanism, there emerged dimly, like the figures in these caves, the divine sermon of love which Brahmanism scorned, and above all the cosmic stoicism to which the poem owes its fame. In the inexorable march of constellations which is the return to the source, man is united with God when he discovers his identity with Him and when he observes the Law, which is caste duty. Action is necessary, because the divine scheme must be fulfilled: it is not you who are about to kill your kinsmen, says Krishna to Arjuna, it is I. And action is purified of life if man is sufficiently in communion with God to offer it up to him as a sacrifice.

... Because they understood this, the ancient seekers for liberation
Could safely engage in action ...
There is nothing, in all the three worlds,
Which I do not already possess;
Nothing I have yet to acquire.
But I go on working, nevertheless ...
Realize that pleasure and pain, gain and loss, victory
And defeat, are all one and the same: then go into battle ...

For my companions, this famous moment was an eternal moment. Yet the sculptures all around me in the shadow, and

the *Gita* itself, expressed not so much the sacred stoicism of
the last verses as the communion with God into which the
metaphysical austerity had transformed itself: the mystique
which Brahmanism, like Buddhism, Christianity and Islam, had
discovered. Even if the verses of communion had not been
recited in another cave, the metamorphosis of faith would have
been present here as palpably as it is in St. Peter's in Rome when
one remembers our cathedrals there. India is obsessed by the
image of the ever-changing waters of the changeless rivers, and
the successive souls of its religion passed before Shiva as did its
ancient armies before the sacrificial pyres. The Old Testament
of the *Upanishads* had become the New Testament of the *Gita*.
In the depths of time, there was the hymn to Kali:

> Thou, Mother of Blessings,
> Thou, terrible Night, Night of delusion, Night of death,
> We greet thee.

And, well after Elephanta, the parable of prayer:

> "I pray in vain," said the daughter of the disciple to the Master.
> "What do you love best in the world?" "My brother's little child."
> "Retire and meditate on him alone, and you will see that he is
> Krishna. Only love can cure the blind."

The meditation of the colossal heads of the *Majesty* on eternity and time, twin prisoners of the Sacred, also seemed like a
meditation on the destiny which guides religions from venera-
tion to love as it guides mortals from birth to death—but
beneath which there remained an inviolable permanence. If the

Bhagavad Gita is present in so many holy places, it is because it expresses this; like the *Majesty*, it is India. Gandhi had tried to translate it. The greatest of the Renouncers of modern times regarded action carried out in the spirit of surrender to his God as the supreme form of renunciation. "My devotion to my people is one of the aspects of the discipline I impose upon myself in order to liberate my soul. I have no need to seek refuge in a cave: I carry my cave inside myself."

> Certain is death for all who shall be born,
> And certain is birth for all who have died . . .

Night falls on the dead of the final combat, after the seventeen-day battle. The few survivors have withdrawn into the forest to die there as ascetics. The patient birds of prey are waiting, and among the fallen swords glittering in the moonlight, monkeys like those which accompanied me at Madurai touch the eyes of the dead with puzzled fingers.

Girls were passing by outside, each with a red flower in her hand. The gulls of Oman still wheeled across the sparkling gulf. A motorboat took us back. Bombay, a crazy bazaar that thinks itself a town, rose little by little above the water, and we made our way toward the enormous archway of the Gateway to the East. Once it watched over the English steamships like a marine temple over a war fleet. Today, ours was the only boat to berth there—back from the India of eternity. On the waterfront, atomic reactors glittered . . .

We were to return to Delhi overnight. For the evening, the

former bungalow of the governor at the tip of the peninsula had been put at my disposal. It was a sad place, like all the uninhabited houses on the shores of the gulf. The garden, still more uninhabited in spite of a few silent gardeners, seemed like a cemetery of Indian Army officers. And the Indian Army was as remote as Akbar's horsemen.

The passion which Asia, vanished civilizations, ethnography have long inspired in me arose from an essential wonderment at the forms which man has been able to assume, but also from the light which every strange civilization threw on my own, that quality of the unusual or the arbitrary which it revealed in one or other of its aspects. I had just relived one of the most profound and complex experiences of my youth. More so than my first encounter with pre-Hispanic America, because England did not destroy the priests and warriors of India, and because temples are still built there to the ancient gods. More so than Islam and Japan, because India is less westernized, because it spreads more widely the nocturnal wings of man; more so than Africa, because of its elaboration, its continuity. Remote from ourselves in dream and in time, India belongs to the Ancient Orient of our soul. The last rajahs are not pharaohs, but the Brahmans of Benares evoke the priests of Isis, the fakirs were there in Alexander's time, and the peacocks in the derelict palaces of Amber had called to my mind the Chaldean multitude, astounded by the ambassadors from the kingdoms of India "whose birds could spread their tails." And this other Egypt, whose people and beliefs had changed little since the time of Ramses, was perhaps the last religious civilization, certainly the last great polytheism. What is Zeus, compared with Shiva? The only god of antiquity whose language is worthy of India is the god without temples—Fate.

What did I really know of this civilization? Its arts, its thought, its history. No more than I knew of the great dead civilizations—except that I had heard its music and had met a few gurus, which was not without importance in a land whose religious thinking expresses a Truth which is not to be understood but lived: "Believe nothing that you have not first experienced." I was not presumptuous enough to "know" (on the way through . . .) a way of thought that had survived seventeen conquests and two millennia; I merely sought to grasp something of its haunting message.

Man can experience the presence of universal Being in all beings, and of all beings in universal Being; he discovers then the identity of all appearances, whether they be pleasure and pain, life and death, outside himself and within Being; he can reach that essence in himself which transcends his transmigrated souls, and experience its identity with the essence of a world of endless returning, which he escapes through his ineffable communion with it. But there is something at once bewitching and bewitched in Indian thought, which has to do with the feeling it gives us of climbing a sacred mountain whose summit constantly recedes; of going forward in darkness by the light of the torch which it carries. We know this feeling through some of our saints and philosophers; but it is in India alone that Being, conquered from universal appearance and metamorphosis, does not part company with them, but often becomes inseparable from them "like the two sides of a medal," to point the way to an inexhaustible Absolute which transcends even Being itself.

Of course, the word "being" is not a satisfactory rendering of the "uncreated" Brahman, the supreme Deity—to which the wise man gains access through what is deepest in his soul, and not through the mind. The gods are merely different means of reaching it, and "each man approaches God through his own gods." It is It that the Buddha seeks to destroy in his earliest teachings, when he gives as the final end of ecstasy what he magnificently calls "the peace of the abyss."

Superstitions swarmed like mayflies around this peak of thought, which animated all the temples I had seen, as well as Benares. But how inadequately it illuminated the vast nation that surrounded me! I had met men of the Brahmin caste, but no priests; intellectuals, artists, diplomats—and their wives; a few great figures, and many politicians, a race unknown at the beginning of the century. Not a single tradesman, not a single peasant. Alone in this melancholy garden of an enormous city looking out over the most religious and surely the most affectionate country in the world, I could recall only an immense and silent multitude—as silent as its friendly animals. A Hindu rather than an Indian crowd: its fields resembled French fields, but its dreams did not resemble French dreams. But what I evoked by way of contrast (more precisely, what was evoked in me), was not a Christian crowd: it was the crowd of the Paris *métro*, and more especially the one I had known best, that of the war. The spirituality of India made me think fleetingly of the Glières chaplain, but the Hindu multitudes, for whom death gives a meaning to life, made me think with bitterness of the men of our own land for whom death has no meaning: the shadowy figures who for centuries had laid a scarlet hibiscus at the foot of a dark god or of a tree reminiscent of a divine benediction, brothers of the peasants in whom I perceived only the sad smile that had perhaps greeted Semiramis, the little tradesmen, brothers of so many other little tradesmen spoke to me of all our own men without caste whom I had seen in the face of death.

Beyond the garden where the sound of the waves was inaudible, the gulf still glittered; the gulls of Oman would wheel back and forth until nightfall. I went inside the deserted bungalow of the last governor of Bombay, to re-read what I wrote in 1940 about my comrades who fought and died in vain . . .

PETER MATTHIESSEN

(1927-)

Born in New York City, Peter Matthiessen was educated at the Sorbonne and Yale University. In 1950, he moved to Paris where he helped found the literary magazine *Paris Review*. Later that same decade, he published *Wildlife in America* (1959). It was the first of many such books he would write on the disastrous effect of human beings upon the natural environment. For the next four decades he explored similar themes in places as diverse as New Guinea, Siberia, and Africa. In 1973, soon after the death of his wife, he traveled to India and Nepal, looking for the rare and elusive snow leopard. The beautifully strange book he published subsequently, *The Snow Leopard* (1978), became something of a cult item. Matthiessen seemed to belong in it to both the great tradition of American transcendentalists, reverential before Indian religion and philosophy, as well as to the more recent and troubled generation of American seekers of Eastern wisdom. He never saw a snow leopard; he wasn't admitted to the Buddhist monastery he badly wanted to see. But these disappointments were more than compensated for, it seems, by the exhilaration of a mind emptied Zen-style, amid the Himalayan vastness, of its usual western concerns. Remarkably, for someone so seemingly self-absorbed, Matthiessen rarely missed anything in the world around him. These excerpts from the beginning of *The Snow Leopard* show him capable of both hard-edged cerebration and lyrical meditation.

from THE SNOW LEOPARD

September 28

At sunrise the small expedition meets beneath a giant fig beyond Pokhara—two white sahibs, four Sherpas, fourteen porters. The Sherpas are of the famous mountain tribe of northeast Nepal, near Namche Bazaar, whose men accompany the ascents of the great peaks; they are Buddhist herders who have come down in recent centuries out of eastern Tibet—*sherpa* is a Tibetan word for "easterner"—and their language, culture, and appearance all reflect Tibetan origin. One of the porters is also a Sherpa, and two are refugee Tibetans; the rest are of mixed Aryan and Mongol stock. Mostly barefoot, in ragged shorts or the big-seated, jodhpur-legged pants of India, wearing all manner of old vests and shawls and headgear, the porters pick over the tall wicker baskets. In addition to their own food and blankets, they must carry a load of up to eighty pounds that is braced on their bent backs by a tump-line around the forehead, and there is much testing and denunciation of the loads, together with shrill bargaining, before any journey in these mountains can begin. Porters are mostly local men of uncertain occupation and unsteadfast habit, notorious for giving trouble. But it is also true that their toil is hard and wretchedly rewarded—about one dollar a day. As a rule, they accompany an expedition for no more than a week away from home, after which they are replaced by others, and the testing and denunciation start anew. Today nearly two hours pass, and clouds have gathered, before all fourteen are mollified, and the tattered line sets off toward the west.

We are glad to go. These edges of Pokhara might be tropical outskirts anywhere—vacant children, listless adults, bent dogs and thin chickens in a litter of sagging shacks and rubble, mud, weeds, stagnant ditches, bad sweet smells, vivid bright broken plastic bits, and dirty fruit peelings awaiting the carrion pig; for want of better fare, both pigs and dogs consume the human excrement that lies everywhere along the paths. In fair weather, all this flux is tolerable, but now at the dreg end of the rainy season, the mire of life seems leached into the sallow skins of these thin beings, who squat and soap themselves and wring their clothes each morning in the rain puddles.

Brown eyes observe us as we pass. Confronted with the pain of Asia, one cannot look and cannot turn away. In India, human misery seems so pervasive that one takes in only stray details: a warped leg or a dead eye, a sick pariah dog eating withered grass, an ancient woman lifting her sari to move her shrunken bowels by the road. Yet in Varanasi there is hope of life that has been abandoned in such cities as Calcutta, which seems resigned to the dead and dying in its gutters. Shiva dances in the spicy foods, in the exhilarated bells of the swarming bicycles, the angry bus horns, the chatter of the temple monkeys, the vermilion tikka dot on the women's foreheads, even in the scent of charred human flesh that pervades the ghats. The people smile—that is the greatest miracle of all. In the heat and stench and shriek of Varanasi, where in fiery sunrise swallows fly like departing spirits over the vast silent river, one delights in the smile of a blind girl being led, of a Hindu gentleman in white turban gazing benignly at the bus driver who reviles him, of a flute-playing beggar boy, of a slow old woman pouring holy water from the Ganga, the River, onto a stone elephant daubed red.

Near the burning ghats, and the industry of death, a river palace has been painted with huge candy-striped tigers.

No doubt Varanasi is the destination of this ancient Hindu at the outskirts of Pokhara, propped up on a basket borne on poles across the shoulders of four servants—off, it appears, on his last pilgrimage to the Mother Ganges, to the dark temples that surround the ghats, to those hostels where the pilgrim waits his turn to join the company of white-shrouded cadavers by the river edge, waits again to be laid upon the stacks of fired wood: the attendants will push this yellow foot, that shriveled elbow, back into the fire, and rake his remains off the burning platform into the swift river. And still enough scraps will remain to sustain life in the long-headed cadaverous dogs that haunt the ashes, while sacred kine—huge white silent things—devour the straw thongs that had bound this worn-out body to its stretcher.

The old man has been ravened from within. That blind and greedy stare of his, that caved-in look, and the mouth working, reveal who now inhabits him, who now stares out.

I nod to Death in passing, aware of the sound of my own feet upon my path. The ancient is lost in a shadow world, and gives no sign.

Grey river road, grey sky. From rock to torrent rock flits a pied wagtail.

Wayfarers: a delicate woman bears a hamper of small silver fishes, and another bends low beneath a basket of rocks that puts my own light pack to shame; her rocks will be hammered to gravel by other women of Pokhara, in the labor of the myriad brown hands that will surface a new road south to India.

Through a shaft of sun moves a band of Magar women, scarlet-shawled; they wear heavy brass ornaments in the left nostril. In the new sun, a red-combed rooster clambers quickly to the roof matting of a roadside hut, and fitfully a little girl starts singing. The light irradiates white peaks of Annapurna marching down the sky, in the great rampart that spreads east and west for eighteen hundred miles, the Himalaya—the *alaya* (abode, or home) of *hima* (snow).

Hibiscus, frangipani, bougainvillaea: seen under snow peaks, these tropical blossoms become the flowers of heroic landscapes. Macaques scamper in green meadow, and a turquoise roller spins in a golden light. Drongos, rollers, barbets, and the white Egyptian vulture are the common birds, and all have close relatives in East Africa, where GS and I first met; he wonders how this vulture would react if confronted with the egg of an ostrich, which was also a common Asian bird during the Pleistocene. In Africa, the Egyptian vulture is recognized as a tool-using species, due to its knack of cracking the huge ostrich eggs by slinging rocks at them with its beak.

Until quite recently, these Nepal lowlands were broadleaf evergreen *sal* forest (*Shorea robusta*), the haunt of elephant and tiger and the great Indian rhinoceros. Forest-cutting and poaching cleared them out; except in last retreats such as the Rapti Valley, to the southeast, the saintly tread of elephants is gone. The last wild Indian cheetah was sighted in central India in 1952, the Asian lion is reduced to a single small population in the Gir Forest, northwest of Bombay, and the tiger becomes legendary almost everywhere. Especially in India and Pakistan, the hoofed animals are rapidly disappearing, due to destruction of habitat by subsistence agriculture, overcutting of the forests, overgrazing by the scraggy hordes of domestic animals, erosion, flood—the whole dismal cycle of events that accompanies over-crowding by human beings. In Asia more than all places on earth, it is crucial to establish wildlife sanctuaries at once, before the last animals are overwhelmed. As GS has written, "Man is modifying the world so fast and so drastically that most animals cannot adapt to the new conditions. In the Himalaya as else-where there is a great dying, one infinitely sadder than the Pleis-tocene extinctions, for man now has the knowledge and the need to save these remnants of his past."

The track along the Yamdi River is a main trading route, passing through rice paddies and villages on its way west to the Kali Gandaki River, where it turns north to Mustang and Tibet. Green village compounds, set about with giant banyans and old stone pools and walls, are cropped to lawn by water buffalo and cattle; the fresh water and soft shade give them the harmony of parks. These village folk own even less than those of Pokhara, yet they are spared by their old economies from modern poverty: one understands why "village life" has been celebrated as the natural, happy domain of man by many thinkers from Lao-tzu to Gandhi. In a warm sun children play, and women roll clothes on rocks at the village fountain and pound grain in stone mortars, and from all sides come reassuring dung smells and chicken clatter and wafts of fire smoke from the low hearths. In tidy yards, behind strong stiles and walls, the clay huts are of warm earthen red, with thatched roofs, hand-carved sills and shutters, and yellow-flowered pumpkin vines. Maize is stacked in narrow cribs, and rice is spread to dry on broad straw mats, and between the banana and papaya trees big calm spiders hang against the sky.

A canal bridged here and there by ten-foot granite slabs runs through a hamlet, pouring slowly over shining pebbles. It is midday, the sun melts the air, and we sit on a stone wall in the cool shade. By the canal is the village tea house, a simple open-fronted hut with makeshift benches and a clay oven in the form of a rounded mound on the clay floor. The mound has a side opening for inserting twigs and two holes on the top for boiling water, which is poured through a strainer of cheap tea dust into a glass containing coarse sugar and buffalo milk. With this *chiya* we take plain bread and a fresh cucumber, while children playing on the shining stones pretend to splash us, and a collared dove sways on a tall stalk of bamboo.

One by one the porters come, turning around to lower their loads onto the wall. A porter of shy face and childlike smile, who looks too slight for his load, is playing comb music on a fig leaf. "Too many hot," says another, smiling. This is the Sherpa porter, Tukten, a wiry small man with Mongol eyes and outsized ears and a disconcerting smile—I wonder why this Tukten is a porter.

I set off ahead, walking alone in the cool breeze of the valley. In the bright September light and mountain shadow—steep foothills are closing in as the valley narrows, and the snow peaks to the north are no longer seen—the path follows a dike between the reedy canal and the green terraces of rice that descend in steps to the margins of the river. Across the canal, more terraces ascend to the crests of the high hills, and a blue sky.

At a rest wall, two figs of different species were planted long ago; one is a banyan, or nigrodha (*Fiscus indica*), the other a pipal (*F. religiosa*), sacred to both the Hindus and the Buddhists. Wild flowers and painted stones are set among the buttressed roots, to bring the traveler good fortune, and stone terraces are built up around the trunks in such a way that the shade-seeking traveler may back up and set down his load while standing almost straight. These resting places are everywhere along the trading routes, some of them so ancient that the great trees have long since died, leaving two round holes in a stonework oval platform. Like the tea houses and the broad stepping-stones that are built into the hills, the rest walls impart a blessedness to this landscape, as if we had wandered into a lost country of the golden age.

Awaiting the line of porters that winds through the paddies, I sit on the top level of the wall, my feet on the step on which the loads are set and my back against a tree. In dry sunshine and the limpid breeze down from the mountains, two black cows are threshing rice, flanks gleaming in the light of afternoon. First the paddy is drained and the rice sickled, then the yoked animals tied by a long line to a stake in the middle of the rice, are driven round and round in a slowly decreasing circle while children fling the stalks beneath their hooves. Then the stalks are tossed into the air, and the grains beneath swept into baskets to be taken home and winnowed. The fire-colored dragonflies in the early autumn air, the bent backs in bright reds and yellows, the gleam on the black cattle and wheat stubble, the fresh green of the paddies and the sparkling river—over everything lies an immortal light, like transparent silver.

In the clean air and absence of all sound, of even the simplest machinery—for the track is often tortuous and steep, and fords too many streams, to permit bicycles—in the warmth and harmony and seeming plenty, come whispers of a paradisal age. Apparently the grove of *sal* trees called Lumbini, only thirty miles south of this same tree, in fertile lands north of the Rapti River, has changed little since the sixth century BC, when Siddhartha Gautama was born there to a rich clan of the Sakya tribe in a kingdom of elephants and tigers. Gautama forsook a life of ease to become a holy mendicant, or "wanderer"—a common practice in northern India even today. Later he was known as Sakyamuni (Sage of the Sakyas), and afterwards, the Buddha—the Awakened One. Fig trees and the smoke of peasant fires, the greensward and gaunt cattle, white egrets and jungle crows are still seen on the Ganges Plain where Sakyamuni passed his life, from Lumbini south and east to Varanasi (an ancient city even when Gautama came there) and Rajgir and Gaya. Tradition says that he traveled as far north as Kathmandu (even then a prosperous city of the Newars) and preached on the hill of Swayambhunath, among the monkeys and the pines.

In Sakyamuni's time, the disciples called yogas were already well evolved. Perhaps a thousand years before, the dark-skinned Dravidians of lowland India had been overcome by nomad Aryans from the Asian steppes who were bearing their creed of sky gods, wind, and light across Eurasia. Aryan concepts were contained in their Sanskrit Vedas, or knowledge—ancient texts of unknown origin which include the Rig Veda and the Upanishads and were to become the base of the Hindu religion. To the wandering ascetic named Sakyamuni, such epic preachments on the nature of the Universe and Man were useless as a cure for human suffering. In what became known as the Four Noble Truths, Sakyamuni perceived that man's existence is inseparable from sorrow; that the cause of suffering is craving; that peace is attained by extinguishing craving; that this liberation may be brought about by following the Eight-fold Path: right attention to one's understanding, intentions, speech, and actions; right livelihood, effort, mindfulness; right concentration, by which is meant the unification of the self through sitting yoga.

The Vedas already included the idea that mortal desire—since it implies lack—had no place in the highest state of being; that what was needed was that death-in-life and spiritual rebirth sought by all teachers, from the early shamans to the existentialists. Sakyamuni's creed was less a rejection of Vedic philosophy than an effort to apply it, and his intense practice of meditation does not content itself with the serenity of yoga states (which in his view falls short of ultimate truth) but goes beyond, until the transparent radiance of stilled mind opens out in *prajna*, or transcendent *knowing*, that higher consciousness or "Mind" which is inherent in all sentient beings, and which depends on the unsentimental embrace of all existence. A true experience of *prajna* corresponds to "enlightenment" or liberation—not change, but transformation—a profound vision of his identity with universal life, past, present, and future, that keeps man from doing harm to others and sets him free from fear of birth-and-death.

In the fifth century BC, near the town of Gaya, south and east of Varanasi, Sakyamuni attained enlightenment in the deep experience that his own "true nature," his Buddha-nature, was no different from the nature of the universe. For half a century thereafter, at such places as the Deer Park in Sarnath, and Nalanda, and the Vulture's Peak near present-day Rajgir, he taught a doctrine based upon the impermanence of individual existence, the eternal continuity of becoming, as in the morning river that appears the same as the river of the night before, now passed away. (Though he preached to women and weakened the caste system by admitting low-born brethren to his order, Sakyamuni never involved himself in social justice, far less government; his way holds that self-realization is the greatest contribution one can make to one's fellow man.) At the age of eighty, he ended his days at Kusinagara (the modern Kusinara), forty miles east of Gorakhpur and just west of the Kali Gandaki River.

This much is true, all else is part of the Buddha legend, which is truth of a different order. In regard to his enlightenment, it is related that this wanderer was in his thirties when he gave up the rigors of the yogi and embraced the "Middle Path" between sensuality and mortification, accepting food in a golden bowl from the daughter of the village headman. Thereupon, he was renounced by his disciples. At dusk he sat himself beneath a pipal tree with his face toward the East, vowing that though his skin and nerves and bones should waste away and his life-blood dry, he would not leave this seat until he had attained Supreme Enlightenment. All that night, beset by demons, Sakyamuni sat in meditation. And in that golden daybreak, it is told, the Self-Awakened One truly perceived the Morning Star, as if seeing it for the first time in his life.

In what is now known as Bodh Gaya—still a pastoral land of cattle savanna, shimmering water, rice paddies, palms, and red-clay hamlets without paved roads or wires—a Buddhist temple stands beside an ancient pipal, descended from that *bodhi* tree, or "Enlightenment Tree," beneath which this man sat. Here in a warm dawn, ten days ago, with three Tibetan monks in maroon robes, I watched the rising of the Morning Star and came away no wiser than before. But later I wondered if the Tibetans were aware that the *bodhi* tree was murmuring with gusts of birds, while another large pipal, so close by that it touched the holy tree with many branches, was without life. I make no claim for this event: I simply declare what I saw there at Bodh Gaya.

W. SOMERSET MAUGHAM

(1874–1966)

The British writer W. Somerset Maugham is best known for his skillful short stories and the novel *Of Human Bondage* (1915), which describes the doomed passion of a medical student not much unlike the one Maugham himself was. Many of his stories are set in Southeast Asia, particularly Malaya, and prefigure the gloomier cosmopolitan fiction of Graham Greene. Strangely, he did not visit India until late in his life—1938—and he took what in many ways was the British Grand Tour of India: Bombay, Benares, Agra, Kerala, Goa. Although a partisan admirer of Kipling, Maugham cast a skeptical eye at the pretensions of empire building. He was interested in exploring the Indian claim to spirituality. He was particularly intrigued by the practice of chastity, perhaps because he found it so difficult to adopt it in his own life. He met a number of Indian holy men. Some of these interests found their way into one of his more famous novels, *The Razor's Edge* (1944), which prefigured the western quest in the 1960s for unwestern forms of personal salvation.

from A WRITER'S NOTEBOOK

Goa. You drive through coconut groves among which you see here and there ruins of houses. On the lagoon sail fishing boats, their lateen sails shining white in the brilliant sun. The churches are large and white, their façades decorated with honey-colored stone pilasters. Inside they are large, bare, spacious, with pulpits in Portuguese baroque carved with the utmost elaboration and altarpieces in the same style. In one, at a side altar, a priest, a native, was saying mass with a dark-faced acolyte to serve him. There was no one to worship. In the Franciscan Church you are shown a wooden Christ on a crucifix and the guide tells you that six months before the destruction of the city it wept tears. In the cathedral they were holding a service, the organ was playing and in the organ loft there was a small choir of natives singing with a harshness in which somehow the Catholic chants acquired a mysteriously heathen, Indian character. It was strangely impressive to see these great empty churches in that deserted place and to know that day by day with not a soul to listen the priests said mass in them.

The priest. He came to see me at the hotel. He was a tall Indian, neither thin nor fat, with good, somewhat blunt features and large dark liquid eyes, with shining whites to them. He wore a cassock. At first he was very nervous and his hands moved restlessly, but I did what I could to put him at his ease, and presently his hands were still. He spoke very good English. He told me that he was of Brahmin family, his ancestor, a Brahmin, having been converted by one of the companions of St. Francis Xavier. He was a man in the early thirties, of powerful physique and of a fine presence. His voice was rich and musical. He had been six years in Rome and during his stay in Europe had traveled much. He wanted to go back, but his mother was old and wished him to remain in Goa till she died. He taught in a school and preached. He spent much of his time converting the Sudras. He said it was hopeless now to try to do anything with the high-caste Hindus. I tried to get him to speak of religion. He told me that he thought Christianity was large enough to embrace all the other faiths, but regretted that Rome had not allowed the Indian Church to develop according to the native inclinations. I got the impression that he accepted the Christian dogmas as a discipline, but without fervor, and I am not sure that if one had been able to get to the bottom of his beliefs one would not have found that they were held with at least a certain skepticism. I had a feeling that even though there were four hundred years of Catholicism behind him he was still at heart a Vedantist. I wondered if to him the God of the Christians was not merged, if not in his mind, at least in some obscure depth of the unconscious, with the Brahman of the Upanishads. He told me that even among the Christians the caste system still obtained to this extent that none of them married out of his own caste. It would be unheard of that a Christian of Brahmin extraction should marry a Christian of Sudra extraction. He was not displeased to tell me that there was not in his veins a drop of white blood; his family had always kept resolutely pure. "We're Christians," he said to me, "but first of all we're Hindus." His attitude to Hinduism was tolerant and sympathetic.

The backwaters of Travancore. They are narrow canals, more or less artificial, that is to say natural stretches of water have been joined up by embanked channels to make a waterway from

Trivandrum to Cochin. On each side grow coconuts, and thatched houses with mud roofs stand at the water's edge, each surrounded by its little compound in which grow bananas, papaya and sometimes a jack tree. Children play; women sit about, or pound rice; in frail boats, sometimes carrying loads of coconuts or leaves or provender for cattle, men and boys slowly paddle up and down; on the banks people fish. I saw one man with a bow and arrow and a little bundle of fish that he had shot. Everyone bathes. It is green, cool and quiet. You get a very curious impression of pastoral life, peaceful and primitive, and not too hard. Now and then a big barge passes, poled by two men from one town to another. Here and there is a modest little temple or a tiny chapel, for a large proportion of the population is Christian.

The river is grown over with the water hyacinth. The plants, with their delicate mauve flowers, rooted not in soil but in water, float along, and as your boat passes through, making a channel of clear water, they are pushed aside; but no sooner has it passed than they drift back with the stream and the breeze, and no trace that you have gone that way remains. So with us who have made some small stir in the world.

The Dewan. I had been told that he was not only an astute but an unscrupulous politician. Everyone agreed that he was as clever as he was crooked. He was a thickset, sturdy man, no taller than I, with alert but not very large eyes, a broad brow, a hooked nose, full lips and a small rounded chin. He had a thick crop of fuzzy hair. He was dressed in a white dhoti, a white tunic fitting close round the neck, and a white scarf; his feet were bare and he wore sandals which he slipped on and off. He had the geniality of the politician who for years has gone out of his way to be cordial with everyone he meets. He talked very good English, fluently, with a copious choice of words, and he put what he had to say plainly and with logical sequence. He had a resonant voice and an easy manner. He did not agree with a good deal that I said and corrected me with decision, but with the courtesy that took it for granted I was too intelligent to be affronted by contradiction. He was of course very busy, having all the affairs of the state in his charge, but seemed to have enough leisure to talk for the best part of an hour on Indian metaphysics and religion as though there were nothing that interested him more. He seemed well read not only in Indian literature, but in English, but there was no indication that he had any acquaintance with the literature or thought of other European countries.

When I began to speak of religion in India as being the basis of all their philosophy, he corrected me. "No," he said, "that is not so; there is no religion in India in your sense of the word; there are systems of philosophy, and theism, Hindu theism, is one of its varieties."

I asked him if educated, cultured Hindus had still an active belief in Karma and transmigration. He answered with emphasis. "I absolutely believe in it myself with all the strength of my being. I am convinced that I have passed through innumerable lives before this one and that I shall have to pass through I do not know how many more before I secure release. Karma and transmigration are the only possible explanations I can see for the inequalities of men and for the evil of the world. Unless I believed in them I should think the world meaningless."

I asked him if, believing this, the Hindu feared death less than the European. He took a little time to think of his answer, and, as I had already discovered was his way, while he was considering it, talked of something else so that I thought he was not going to answer. Then he said: "The Indian is not like the Japanese who has been taught from his earliest years that life is of no value and that there are a number of reasons for which he must not hesitate for an instant to sacrifice it. The Indian does not fear death because it will take him away from life, he fears it because there is uncertainty in what condition he may be born next. He can have no assurance that he will be born a Brahmin, an angel or even a God, he may be born a Sudra, a dog or a worm. When he thinks of death it is the future he fears."

The viña-player. He was a stoutish man of forty, clean-shaven, with all the front part of his head shaven too; his hair, long at the back, was tied in a knot. He was dressed in a dhoti and a collarless shirt. He sat on the floor to play. His instrument was highly decorated, carved in low relief and ending in a dragon's head. He played for a couple of hours, now and then breaking into a few bars of song, music hundreds of years old, but some much less, music of the last century when under a Maharajah of Travancore, himself an accomplished musician, there was great enthusiasm for the art. It is elaborate music, which requires all your attention, and I do not think I could have followed it at all if I hadn't had some acquaintance with modern music. It is slowly rhythmical and when your ear gets accustomed to it various and tuneful. Of late years the composers have been not a little influenced by modern music, European music, and it is queer in these Eastern melodies to discern a faint recollection of the bagpipes or the martial din of a military band.

A Hindu house. The owner was a judge who had inherited it from his fathers. He was dead, and I was received by his widow, a stout woman in white with white curly hair hanging down her back, and bare feet. You entered by a door in a blank wall and found yourself in a sort of loggia with a carved wooden ceiling of jackwood. It was decorated with lotus leaves and in the center a bas-relief of Siva dancing. Then came a small dusty courtyard in which were growing crotons and cassias. Then the house. In front was a veranda with hanging eaves, showing the open woodwork of the roof, beautifully joined, and with a carved ceiling of a rich brown like that of the loggia. At each end was a raised part under which were receptacles in which the owner normally kept his clothes and which served as seats. Here he received his guests. At the back were two doors with rich locks and hinges of decorated brass; they led to two small dark rooms, with one bed in each, and in one of which the master of the house had slept. At one side was a closed aperture which led to a space in which the grain was kept. Going through a small door at the side you came into another courtyard; at the back of this were the women's apartments and on the sides the kitchen and other small rooms. I was shown into one room in which was some poor, shabby and old-fashioned European furniture.

The first courtyard at night would surely lose its dusty neg-lected aspect, and under the moon and the stars, cool and silent, form a romantic setting. I should have liked to listen there to the viña-player, his absorbed and serious face lit by the smoky flame of a brass lamp, its wick floating in coconut oil.

VED MEHTA

(1 9 3 4 –)

Ved Mehta was born in what is now Pakistan. An attack of meningitis left him completely blind at four. He left India when he was sixteen years old to go to a school for the blind in the United States. He was educated at Oxford and Harvard and went on to live in New York. His many memoirs describe in detail these physical and emotional displacements. During the last four decades, he has returned often to India, researching reports for *The New Yorker* that have now gone into several books and form one of the most substantial journalistic engagements with contemporary India. The earliest of these pieces excerpted here describe his visit in 1966 to the Kumbha Mela, a once-in-twelve-years gathering of devout Hindus at the confluence of the rivers Ganges and Yamuna. Celebrities and glossy magazines in the West have recently discovered the Kumbha Mela. At the time of Mehta's visit, it was a less glamorous affair, notable mostly for its bewildering variety of Hindu sects and sadhus (mendicants). Mehta met, among other Hindu religious entrepreneurs, Maharishi Mahesh Yogi, who, though then still some years away from worldwide fame as the guru of the Beatles, had, as the excerpt demonstrates, carefully distilled his wisdom into a vagueness that could both confuse and console.

from PORTRAIT OF INDIA

THE LOINS OF THE EARTH ARE BETWIXT
THE GANGA AND THE YAMUNA

Today, I am in Allahabad, which, like the other Indian cities, is a jumble of British, Muslim, and Hindu influences. The British Allahabad, which now exists only for the benefit of a few educated Indians, takes in the military and civil cantonments, the racecourse, the clubs, and the university. The Muslim Ilahabas is well represented by Akbar's great fort, which lies three miles to the east of the city, but the wedge of land has by now been so eroded that the water flows very close to the embankment, leaving a correspondingly larger sand bank at Jhusi, across the Ganga. The ancient Hindu Prayaga can be observed in the parched, dusty, but joyful faces of tens of thousands of pilgrims coming to the city on the Grand Trunk Road—some in buses, tongas, ekkas, and bullock carts, some on bicycles, horses, and even elephants, but most on foot, patiently trudging, with loads on their heads, as if they had been walking for years.

The country is in mourning for the death of Prime Minister Shastri, at Tashkent, but the *mela* goes on, and at one point on the day before Amavasya I find myself resting in a tent—pitched near the *sangam*—which I have reserved in advance, and composing a letter to Roy and Miss Devi, who print in *Kumbha* a letter to a friend relating some of their experiences at the Purna Kumbha *mela* of 1954:

I have heard from you such a lot about the *sadhus* you have met [their letter says] that I may as well return the compliment by telling you about a few *we* have had the good fortune to contact here—at the Kumbha *mela*.

What we have seen at this great congregation of *sadhus* and pilgrims has moved us to our depths. We were given, as it were, a glimpse into the heart of Reality, the Great Reality that *is* India— where dreams come true and the dynasty of the holy still abides! We may well be proud. But to begin . . .

And my letter, never sent, begins, "Once, in your book, you resorted to a letter, as though that perfunctory but intimate form were the best you had at your disposal for conveying an impression of the *mela*. I have just spent some time at Jhusi, which is one vast stretch of saffron tents interrupted by straw huts, by sheds roofed with sheets of corrugated iron, by bamboo towers, and by bamboo poles flying the flags or signs of every imaginable sect of *sadhus*. And though I am not clear yet about what those dreams are that come true here, at times I did feel as though I were sleepwalking through some celestial bazaar. Or was it a medieval battlefield with hordes of Saracens in disarray? No, perhaps it was an ancient camp of Hannibal. Every man or beast was covered with dust. In front of the tents, which seemed to extend nearly to the horizon, camp fires burned. By the camp fires, beneath the open sky, were huddles of squatting *sadhus* and milling or motionless crowds of pilgrims. Now and again, I passed an elephant, festooned with flower garlands and embroidered rugs. All along the way, beggars held out their bowls, into which pilgrims dropped coins or grain. There were naked *sadhus* and *sadhus* opulently robed. There were *sadhus* wearing *dhotis* and marigolds, with horizontal stripes of ash on their foreheads. There were *sadhus* with ash-

smeared naked bodies, offering *ghi, jaggery,* and *sesamum* to a sacrificial fire that crackled in a brazier, and chanting, '*Hare Ram.
Hare Krishna. Hare Om.*' Elsewhere, *sadhus* were shaking bells or
clapping tongs or cymbals, or were singing or haranguing crowds
over loudspeakers, or were leaping up and down, or were hanging by their feet from trees. Here was a *sadhu* reclining on a bed
of thorns; there was a *sadhu* waist-deep in mud; near by, a *sadhu*
stood on one foot, and opposite him another balanced himself
on one arm; farther along were *sadhus* fixed in still other yogic
contortions. Beyond, a man wearing a skimpy loincloth was in
the middle of a ritualistic dance to the music of a harmonium.
Then, there was a group of seated men, each with a finger
pressed to his lips. Opposite them sat other men, each with his
forefingers in his ears. The names of the sects of *sadhus* were as
endless as the ways they conceived of God: for the Vedantists,
it was as the One; for the Vaishnavas, as all things; for the
Shankarites, as the self; for the Tantriks, as the doctrines in their
sacred books; for the Shaktas, as Kali; for the Shaivas and Ava-
dhutas, as Mother Ganga—all, of course, overlapping even as
they asserted their contradictions."

Since at the *mela* anyone can go anywhere and talk to anyone,
I visit a number of the *sadhus'* camps at Jhusi. On a *gaddi* (Hindi
for "cushion") of straw in one tent, pitched a little apart from
the others, a man sits silent and withdrawn, like a *guru.* Near him
sits a fast-talking man who is answering questions addressed to
the silent man by an Indian filmmaker.

"Looking at your face, I get the impression you have achieved
great peace," the filmmaker is saying, in Urdu. "In your eyes
there is this wonderful glow of happiness. How do you achieve
this peace?" He adds, "This question may seem very foolish to

you, but I would like to know if you encounter any difficulty in keeping your vow of celibacy."

"How do I know you're not a spy?" the fast-talking man asks.

"Spy for what?" the filmmaker cries.

The man on the *gaddi* seems about to say something, but the fast-talking man speaks up again. "You could be a spy for another *akhara*, or a spy for the government," he says.

The filmmaker courteously identifies himself as Habib Tanvir and explains that he is shooting a documentary on the Kumbha *mela*, which he hopes to sell to the BBC.

The fast-talking man listens warily, and then says, "The question you ask about peace would take months to answer, because the answer is very difficult, and I would have to go through many highways and byways. As for the other matter, if you have had that experience, it's much more difficult. It's not at all difficult for us, because we have never had that experience."

One large colony of tents is marked by a sign that reads, "Spiritual Regeneration Movement Foundation of India." This is the headquarters of Maharishi Mahesh Yogi. I know of him, or know the few available facts about him (all uncorroborated): that he was born around 1910; that his father was a revenue inspector; that he attended Allahabad University; that he worked in a factory for a time; that for some years he studied in the Himalayas with the *jagadguru* Shankaracharya of Badi ka Ashram; and that, unlike most Indian sages, who use one religious title, he prefers to use two—Maharishi, which is Sanskrit for "great seer," and Yogi, which is from the Sanskrit "*yoga*," meaning "effort." Inside the first tent, which is packed with such items as tomato sauce, cornflakes, soap, toothpaste, and chewing gum—

all imports, to judge from the labels—a man in a brown lounge
suit and with a vermilion mark on his forehead comes up to me.
He tells me his name and continues, in English, "I am America-
returned. I am M.A. and Ph.D. in public administration from the
States. Guruji has fifty-four *chelas* from distant foreign lands here
at Kumbha. I myself am going to be initiated on this Amavasya,
when Guruji will recite some *mantras* to me by the side of
Mother Ganga, and I will recite them back. I met the Guruji
only a month ago. After I set my eyes on Guruji, I left my five
children to follow him."

He takes me to an open area among the tents, where many
Westerners, some in Indian dress, are standing around a serving
table finishing a meal of macaroni and custard. I accept a small
dish of custard from a girl in Western dress. She has very long
eyelashes and the slightly bored expression of a fashion model.

"Where are you from?" I ask her.

"From Canada," the girl replies. "Guruji is a fact, and, like a
fact, he manifested himself to me in Canada."

When I ask her to tell me something about the Spiritual
Regeneration Movement, she says tersely, "You must address
any questions you have to Guruji himself."

An Englishwoman joins us. "Guruji has been around the
world six times, and now we have a half-dozen Spiritual Regeneration Movement centers in Britain," she says. "They teach
Guruji's simple technique of meditation."

The members of the group start moving into a tent. They
arrange themselves as best they can on the floor in front of
Maharishi Mahesh Yogi, a merry-looking little man with smooth
skin, blunt features, and long, well-oiled hair. He is dressed

in a flowing cream-colored silk robe. Three tape recorders stand near him on the floor, as sacred books might surround another *guru*.

Maharishi Mahesh Yogi urges the audience to ask questions, and I ask a general question about the nature of his movement.

He asks me to identify myself, and when I do, he says, in English, in a soft, rich, bemused voice, "All I teach is a simple method of meditation. We are all conscious on a mundane level, but beneath that consciousness, in each one of us, there is an ocean vaster than any in the world. It's there that most new thoughts originate. The bridge between the mundane level of consciousness and the ocean is meditation—not reading, because if you read you can have only secondhand thoughts. Meditation expands the consciousness and leads to the greatest production of goods and services. The ultimate test of my method of meditation is therefore its utility—the measure of the usefulness of people to society. Through my method of meditation, the poor can become as rich as the rich, and the rich can become richer. I taught my simple method of meditation to a German cement manufacturer. He taught the method to all his employees and thereby quadrupled the production of cement. As I said when addressing a meeting in the Albert Hall, in London, my technique does not involve withdrawal from normal material life. It enhances the material values of life by the inner spiritual light. My method is, in my London example, 'like the inner juice of the orange, which can be enjoyed without destroying the outer beauty of the fruit. This is done simply by pricking the orange with a pin again and again, and extracting the juice little by little, so that the inner juice is drawn out on the surface, and both are enjoyed simultaneously.'"

During the rest of the session, which goes on for a few hours, with the tape recorders running, Maharishi Mahesh Yogi expounds on his simple method of meditation. He has a way of dismissing everything. Not only does he rule out at the start all questions concerning morality, theology, and philosophy—implying at one point that men are free to do anything in their personal lives, to themselves or to others, as long as, by the technique of meditation, they experience the bliss that is within themselves—but he seems to remove himself from the whole process of intellectual discourse by giggling at every question put to him and then at his own answer to the question, so one feels that no matter how long one talked to him one would come away with, at worst, chagrin at having been ridiculed and, at best, vague excitement at having been tantalized. He does not satisfactorily answer any question. (If by a few minutes of meditation a day the poor can become rich, why do they continue to be poor? Maharishi Mahesh Yogi's answer is that they are too indolent to master his simple method of meditation.)

JAN MORRIS

(1926–)

Jan Morris was born in Wales, where she presently lives, and was known as James Morris until her sex-change operation in the 1970s. She has published a historical trilogy on the British empire, *Heaven's Command*, *Rule Britannica*, and *Farewell the Trumpets*; a book on colonial architecture in India; and also biographies of Venice, Trieste, Sydney, and New York. As a travel writer, she is a connoisseur of people, places, individual and national eccentricities, and her essays seem driven by sheer enthusiasm. But there is a calm, discerning eye beneath the bubbly adjective-laden prose; she seems constantly working to make palpable that elusive special essence of a place. Her powers of evocation and sympathy are matched by her vivid historical imagination—qualities that are immediately striking in the following essay on Delhi, that most antique and intractable of Indian metropolises.

MRS. GUPTA NEVER RANG

Delhi, 1975

Indira Gandhi was in power in Delhi in 1975, but though she had clamped the country under a State of Emergency, harshly limiting the press and imprisoning much of the opposition, to the stranger the Indian capital felt much the same as ever. There is not much in this essay to reveal which particular regime governed India at the time of its writing: Delhi is one of those cities whose age, manner and disposition easily absorb the styles of its successive rulers.

"You see," said the government spokesman, "you may liken Delhi to the River Ganges, it twists and turns, many other streams join it, it divides into many parts, and it flows into the sea in so many channels that nobody may know which is the true river. You follow my train of thought? It is a metaphysical matter, perhaps. You will do best to burrow under the surface of things and discover what is not revealed to us ordinary mortals! In the meantime, you will take a cup of tea, I hope?" I took a cup of tea, milkless, very sweet, brought by a shuffling messenger in a high-buttoned jacket with a scarf around his neck, and between pleasantries I pondered the spokesman's advice. Indians, of course, love to reduce the prosaic to the mystic. It is part of their Timeless Wisdom. For several centuries the tendency has variously baffled, infuriated, amused and entranced travelers from the West, and India is full of pilgrims still, come from afar to worship at the shrines of insight. But *Delhi*? Delhi is not just a national capital, it is one of the political ultimates, one of the prime movers. It was born to power, war and glory. It rose to greatness not because holy men saw visions there but because it commanded the strategic routes from the Northwest, where the conquerors came from, into the rich flatlands of the Ganges delta. Delhi is a soldiers' town, a politicians' town, a journalists', a diplomats' town. It is Asia's Washington, though not so picturesque, and lives by ambition, rivalry and opportunism.

"Ah yes," he said, "what you are thinking is quite true, but that is the *surface* of Delhi. You are an artist, I know, you should look *beyond*! And if there is anything we can do to help your inquiries," he added with an engaging waggle of his head, "you have only to let us know. You may telephone us at any time and we will ring you back with the requisite information in a moment or two. We are here to help! That is why we are here! No, no, that is our duty!"

Certainly Delhi is unimaginably antique, and age is a metaphysic, I suppose. Illustrations of mortality are inescapable there, and do give the place a sort of nagging symbolism. Tombs of emperors stand beside traffic junctions, forgotten fortresses command suburbs, the titles of lost dynasties are woven into the vernacular, if only as street names.

One of the oldest and deadest places I know, for a start, is the crumbled fortress-capital of Tughluqabad in the city's southern outskirts. For a single decade it was a place of terrific consequence, for nearly seven centuries since it has been a grey wasteland of piled stones and ruined alleyways, a *memento mori* by any standard, inhabited only by the disagreeable monkeys which are the familiars of Delhi, and by a melancholy watchman who, recently transferred by the Archaeological Survey from some more frequented historical monument, now sees nobody but the apes from one day to the next.

Or consider, in another kind of allegory, the Lodi Gardens. These are popular promenades, but they are also the cemetery of the Lodi kings who thrived in the early sixteenth century. Here death and life consort on familiar terms, and especially in the early morning, when Delhi people go out for some fresh air before the sun comes up, they offer some piquant juxtapositions. All among the memorials the citizens besport themselves, pursuing their Yogic meditations in the tomb of Sikander Lodi, jogtrotting among the funerary domes, exercising their pampered dachshunds beside the Bara Gumbad Mosque or pissing, in the inescapable Delhi manner, behind the mausoleum of Mohammed Shah.

They used to say, to express the marvelous continuity of Delhi, that seven successive capitals existed here, each superimposed upon the last. Nowadays they are always finding new ones, and the latest tally seems to be fourteen. Few foreigners and still fewer Indians have ever heard of most of the dynasties represented, but here and there across the capital some of them have left not merely tombs or ruins but living remnants of themselves. Embedded, for instance, in one of Delhi's smarter quarters, almost within sight of the Oberoi Intercontinental, is the Moslem village shrine of Nizamuddin, built in the time of the fourteenth-century Sultan Ghiyasuddin Tughluq and still as holy as ever.

Through tortuous mucky lanes one approaches it from the busy highway, past the statutory Indian lines of beggars, crones and sadhus, through the spittle-stained portals where the old men stare, and into the intricate jumble of courts, tombs and arcades that surrounds the mosque of Nizamuddin and its sacred pool. Here mendicants lope around on knobbly staves, saintly scholars are at their books, sweet old ladies sit outside tombs (they are not allowed in, being female), and in the mosque there hustles and brushes the muezzin, an indefatigable goblin figure with white eyebrows and dainty tread. Nothing here is unpremeditated. All moves, though you might not guess it, to an immemorial schedule: the prayer call comes precisely to time, the rituals are meticulously ordered, even the whining beggars have their appointed place in the hierarchy, and when I left the precincts the imam gave me his visiting card—his name is Al Haj Hazrat Peer Qazi Syed Safdar Ali Nizami, and his cable address is HEADPRIEST DELHI.

Even more a living relic, so to speak, is the Begum Timur Jehan Shahzadi of Darya Ganj, in the old walled city of Delhi. This lady is a Moghul princess of the dynasty which made Delhi its capital in the seventeenth century and built the very city, Shahjehanabad, in whose labyrinthine recesses she lives now. Just go to the Old City, her son-in-law had assured me, and ask for the Begum Jehan's house: and though in the event this proved insufficient advice, and I spent half an afternoon stumbling through the high-walled maze of Shahjehanabad, vainly presenting the inquiry, still I relished the form of it, and thought it was rather like knocking on the door of the Great Pyramid, asking for Cheops.

I found her in the end anyway, ensconced in her front sitting room between portraits of her imperial forebears: a short, decisive old lady with a brief mischievous smile and an air of totally liberated self-possession. There is no pretending that this princess lives much like a princess. Her old house, into which her family moved when they were ejected by later conquerors from their imperial palace, is a beguiling shambles in the old Islamic style: a couple of rooms in the Western manner for the convenience of visitors, the rest more or less medieval—a wide decrepit courtyard, a dusty trellised vine, thickly populated chambers all around. There are granddaughters and sons-in-law and undefined connections; there are skivvies and laundrymen and assorted sweepers; there are children and dogs and unexplained loiterers in doorways. Forty or fifty souls constitute the tumbled court of the Begum Timur Jehan, and through it she moves commandingly in green trousers, issuing instructions, reminiscing about emperors, traitors or ladies of the harem, and frequently consulting her highly organized notebook, all asterisks and cross-references, for addresses or reminders.

Like HEADPRIEST DELHI she lives very near the earth, close to the muck and the spittle, close to the mangy dogs and the deformed indigents in the street outside. Delhi is scarcely an innocent city, for on every layer it is riddled with graft and intrigue, but it is distinctly organic, to an atavistic degree. An apposite introduction to the city, I think, is provided by Map Eight of the *Delhi City Atlas*, which marks a substantial slab of the municipal area as being Dense Jungle: though this is now a city of a million inhabitants, it feels near the bush still. From many parts of it the open plain is in sight, and the country trees of India, the feathery tamarisks and ubiquitous acacias, invade every part of it—the animals too, for squirrels are everywhere and monkeys, buffalos, cows, goats and a million pye-dogs roam the city streets peremptorily.

There is simplicity everywhere, too, for rural people from all India flock into Delhi for jobs, for help, to see the sights. There are Sikhs and sleek Bengalis, Rajputs ablaze with jewelry, smart Gujaratis from the western coast, beautiful Tamils from the south, cloaked Tibetans smelling of untanned leather, clerks from Bombay smelling of aftershave, students, wandering sages, clumping soldiers in ammunition boots, black-veiled Moslem women, peasants in for the day from the scorched and desiccated Punjab plains. Endearingly they trail through their national

monuments, awestruck, and the attendants intone their mono-
logues hoping for tips, and the tourist buses line up outside the
Presidential Palace, and the magicians prepare their levitations
and inexplicable disappearances in the dusty ditch below the
ramparts of the Red Fort.

This is the Gandhian truth of India, expressed in Delhi chiefly
by such reminders of an earthier world beyond the city limits.
Though I fear I might not give up my electric typewriter without
a struggle, still I am a Gandhian myself in principle, and respond
easily to this suggestion of a vast Indian *naïveté*, stretching away
from Delhi like a limitless reservoir, muddied perhaps but
deeply wholesome. The Gandhian ethic is rather outmoded in
India, in fact, and the Mahatma himself seems to be losing
his charismatic appeal, but still I liked the inscriptions in the
visitors' book at Birla House, where he died in 1948 (his body
was displayed to the public on the roof, illuminated by search-
light), and where many a country pilgrim reverently pauses.
"My heart heaving with emotion," wrote P. H. Kalaskar. "Moving indeed," thought A. K. Barat. Several people wrote "Felt
happy." One said "Most worth seeing place in Delhi," and when,
quoting from the master himself, I contributed "Truth is God,"
the inevitable onlookers murmured, "Very good, very good,"
nodded approvingly to each other and touched my hand in
sympathy.

Delhi is a city of basic, spontaneous emotions: greed, hate,
revenge, love, pity, kindness, the murderous shot, the touch of
the hand. Its very subtleties are crude: even its poverty is black
and white. On the one side are the organized beggar children
who, taught to murmur a few evocative words of despair like

"hungry," "baby" or "mummy," succeed all too often in snaring the susceptible stranger. On the other are the courtly thousands of the jagghis, the shantytowns of matting, tentage and old packing cases which cling like black growths to the presence of Delhi.

There are beggars in Delhi who are comfortably off, and people too proud to beg who possess nothing at all, not a pot or a pan, not a pair of shoes. I saw one such man, almost naked, shivering with the morning cold and obviously very ill, huddled against a lamppost in Janpath early one morning. He asked for nothing, but I felt so sorry for him, and for a moment so loved him for his suffering, that I gave him a ten-rupee note, an inconceivable amount by the standards of Indian indigence. He looked at it first in disbelief, then in ecstasy and then in a wild gratitude, and I left him throwing his hands to heaven, singing, praying and crying, still clinging to his lamppost, and sending me away, slightly weeping myself, to coffee, toast and orange juice ("You'll be sure it's chilled, won't you?") at my hotel.

The voice of the people, Gandhi used to say, is the voice of God. I doubt it, but I do recognize a divine element to the Indian poverty, ennobled as it is by age and sacrifice. Indians rationalize it by the concept of reincarnation, and I see it too as a halfway condition, a station of the cross. "In the next world," I suggested to my driver after a long and exhausting journey into the country, "I'll be driving and you'll be lying on the backseat," but he answered me with a more elemental philosophy. "In the next world," he replied, "we'll *both* be lying on the backseat!" For even the inegality of Delhi, even the pathos, often has something robust to it, a patient fatalism that infuriates many modernists but is a solace to people like me. It is disguised often in Eastern mumbo-jumbo, preached about in ashrams to gullible Californians and exploited by swamis from the divine to the absurd: but it is really no more than a kindly acceptance of things as they are, supported by the sensible thesis that things are not always what they appear to be.

But pathos, yes. Delhi is the capital of the losing streak. It is the metropolis of the crossed wire, the missed appointment, the puncture, the wrong number. Every day's paper in Delhi brings news of some new failure, in diplomacy, in economics, in sport: when India's women entered the world table-tennis tournament during my stay in Delhi, not only were they all beaten but one actually failed to turn up for the match. I was pursued in the city by a persistent and not unattractive Rajput businessman. I thought him rather suave as I fended him off, in his well-cut check suit and his trendy ties, confident of manner, worldly of discourse: but one day I caught sight of him *hors de combat*, so to speak, muffled in a threadbare overcoat and riding a battered motor scooter back to his suburban home—and suddenly saw him, far more endearingly if he did but know it, as he really was, smallish, poorish, struggling and true.

He dropped me in the end anyway, perhaps because I developed an unsightly boil in my nose—men seldom send roses to girls with red noses. The side of my face swelled up like a huge bunion, and I was half red and half white, and sniffly and sad and sorry for myself. In this condition, self-consciously, I continued my investigations, and at first I was touched by the tact with which Indians in the streets pretended not to notice. After a day or two, though, I realized that the truth was more affecting still. They *really* did not notice. They thought my face quite normal. For what is a passing grotesquerie, in a land of deformities?

"Certainly," said the government spokesman, perusing my list of questions, "by all means, these are all very simple matters. We can attend to them for you at once. As I told you, it is our duty! It is what we are paid for! I myself have to attend an important meeting this afternoon—you will excuse me I hope?—but I will leave all these little matters with our good Mrs. Gupta and all will be taken care of. I will telephone you with the answers myself without fail—or if not I myself, then Mrs. Gupta will be sure to telephone you either today or tomorrow morning. Did you sign our register? A duplicate signature here if you would not mind, and the lady at the door will issue you with the requisite application form for a pass—it will make everything easier for you, you see. Have no fear, Mrs. Gupta will take care of everything. But mark my words, you will find the spiritual aspects of our city the most rewarding. Remember the River Ganges! As a student of history, you will find that I am right! Ha ha! Another cup of tea? You have time?"

Even he would agree, though, that the spiritual aspect is hardly predominant in New Delhi, the headquarters of the Indian government and the seat of Indian sovereignty—the newest and largest of Delhi's successive capitals. This was built by the British, and despite one or two sententious symbolisms and nauseating texts—"Liberty Will Not Descend to a People, A People

Must Raise Themselves to Liberty"—it is a frank and indeed noble memorial to their own imperial Raj. It is not anomalous even now. For one thing it was built in a hybrid style of East and West, to take care of all historical contingencies, and for another, Britishness is far from dead in Delhi. Delhi gentlemen, especially of the sporting classes, are stupendously British still. Delhi social events can be infinitely more English than Ascot or Lords. The following scrambled-names puzzle appeared recently in a Delhi magazine: LIWL EFFEY (a comedian); UALNIJ YHLXEU (a zoologist); ARMY SHES (a pianist); HIIPPLL LLEGAADU (a historian). Only two classes of people on earth could solve this riddle without reference books: Britons of a certain age, Indians of a certain class.

Besides, the grand ensemble of New Delhi, the Presidential Palace flanked by the two wings of the Secretariat, has adapted easily to the republican style. It was the greatest single artifact of the British Empire, perhaps its principal work of art, and there are men still alive in Delhi who spent all their working lives building it. I met one, a rich and venerable Sikh contractor, and he recalled the great work with immense pride, and spoke affectionately of its English architects, and said it never once occurred to him to suppose, during all the years he worked upon it, that an Indian would ever be sitting in the halls of the Viceroy's Lodge.

Seen early on a misty morning from far down the ceremonial mall, Rajpath, New Delhi is undeniably majestic—neither Roman, its architects said, nor British, nor Indian, but *imperial*. Then its self-consciousness (for its mixture of styles is very contrived) is blurred by haze and distance and by the stir of awakening Delhi—the civil servants with their bulging briefcases, the multitudinous peons, the pompous early-morning policemen, the women sweepers elegant in primary colors, the minister perhaps (if it is not *too* early) in his chauffeur-driven, Indian-built limousine, the stocky Gurkha sentries at the palace gates, the first eager tourists from the Oberoi Intercontinental, the entertainer with his dancing monkeys, the snake charmer with his acolyte children, the public barber on the pavement outside Parliament, the women preparing their washing beside the ornamental pools, the man in khaki who, approaching you fiercely across the formal gardens, asks if you would care for a cold drink.

Then the power of India, looming above these dusty complexities, is unmistakable: not only created but instinctive, sensed by its foreign rulers as by its indigenous, and aloof to history's permutations. Of all the world's countries, India is the most truly prodigious, and this quality of astonishment displays itself afresh every day as the sun comes up in Delhi. Five hundred and eighty million people, three hundred languages, provinces from the Himalayan to the equatorial, cities as vast as Bombay and Calcutta, villages so lost in time that no map marks them, nuclear scientists and aboriginal hillmen, industrialists of incalculable wealth and dying beggars sprawled on railway platforms, three or four great cultures, myriad religions, pilgrims from across the world, politicians sunk in graft, the Grand Trunk Road marching to Peshawar, the temples of Madras gleaming in the sun, an inexhaustible history, an incomprehensible social system, an unfathomable repository of human resource, misery, ambiguity, vitality and confusion—all this, the colossal corpus of India, invests, sprawls around, infuses, elevates, inspires and very nearly overwhelms New Delhi.

Searching for a corrective to such cosmic visions, I thought I would investigate the roots or guts of New Delhi, instead of contemplating its tremendous aura, so I inveigled my way not into the State Hallroom or the Durbar Hall but into the kitchens of the Presidential Palace, by way of an obliging aide-de-camp and a compliant housekeeper (for as dubious flunkies repeatedly murmured as I made my way downstairs, "It is not allowed to visitors"). At first I thought I had succeeded in finding humanity among that majesty, for the way to the kitchens passed through a labyrinth of homely offices, workshops and storerooms and cupboards, supervised by smiling and apparently contented domestics. Here were the Pot Cleaners, scouring their big copper pans. Here were the Linen Keepers, standing guard on their pillowslips. Here were the Washing Up Men, ankle deep in suds themselves, and here the Bakers invited me to taste the morning's loaf. I felt I was passing through some living exhibition of Indian Crafts, diligent, chaste and obliging.

But even before I entered the kitchen proper, a clanking and grand aroma brought me back to the realities of New Delhi, for in the palace of Rashtrapati Bhavan, Downstairs is scarcely less consequential than Up. These kitchens are imperial institutions themselves, half Western, half Eastern, colossal in scale, lordly in pretension. Armies of cooks seemed to be laboring there. Foods of a dozen cuisines seemed to be in preparation. Batteries of aged electric ovens hummed and whirred. There were squadrons of deep freezers and battalions of chopping boards and armories of steel choppers. The cooks and their underlings bowed to me as I passed, but not obsequiously. It was with condescension that they greeted me, one by one along the preparation tables, and when at last I reached the sizzling center of that underworld, I felt myself to be more truly at a crossroad of the empires than anywhere else in Delhi—for there, just around the corner from the English ovens of the viceroys, they were smoking over charcoal braziers, scented with wheat grain, the aromatic yellow pomfrets that were a grand delicacy of the Moghuls.

So even in the kitchens power presides, in a traditional, ample sense. Delhi is full of it, for this republic, which came to office in a loincloth, rules in a gaudier uniform. Nehru said that modern Western civilization was ersatz, living by ersatz values, eating ersatz food: but the ruling classes of Delhi, the politicians, the businessmen, the military, have mostly adopted those values without shame. Gandhi said that his India would have "the smallest possible army," but Delhi is one of the most military of all capitals: when I looked up some friends in the Delhi telephone book, I found that under the name Khanna there were four generals, an air commodore, twelve colonels, a group captain, twelve majors, three wing commanders, four captains, one commander, three lieutenant commanders and a lieutenant.

Nor is Delhi's display just a façade or a bluff. India often seems to outsiders a crippled country, emaciated by poverty and emasculated by philosophy, but it is only a half-truth. We are told that half India's population is undernourished and three quarters illiterate: that leaves nearly 180 million people who are well fed and literate. The Indian gross national product is the tenth largest on earth. The armies of India are very strong and are largely equipped from Indian factories. I went one day to the Delhi Industrial Fair, housed in a series of modernist ziggurats directly across the street from the gateway of the ruined city Purana Qila, and there I discovered that India makes not only warships, railway engines and aircraft, but Carbicle Grinders too, Lapping Machines and Micro-Fog Lubricators ("I'll take that one," said I flippantly, pointing to an electric transformer as big as a cottage, "please send it to my hotel"—and diligently the salesman took out his order form).

Power corrupts, of course, and in India it corrupts on a grand scale. At the top, the whisper of nepotism or opportunism repeatedly approaches Central Government itself. At the bottom, graft harasses the street hawkers of the city, who can scarcely afford the protection money demanded by the police. Even the stranger to Delhi feels the rot: in the arrogant petty official declining to look up from his newspaper, in the stifling addiction to red tape and precedent, in the affectations and snobberies which, as they thrive in Washington's Georgetown, flourish here too in the districts south of Rajpath.

As it happens, I am rather an addict of power. I do not much enjoy submitting to it or even exerting it, but I do like observing it. I like the aesthetics of it, colored as they so often are by pageantry and history. I am everybody's patriot, and love to see the flags flying over palace or parliament, Westminster or Quai d'Orsay. I am very ready to be moved by the emanations of power in Delhi—the sun setting behind the Red Fort, the grand mass of New Delhi seen across the dun plateau or the ceremony of Beating Retreat on Vijay Chowk, when a dozen military bands pluck at the heart with the Last Post and "Abide with Me."

Nobody cries more easily than I do, when the bugle sounds or the flag comes down, but somehow I do not respond to the old magic in India. The British, rationalizing their own love of imperial pomp, used to claim that it was necessary to retain the respect of Asiatics. It availed them nothing, though, against the "half-naked fakir," as Churchill called Gandhi, and now too the magnificence of Delhi seems paradoxically *detached* from India. How remote the great ensigns which, enormously billowing above their embassies in the diplomatic enclave, testify to the presence of the plenipotentiaries! How irrelevant the posturings of the grandees, hosts and guests alike, the Polish defense minister greeted by epauletted generals, the Prince of Wales inevitably winning his polo match, the resident Congress party spokesman puffed up at one press conference, the visiting minister of national reorientation condescending at the next.

And most detached of all seems the unimaginable bureaucracy of Delhi, battening upon the capital—a power sucker, feeding upon its own consequence or sustained intravenously by interdepartmental memoranda, triplicate applications, copies and comments and addenda and references to precedent—a monstrous behemoth of authority, slumped immovable among its files and tea trays. Much of it is concerned not with practical reality at all but with hypotheses or dogma. Forty government editors are engaged in producing the collected works of Gandhi, down to the last *pensée*—they have got to volume fifty-four. Hundreds more are concerned with plans, for there was never a capital like Delhi for planners—the Multilevel Planning Section, the Plan Coordination Division, the Plan Information Unit, the Social Planning Unit, the Project Appraisal Unit, the Socio-Economic Research Unit, the Program Evaluation Organization, the National Sample Survey Organization, the National Survey Organization, the Central Statistical Organization. Big Brother is everywhere, with a slide rule, a clipboard and a warning in small print. "This map," says one Delhi tourist publication severely, "is published for tourists as a master guide and *not as legal tender*"—and there, in its mixture of the interfering, the pedantic, the unnecessary and the absurd, speaks the true voice of Indian officialdom.

But this is an essential part of the Indian mystery, always has been, probably always will be. Delhi is too old to care anyway, and takes the system as it comes. Which viceroy or president had he most enjoyed serving, I asked one antediluvian retainer at Rashtrapati Bhavan. He shrugged his shoulders with an almost perceptible creak. "I serve the government," he said. "It is all the same to me." With this indifference in mind I went that afternoon to a murder trial which, to much publicity, was proceeding then in the New District Court, a kind of permanent bad dream in concrete in the northern part of the city—filthy, cramped, dark and suffocatingly overcrowded. Here authority was at its most immediate and most awful. The case concerned the alleged murder of a well-known south-of-Rajpath lady by her husband, a fashionable eye surgeon, assisted by his mistress and an assortment of vagabond accomplices. It was a true *crime passionel* with thuggish overtones, and at least five people faced, there and then, the ultimate penalty. The judge was a grave and clever Sikh, turbaned and spectacled. The court was jammed with a festering, jostling audience, hungry for the salacious, the macabre and the terrible. The white-tabbed attorneys droned and argued, the watchmen barred the door with staves, the accused sat in chains along the side of the court, shackled to their guards.

Yet fearful though their predicament was, they did not seem awestruck nor even alarmed. They were like sightseers themselves, of their own tragedy. They yawned occasionally. They exchanged comments. They laughed at the legal jokes. And sometimes, feeling the strain of the long day, they raised their manacled wrists to their warders' shoulders and, placing their cheeks upon their hands like sleepy children, dozed through destiny for a while.

"I will find that out for you, of course," said the government spokesman. "It will be no problem at all. You see, it is something I am not exactly sure of myself, but we have many sources of information. Do we have your telephone number? Ah yes. I have temporarily mislaid it. Would you give it to me again? Rest assured, dear lady, I shall find out this information, together with the answers to your earlier questions, and shall telephone you for certain, if not this afternoon, then tomorrow morning first thing.

"I don't know if you are familiar, you see, with the *Bhagavad Gita*? As a student of the Gandhian philosophy you would find it very beautiful: and you would find it exceedingly relevant to your article about Delhi. It is self-awareness, you see, that is the key. Oh madam, you are laughing at me! You are very wicked! But never mind, you will see, you will see! And in the meantime you may be quite sure," he concluded with his usual charming smile and reassuring shake of the head, "that I will be telephoning you with this information, or if not I myself, then our good Mrs. Gupta is sure to. It is not very spiritual but we must do our duty!"

There is a species of telephone operators' English, often heard in Delhi, which is not exactly an articulated language at all, but a sort of elongated blur. Indian English proper, of course, is one of India's cruellest handicaps, for it is so often imperfect of nuance and makes for an unreal relationship between host and visitor, besides often making highly intelligent people look foolish ("CHINESE GENERALS FLY BACK TO FRONT," said a celebrated Indian headline long ago). But the elliptical, slithery kind is something else again, and has another effect on its hearers. It makes one feel oddly opaque or amorphous oneself, and seems to clothe the day's arrangements in a veil of uncertainty.

This is proper. One should not go fighting into Delhi, chin up and clear eyed. Here hopes are meant to wither and conceptions adjust. A single brush with a noseless beggar is enough to change your social values. Just one application for an import license will alter your standards of efficiency. After a while graver mutations may occur, and you will find yourself questioning the Meaning of It All, the Reality of Time and other old Indian specialties. "You will see, you will see!" Most disconcerting of all, you may well come to feel that the pomp and circumstance of Delhi, which struck you at first as illusory display, is in fact the only reality of the place! All the rest is mirage. Everything else in the Indian presence, north, east, south, west, across the Rajasthani deserts, down to the Coromandel beaches, far away to the frontiers of Tibet, everything else is suggestion, never to be substance.

I pick a Delhi newspaper at random. Crowd Loots Colliery. Police Kill Dacoits. Dacoits Loot Pilgrims. Students Raid Cinema. Farmers Arrested during Agitation. Teachers Boycott Examination. Police Fire on Crowd. Mizo Rebels Spotted. Peace Feelers for Naga Rebels. A State of Emergency exists in India, but one is hardly aware of it, for this is a country always in emergency, crossed perpetually by dim figures of faith and violence, prophets of revolution, priests of reaction, saints and spies and fanatics, moving here and there through a haze of hatred, idealism and despair. Experts Visit Bomb Blast Site. Police Charge Crowd. 600 Arrested. Government Minister Has Asthma.

Sometimes these shadows reach into Delhi itself, and chaos feels uncomfortably close. While I was there the hereditary Imam of the Jama Masjid, the greatest mosque in India, was engaged in a quarrel with the government. He was even heard inciting his congregation to political dissent over the loudspeakers of his minaret during a visit to the neighborhood by Mrs. Gandhi herself. His family have been incumbents of the Imamate since the mosque was founded by Shah Jehan in 1650, and are great figures in the Muslim community: nevertheless he was arrested, and in the ensuing riots at least six people were killed (always add a zero, an Indian acquaintance nonchalantly told me, if you want the true figure) and at least six hundred locked away for safety's sake.

It happened that I was wandering around the purlieus of the mosque on the day of the arrest, and bleak was the sensation of *déjà vu* with which I watched the riot police, brandishing their guns and batons, heavily clambering out of their trucks. But more ominous still, I thought, was the spectacle of the mosque itself a few days later. They slapped a curfew on the area, and when I next passed its outskirts, along the crammed and filthy pavements of Netaji Subhash Marg, where the beggar families crouch day and night beneath their sacking shelters and the teeming junk bazaars crowd around the Chadni Chowk—when I looked across to the Jama Masjid, I saw its great shape there silent and eerily deserted—gone the milling figures of the faithful on its steps, gone the stir of commerce and devotion that habitually surrounds it, empty all the stalls and shops, the kebab restaurants, the fortune-tellers, the silversmiths, the tanners and the cobblers. All were empty, and the mosque looked like some immense captive champion, brooding there in solitary confinement.

Yet even this all-too-real reality seemed a deception upon the composure of Delhi. I never feel insecure there, even when the riot police are storming by. The only citizens who frighten me are those damned monkeys, so beguiling of motion, so threatening of grimace. Delhi people treat these beasts with distinct circumspection, crossing roads to avoid them or bribing them with peanuts to go away, and in this, it seemed to me, poor Indians behave toward monkeys much as Europeans behave toward poor Indians—especially as, the monkey god Hanuman being an important figure of the Hindu pantheon, some element of conscience is presumably involved. This disconcerting parallel gave me an unexpected sense of membership, and every time a monkey bared its teeth at me I felt like saying, "Wait, friend, wait—I'm the European, it's the poor Indian you want!"

For the Indian sense of hierarchy, which so contributes to the bafflement of India, provides for each rank of society a kind of comradeship; and in Delhi especially, which is like a shadow play of India, one senses the hidden force of it. The Untouchables of the capital—Harijans, Children of God, as Gandhi called them—live in well-defined colonies on the edge of the city. Though I knew better intellectually, emotionally I somehow expected, when I drove out there one afternoon, to find them a people made morose and hangdog by their status. In fact they turned out to be a very jolly lot, welcoming and wreathed in smiles, and looking at least as cheerful as the average member of the Socio-Economic Research Unit, say. Why not? They might be Harijans to the world outside, but they were doubtless Brahmins to each other.

In the same way Delhi, preoccupied with its own diurnal round of consequence and command, is paradoxically protected against that dust storm of controversy, threat and misfortune which hangs always, dark and ill-defined, over the Indian horizons. That blur or slither of Delhi, which begins as a mystery and develops into an irritation, becomes in the end a kind of reassurance. After trying three times, you give up gratefully. After expostulating once or twice, it is a pleasure to accede. You think you can change the system? Try it, try it, and when the elaborations of Delhi have caught up with you, when you realize the tortuous significances of the old method, when it has been explained to you that only Mrs. Gupta is qualified to take the money, that Mr. Mukerjee is prevented by custom from working beside Mr. Mukhtar Singh and that Mr. Mohammed will not of course be at work on Fridays, when it dawns upon you gradually that it has been done more or less this way, come conqueror, come liberation, since the early Middle Ages, with a relieved and affectionate smile you will probably agree that perhaps it had better be left as it is.

As it is! India is always as it is! I never despair in Delhi, for I feel always all around me the fortification of a profound apathy. The capital is essentially apathetic to the nation: the nation is aloof to the capital. By the end of the century there will be, at the present rate of increase, nearly 1,000 million people in India, and I think it very likely that there will have been a revolution of one complexion or another. But the traveler who returns to

Delhi then will find the city much the same, I swear, will respond to much the same emotions, indulge in just the same conjectures, bog down in just the same philosophical quagmires, and reach, if he is anything like me, about the same affectionate and inconclusive conclusions.

"You see? You see? Did I not say so? You are thinking metaphysically, as I foretold!" Well, perhaps. But the government spokesman proved his point better himself, for neither he nor Mrs. Gupta ever did ring.

V. S. NAIPAUL
(1 9 3 2 -)

In 1962, V. S. Naipaul first traveled to India, the land that his ancestors had left as indentured laborers in the late nineteenth century. Naipaul took with him the conventional ideas of India—the India people then knew as the land of Gandhi and Nehru, the India of the glittering classical past, which had been meticulously dredged up by European Indologists in the nineteenth century. He took with him his own childhood memories of an old India, the Brahmanic world of rituals and myths that had been carefully preserved in Trinidad, where he spent the first eighteen years of his life. But the poverty and wretchedness Naipaul encountered in India revived all the fears and insecurities he had known as a child. An anguished, often angry, perception of Indian realities drives *An Area of Darkness*, the book he wrote about his yearlong travels in India. Its sentences surge forward with a kind of nervous urgency, examining, refining, rejecting. But there are moments of calm and acceptance; and in the long section in the middle of the book where Naipaul describes his stay in Kashmir, you see the writer yield to an almost childlike wonder for his surroundings.

from AN AN AREA OF DARKNESS

HOTEL LIWARD
Prop: Flush System M. S. Butt

The sign came later, almost at the end of our stay. "I am honest man," the owner of the C-class houseboat had said, as we stood before the white bucket in one of the mildewed and tainted rooms of his rotting hulk. "And flush system, this is not *honest*." But Mr. Butt, showing us his still small sheaf of recommendations in the sitting room of the Liward Hotel, and pointing to the group of photographs on the pea-green walls, had said with a different emphasis, "*Before* flush." We looked at the laughing faces. At least a similar betrayal could not be ours. The sign, dispelling conjecture, was placed high on the pitched roof and lit by three bulbs, and could be seen even from Shankaracharya Hill.

It seemed an unlikely amenity. The hotel stood in the lake, at one end of a plot of ground about eighty feet long by thirty wide. It was a rough two-storeyed structure with ochre concrete walls, green and chocolate woodwork, and a roof of unpainted corrugated iron. It had seven rooms altogether, one of which was the dining room. It was in reality two buildings. One stood squarely in the angle of the plot, two walls flush with the water; it had two rooms up and two rooms down. A narrow wooden gallery went right around the top floor; around two sides of the lower floor, and hanging directly above the water, there was another gallery. The other building had one room down and two up, the second of which was a many-sided semicircular wooden projection supported on wooden poles. A wooden staircase led to the corridor that linked the two buildings; and the whole structure was capped by a pitched corrugated-iron roof of complex angular design.

It had a rough-and-ready air, which was supported by our first glimpse of Mr. Butt, cautiously approaching the landing stage to welcome us. He wore the Kashmiri fur cap, an abbreviation of the Russian. His long-tailed Indian-style shirt hung out of his loose trousers and dangled below his brown jacket. This suggested unreliability; the thick frames of his spectacles suggested abstraction; and he held a hammer in one hand. Beside him was a very small man, bare-footed, with a dingy grey pullover tight above flapping white cotton trousers gathered in at the waist by a string. A touch of quaintness, something of the Shakespearean mechanic, was given him by his sagging woollen nightcap. So misleading can first impressions be: this was Aziz. And flush was not yet finally installed. Pipes and bowls had been laid, but cisterns were yet to be unwrapped.

"One day," Aziz said in English. "Two days."

"I like flush," Mr. Butt said.

We read the recommendations. Two Americans had been exceedingly warm; an Indian lady had praised the hotel for providing the "secrecy" needed by honeymoon couples.

"*Before* flush," Mr. Butt said.

With this his English was virtually exhausted, and thereafter we dealt with him through Aziz.

We bargained. Fear made me passionate; it also, I realized later, made me unnaturally convincing. My annoyance was real; when I turned to walk away I was really walking away; when I was prevailed upon to return—easy, since the boatman refused to ferry me back to the road—my fatigue was genuine. So we agreed. I was to take the room next to the semicircular sitting room, of which I was also to have exclusive use. And I needed a reading lamp.

"Ten-twelve rupees, what is that?" Aziz said.

And, I would need a writing table.

He showed me a low stool.

With my hands I sketched out my larger requirements.

He showed me an old weathered table lying out on the lawn.

"We paint," he said.

I rocked the table with a finger.

Aziz sketched out two timber braces and Mr. Butt, understanding and smiling, lifted his hammer.

"We fix," Aziz said.

It was then that I felt they were playing and that I had become part of their play. We were in the middle of the lake. Beyond the alert kingfishers, the fantastic hoopoes pecking in the garden, beyond the reeds and willows and poplars, our view unbroken by houseboats, there were the snow-capped mountains. Before me a nightcapped man, hopping about restlessly, and at the end of the garden a new wooden shed, his home, unpainted and warm against the gloom of low-hanging willows. He was a man skilled in his own way with hammer and other implements, anxious to please, magically improvising, providing everything. The nightcap did not belong to a Shakespearean mechanic; it had a fairy-tale, Rumpelstiltskin, Snow White-and-the-seven-dwarfs air.

"You pay advance and you sign agreement for three months."

Even this did not break the spell. Mr. Butt wrote no English. Aziz was illiterate. I had to make out my own receipt. I had to write and sign our agreement in the back of a large, serious-looking but erratically filled ledger which lay on a dusty shelf in the dining room.

"You write three months?" Aziz asked.

I hadn't. I was playing safe. But how had he guessed?

"You write three months."

The day before we were to move in we paid a surprise visit. Nothing appeared to have changed. Mr. Butt waited at the landing stage, dressed as before and as seemingly abstracted. The table that was to have been painted and braced remained unpainted and unbraced on the lawn. There was no sign of a reading lamp. "Second coat," Aziz had said, placing his hand on the partition that divided bathroom from bedroom. But no second coat had been given, and the bright blue paint lay as thin and as scabrous on the new, knot-darkened wood. Dutifully, not saying a word, Mr. Butt examined with us, stopping when we stopped, looking where we looked, as though he wasn't sure what, in spite of his knowledge, he might find. The bathroom was as we had left it: the lavatory bowl in position, still in its gummed paper taping, the pipes laid, the cistern absent.

"Finish," I said. "Finish. Give back deposit. We go. No stay here."

He made no reply and we went down the steps. Then across the garden, from the warm wooden shack, embowered in willows, Aziz came tripping, nightcapped and pullovered. Blue paint spotted his pullover—a new skill revealed—and there was a large spot on the tip of his nose. He was carrying, as if about to offer it to us, a lavatory cistern.

"Two minutes," he said. "Three minutes. I fix."

One of Snow White's own men in a woollen nightcap: it was impossible to abandon him.

Three days later we moved in. And it had all been done. It was as if all the folk at the bottom of the garden had lent a hand with broom and brush and saw and hammer. The table had been massively braced and tremendously nailed together; it was covered with an already peeling skin of bright blue paint. A large bulb, fringed at the top with a small semi-spherical metal shade, was attached to a stunted flexible arm which rested on a chromium-plated disc and was linked by incalculable tangled yards of flex—I had specified length and maneuverability—to the electric point: this was the lamp. In the bathroom the lavatory cistern had been put in place. Aziz, like a magician, pulled the chain; and the flush flushed.

"Mr. Butt he say," Aziz said, when the waters subsided, "this is not his hotel. This is *your* hotel."

There were others beside Aziz and Mr. Butt. There was the sweeper boy in flopping garments of requisite filth. There was Ali Mohammed. He was a small man of about forty with a cadaverous face made still more so by ill-fitting dentures. His duty was to entice tourists to the hotel, and his official dress consisted of a striped blue Indian-style suit of loose trousers and lapel-less jacket, shoes, a Kashmiri fur cap and a silver watch and chain. So twice a day he came out of the hut at the bottom of the garden and, standing with his bicycle in the *shikara*, was paddled past the tailor's one-roomed wooden shack, high and crooked above the water, past the poplars and the willows, past the houseboats, past Nehru Park, to the *ghat* and the lake boulevard, to cycle to the Tourist Reception Center and stand in the shade of chenars outside the entrance, with the tonga-wallahs, houseboat-owners or their agents, below the hoarding with Mr. Nehru's portrait. And there was the *khansamah*, the cook. He was older than Aziz or Ali Mohammed, and more nobly built. He was a small man, but he was given height by the rightness of his proportions, his carriage, his long-tailed shirt and the loose trousers that tapered down to his well-made feet. He was a brooder. His regular features were tormented by nervousness and irritability. He often came out of the kitchen and stood for minutes on the veranda of the hut, gazing at the lake, his bare feet beating the floorboards.

Our first meal was all ritual. The concrete floor of the dining room had been spread with old matting; and on the table two small plastic buckets sprouted long-stemmed red, blue, green and yellow plastic daisies. "Mr. Butt he buy," Aziz said. "Six rupees." He went out for the soup; and presently we saw him and Ali Mohammed, each holding a plate of soup, coming out of the hut and walking carefully, concentrating on the soup, down the garden path.

"Hot box coming next week," Aziz said.

"Hot box?"

"*Next* week." His voice was low; he was like a sweet-tempered nurse humoring a spoilt and irascible infant. He took a napkin off his shoulder and flicked away tiny flies. "This is *nothing*. Get little hot, little flies dead. Big flies come chase little flies. Then mosquito come bite big flies and *they* go away."

And we believed him. He withdrew and stood outside below the projecting sitting room; and almost immediately we heard him shouting to the kitchen or to some passing lake dweller in a voice that was entirely altered. Through the windows at our back we had a view of reeds, mountains, snow and sky; before us from time to time we had a glimpse of Aziz's night-capped head as he peered through the as yet glassless window-frame. We were in the middle of the unknown, but on our little island we were in good hands; we were being looked after; no harm could come to us; and with every dish that came out of the hut at the end of the garden our sense of security grew.

Aziz, his delight matching ours, shouted for the *khansamah*. It seemed an impertinent thing to do. A grumble, a silence, a delay showed that it was so taken. When at last the *khansamah* appeared he was without his apron; he was nervous and bashful. What would we like for dinner? What would we like for dinner? "You want scones for tea? And pudding, what you want for pudding? Tipsy pudding? Trifle? Apple tart?"

Snow White had gone, but her imparted skills remained.

It was only early spring, and on some mornings there was fresh snow on the mountains. The lake was cold and clear; you could see the fish feeding like land animals on the weeds and on the lake bed, and when the sun came out every fish cast a shadow. It could be hot then, with the sun out, and woollen clothes were uncomfortable. But heat presently led to rain, and then the temperature dropped sharply. The clouds fell low over the mountains, sometimes in a level bank, sometimes shredding far into the valleys. The temple at the top of Shankaracharya Hill, one thousand feet above us, was hidden; we would think of the lonely brahmin up there, with his woollen cap and his small charcoal brazier below his pinky-brown blanket. When the wind blew across the lake the young reeds swayed; on the rippled water reflections were abolished; the magenta discs of the lotus curled upwards; and all the craft on the lake made for shelter. Some pulled in at the hotel landing-stage; occasionally their occupants went to the hut to get charcoal for their hookahs or for the mud-lined wicker braziers which they kept below their blankets. And immediately after rain the lake was as glassy as could be.

The hotel stood on one of the main *shikara* lanes, the silent highways of the lake. The tourist season had not properly begun and about us there still flowed only the life of the lake. In the morning the flotilla of grass-laden *shikaras* passed, paddled by women sitting cross-legged at the stern, almost level with the water. The marketplace shifted, according to custom, from day to day. Now it was directly in front of the hotel, beyond the lotus patch; now it was farther down the lane, beside the old boat that was the pettiest of petty lake shops. Often it seemed that buyer and seller would come to blows; but the threatening gestures, the raised voices, the paddling away, abuse hurled over the shoulder, the turning back, abuse continuing, all this was only the lake method of bargaining. All day the traffic continued. The cheese man, priestlike in white, sat before white conical mounds of cheese and rang his bell, he and his cheese sheltered by an awning, his paddler exposed at the stern. The milk-lady was fearfully jeweled; silver earrings hung from her distended lobes like keys from a key ring. The confectioner's goods were contained in a single red box. The "Bread Bun & Butter" man called every day at the hotel; on his *shikara* board *N* was written back to front. "Beau-ti-ful! Mar-velous! Lover-ly!" This was the cry of Bulbul, the flower seller. His roses sweetened our room for a week; his sweet peas collapsed the day they were bought. He suggested salt; his sweet peas collapsed again; we quarreled. But his *shikara* continued to be a moving bank of bewitching color in the early mornings, until the season was advanced and he left us to work the more profitable A-class houseboats on Nagin Lake. The police *shikara* passed often, the sergeant paddled by constables. In the post office *shikara*, painted red, the clerk sat cross-legged at a low desk, selling stamps, canceling letters and ringing his bell. Every tradesman had his paddler; and the paddler might be a child of seven or eight. It did not look especially cruel. Here children were, as they have until recently been elsewhere, miniature adults in dress, skills and appearance. Late at night we would hear them singing to keep their spirits up as they paddled home.

So quickly we discovered that in spite of its unkempt lushness, its tottering buildings and the makeshift instincts of its inhabitants, the lake was charted and regulated; that there were divisions of labor as on land; and that divisions of water space were to be recognized even if marked by no more than a bent and sagging length of wire. There were men of power, with areas of influence; there were regional elected courts. And such regulations were necessary because the lake was full of people and the lake was rich. It provided for all. It provided weeds and mud for vegetable plots. A boy twirled his bent pole in the water, lifted, and he had a bundle of rich, dripping lake weed. It provided fodder for animals. It provided reeds for thatching. It provided fish, so numerous in the clear water that they could be seen just below the steps of the busy *ghat*. On some days the lake was dotted with fishermen who seemed to be walking on water: they stood erect and still on the edge of their barely moving *shikaras*, their tridents raised, their eyes as sharp as those of the kingfishers on the willows.

GEORGE ORWELL

(1903–50)

George Orwell, the iconic author of *1984* (1945) and *Animal Farm* (1949), was born as Eric Arthur Blair in Motihari, Bengal, at a time when the sun did not seem to set on the British Empire. He spent his first four years in India before being sent, as was usual in those days, to England, where he was educated at Eton. He returned to the subcontinent as an officer in the Imperial Police Service. The essay "Shooting an Elephant" describes the absurdity of the role of the imperial master he found himself in. Eventually, the experience of carrying out his duties of an imperial factotum convinced him of the "evil" of imperialism and of the necessity of social and economic justice. It became an important marker in his intellectual journey through the turbulent Europe of the 1930s and 1940s where many writers found themselves gravitating toward either Fascism or Communism. His unsentimental knowledge of oppressed peoples was what gave his voice, almost alone among the British and American intellectuals, its peculiar honesty and conviction.

SHOOTING AN ELEPHANT

In Moulmein, in Lower Burma, I was hated by large numbers of people—the only time in my life that I have been important enough for this to happen to me. I was sub-divisional police officer of the town, and in an aimless, petty kind of way anti-European feeling was very bitter. No one had the guts to raise a riot, but if a European woman went through the bazaars alone somebody would probably spit betel juice over her dress. As a police officer I was an obvious target and was baited whenever it seemed safe to do so. When a nimble Burman tripped me up on the football field and the referee (another Burman) looked the other way, the crowd yelled with hideous laughter. This happened more than once. In the end the sneering yellow faces of young men that met me everywhere, the insults hooted after me when I was at a safe distance, got badly on my nerves. The young Buddhist priests were the worst of all. There were several thousands of them in the town and none of them seemed to have anything to do except stand on street corners and jeer at Europeans.

All this was perplexing and upsetting. For at that time I had already made up my mind that imperialism was an evil thing and the sooner I chucked up my job and got out of it the better. Theoretically—and secretly, of course—I was all for the Burmese and all against their oppressors, the British. As for the job I was doing, I hated it more bitterly than I can perhaps make clear. In a job like that you see the dirty work of Empire at close quarters. The wretched prisoners huddling in the stinking cages of the lock-ups, the grey, cowed faces of the long-term convicts, the scarred buttocks of the men who had been flogged with bamboos—all these oppressed me with an intolerable sense of guilt. But I could get nothing into perspective. I was young and ill-educated and I had had to think out my problems in the utter silence that is imposed on every Englishman in the East. I did not even know that the British Empire is dying, still less did I know that it is a great deal better than the younger empires that are going to supplant it. All I knew was that I was stuck between my hatred of the empire I served and my rage against the evil-spirited little beasts who tried to make my job impossible. With one part of my mind I thought of the British Raj as an unbreakable tyranny, as something clamped down, *in saecula saeculorum*, upon the will of prostrate peoples; with another part I thought that the greatest joy in the world would be to drive a bayonet into a Buddhist priest's guts. Feelings like these are the normal by-products of imperialism; ask any Anglo-Indian official, if you can catch him off duty.

One day something happened which in a roundabout way was enlightening. It was a tiny incident in itself, but it gave me a better glimpse than I had had before of the real nature of imperialism—the real motives for which despotic governments act. Early one morning the sub-inspector at a police station on the other end of the town rang me up on the phone and said that an elephant was ravaging the bazaar. Would I please come and do something about it? I did not know what I could do, but I wanted to see what was happening and I got on to a pony and started out. I took my rifle, an old .44 Winchester and much too small to kill an elephant, but I thought the noise might be useful *in terrorem*. Various Burmans stopped me on the way and told me about the elephant's doings. It was not, of course, a wild elephant, but a tame one which had gone "must." It had been chained up as tame elephants always are when their attack of "must" is due, but on the previous night it had broken its chain and escaped. Its mahout, the only person who could manage it when it was in that state, had set out in pursuit, but he had taken the wrong direction and was now twelve hours' journey away, and in the morning the elephant had suddenly reappeared in the town. The Burmese population had no weapons and were quite helpless against it. It had already destroyed somebody's bamboo hut, killed a cow and raided some fruit-stalls and devoured the stock; also it had met the municipal rubbish van, and, when the driver jumped out and took to his heels, had turned the van over and inflicted violence upon it.

The Burmese sub-inspector and some Indian constables were waiting for me in the quarter where the elephant had been seen. It was a very poor quarter, a labyrinth of squalid bamboo huts, thatched with palm-leaf, winding all over a steep hillside. I remember that it was a cloudy stuffy morning at the beginning of the rains. We began questioning the people as to where the elephant had gone, and, as usual, failed to get any definite information. That is invariably the case in the East; a story always sounds clear enough at a distance, but the nearer you get to the scene of events the vaguer it becomes. Some of the people said that the elephant had gone in one direction, some said that he had gone in another, some professed not even to have heard of any elephant. I had almost made up my mind that the whole story was a pack of lies, when we heard yells a little distance away. There was a loud, scandalized cry of "Go away, child! Go away this instant!" and an old woman with a switch in her hand came round the corner of a hut, violently shooing away a crowd of naked children. Some more women followed, clicking their tongues and exclaiming; evidently there was something there that the children ought not to have seen. I rounded the hut and saw a man's dead body sprawling in the mud. He was an Indian, a black Dravidian coolie, almost naked, and he could not have been dead many minutes. The people said that the elephant had come suddenly upon him round the corner of the hut, caught him with its trunk, put its foot on his back and ground him into the earth. This was the rainy season and the ground was soft, and his face had scored a trench a foot deep and a couple of yards long. He was lying on his belly with arms crucified and head sharply twisted to one side. His face was coated with mud, the eyes wide open, the teeth bared and grinning with an expression of unendurable agony. (Never tell me, by the way, that the dead look peaceful. Most of the corpses I have seen looked devilish.) The friction of the great beast's foot had stripped the skin from his back as neatly as one skins a rabbit. As soon as I saw the dead man I sent an orderly to a friend's house near by to borrow an elephant rifle. I had already sent back the pony, not wanting it to go mad with fright and throw me if it smelled the elephant.

The orderly came back in a few minutes with a rifle and five cartridges, and meanwhile some Burmans had arrived and told us that the elephant was in the paddy fields below, only a few hundred yards away. As I started forward practically the whole population of the quarter flocked out of their houses and followed me. They had seen the rifle and were all shouting excitedly that I was going to shoot the elephant. They had not shown much interest in the elephant when he was merely ravaging their homes, but it was different now that he was going to be shot. It was a bit of fun to them, as it would be to an English crowd; besides, they wanted the meat. It made me vaguely uneasy. I had no intention of shooting the elephant—I had merely sent for the rifle to defend myself if necessary—and it is always unnerving to have a crowd following you. I marched down the hill, looking and feeling a fool, with the rifle over my shoulder and an ever-growing army of people jostling at my heels. At the bottom when you got away from the huts there was a metalled road and beyond that a miry waste of paddy fields a thousand yards across, not yet ploughed but soggy from the first rains and dotted with coarse grass. The elephant was standing eighty yards from the road, his left side toward us. He took not the slightest notice of the crowd's approach. He was tearing up bunches of grass, beating them against his knees to clean them and stuffing them into his mouth.

I had halted on the road. As soon as I saw the elephant I knew with perfect certainty that I ought not to shoot him. It is a serious matter to shoot a working elephant—it is comparable to destroying a huge and costly piece of machinery—and obviously one ought not to do it if it can possibly be avoided. And at that distance, peacefully eating, the elephant looked no more dangerous than a cow. I thought then and I think now that his attack of "must" was already passing off; in which case he would merely wander harmlessly about until the mahout came back and caught him. Moreover, I did not in the least want to shoot him. I decided that I would watch him for a little while to make sure that he did not turn savage again, and then go home.

But at that moment I glanced round at the crowd that had followed me. It was an immense crowd, two thousand at the least and growing every minute. It blocked the road for a long distance on either side. I looked at the sea of yellow faces above the garish clothes—faces all happy and excited over this bit of fun, all certain that the elephant was going to be shot. They were watching me as they would watch a conjurer about to perform a trick. They did not like me, but with the magical rifle in my hands I was momentarily worth watching. And suddenly I realized that I should have to shoot the elephant after all. The people expected it of me and I had got to do it; I could feel their two thousand wills pressing me forward, irresistibly. And it was at this moment, as I stood there with the rifle in my hands, that I first grasped the hollowness, the futility of the white man's dominion in the East. Here was I, the white man with his gun, standing in front of the unarmed native crowd—seemingly the leading actor of the piece; but in reality I was only an absurd puppet pushed to and fro by the will of those yellow faces behind. I perceived in this moment that when the white man turns tyrant it is his own freedom that he destroys. He becomes a sort of hollow, posing dummy, the conventionalized figure of a sahib. For it is the condition of his rule that he shall spend his life in trying to impress the "natives" and so in every crisis he has got to do what the "natives" expect of him. He wears a mask, and his face grows to fit it. I had got to shoot the elephant. I had committed myself to doing it when I sent for the rifle. A sahib has got to act like a sahib; he has got to appear resolute, to know his own mind and do definite things. To come all that way, rifle in hand, with two thousand people marching at my heels, and then to trail feebly away, having done nothing— no, that was impossible. The crowd would laugh at me. And my whole life, every white man's life in the East, was one long struggle not to be laughed at.

But I did not want to shoot the elephant. I watched him beating his bunch of grass against his knees, with that preoccupied grandmotherly air that elephants have. It seemed to me that it would be murder to shoot him. At that age I was not squeamish about killing animals, but I had never shot an elephant and never wanted to. (Somehow it always seems worse to kill a *large* animal.) Besides, there was the beast's owner to be considered. Alive, the elephant was worth at least a hundred pounds; dead, he would only be worth the value of his tusks—five pounds, possibly. But I had got to act quickly. I turned to some experienced-looking Burmans who had been there when we arrived, and asked them how the elephant had been behaving. They all said the same thing: he took no notice of you if you left him alone, but he might charge if you went too close to him.

It was perfectly clear to me what I ought to do. I ought to walk up to within, say, twenty-five yards of the elephant and test his behavior. If he charged I could shoot, if he took no notice of me it would be safe to leave him until the mahout came back. But also I knew that I was going to do no such thing. I was a poor shot with a rifle and the ground was soft mud into which one would sink at every step. If the elephant charged and I missed him, I should have about as much chance as a toad under a steam-roller. But even then I was not thinking particularly of my own skin, only the watchful yellow faces behind. For at that moment, with the crowd watching me, I was not afraid in the ordinary sense, as I would have been if I had been alone. A white man mustn't be frightened in front of "natives"; and so, in general, he isn't frightened. The sole thought in my mind was that if anything went wrong those two thousand Burmans would see me pursued, caught, trampled on and reduced to a grinning corpse like that Indian up the hill. And if that happened it was quite probable that some of them would laugh. That would never do. There was only one alternative. I shoved the cartridges into the magazine and lay down on the road to get a better aim.

The crowd grew very still, and a deep, low, happy sigh, as of people who see the theater curtain go up at last, breathed from innumerable throats. They were going to have their bit of fun after all. The rifle was a beautiful German thing with cross-hair sights. I did not then know that in shooting an elephant one should shoot to cut an imaginary bar running from ear-hole to ear-hole. I ought therefore, as the elephant was sideways on, to have aimed straight at his ear-hole; actually I aimed several inches in front of this, thinking the brain would be further forward.

When I pulled the trigger I did not hear the bang or feel the kick—one never does when a shot goes home—but I heard the devilish roar of glee that went up from the crowd. In that instant, in too short a time, one would have thought, even for the bullet to get there, a mysterious, terrible change had come over the elephant. He neither stirred nor fell, but every line of his body had altered. He looked suddenly stricken, shrunken, immensely old, as though the frightful impact of the bullet had paralyzed him without knocking him down. At last, after what seemed a long time—it might have been five seconds, I dare say—he sagged flabbily to his knees. His mouth slobbered. An enormous senility seemed to have settled upon him. One could have imagined him thousands of years old. I fired again into the same spot. At the second shot he did not collapse but climbed with desperate slowness to his feet and stood weakly upright, with legs sagging and head drooping. I fired a third time. That was the shot that did for him. You could see the agony of it jolt his whole body and knock the last remnant of strength from his legs. But in falling he seemed for a moment to rise, for as his

hind legs collapsed beneath him he seemed to tower upwards
like a huge rock toppling, his trunk reaching skyward like a tree.
He trumpeted, for the first and only time. And then down he
came, his belly toward me, with a crash that seemed to shake the
ground even where I lay.

I got up. The Burmans were already racing past me across the
mud. It was obvious that the elephant would never rise again,
but he was not dead. He was breathing very rhythmically with
long rattling gasps, his great mound of a side painfully rising and
falling. His mouth was wide open—I could see far down into
caverns of pale pink throat. I waited a long time for him to die,
but his breathing did not weaken. Finally I fired my two remain-
ing shots into the spot where I thought his heart must be. The
thick blood welled out of him like red velvet, but still he did not
die. His body did not even jerk when the shots hit him, the tortured breathing continued without a pause. He was dying, very
slowly and in great agony, but in some world remote from me
where not even a bullet could damage him further. I felt that I
had got to put an end to that dreadful noise. It seemed dreadful
to see the great beast lying there, powerless to move and yet
powerless to die, and not even to be able to finish him. I sent
back for my small rifle and poured shot after shot into his heart
and down his throat. They seemed to make no impression. The
tortured gasps continued as steadily as the ticking of a clock.

In the end I could not stand it any longer and went away. I
heard later that it took him half an hour to die. Burmans were
arriving with dahs and baskets even before I left, and I was told
they had stripped his body almost to the bones by the afternoon.

Afterwards, of course, there were endless discussions about
the shooting of the elephant. The owner was furious, but he was

only an Indian and could do nothing. Besides, legally I had done the right thing, for a mad elephant has to be killed, like a mad dog, if its owner fails to control it. Among the Europeans opinion was divided. The older men said I was right, the younger men said it was a damn shame to shoot an elephant for killing a coolie, because an elephant was worth more than any damn Coringhee coolie. And afterwards I was very glad that the coolie had been killed; it put me legally in the right and it gave me a sufficient pretext for shooting the elephant. I often wondered whether any of the others grasped that I had done it solely to avoid looking a fool.

PIER PAOLO PASOLINI

(1922–75)

Pier Paolo Pasolini, who along with Fellini and Antonioni was one of the great film directors to have emerged from Italy in the post–World War II years, was also a writer of considerable talent; he is best known for his short stories. He went to India in 1961, accompanied by the novelists Alberto Moravia and Elsa Morante. Although attracted by socialism, Pasolini expressed in his films a profound ambivalence toward modern civilization. He was among many Italian intellectuals who felt alienated by the rapid postwar reconstruction and modernization of Italy. India seems to have intensified his feelings of distrust and scorn. Like many European travelers, he became obsessed with poverty and often saw little else but the physical wretchedness of the places he visited. He also brought his suspicion of the postwar Italian middle class to India. The following pages describe his vivid sense of the uncertainties of the semi-westernized Indian middle class.

from THE SCENT OF INDIA

It seemed like the face of San Sebastian: inclined a little toward one shoulder, the lips swollen and almost white, the eyes as if glazed with a frozen lament, and an upper lid drawn back and red. He was walking along the edge of a shady street on the periphery of Gwalior and, having noticed that I observed him for a moment, he now followed us with a sad smile.

He was covered with the usual white rags: while around him, along that street on the periphery (if periphery and center have any meaning for Indian cities), the usual lugubrious misery, the usual shops little more than boxes, the usual little houses in ruins, the usual stores worn down by the breath of the monsoons, the usual high stench which smothers breathing. That smell of poor food and of corpses which in India is like a continuous powerful air current that gives one a kind of fever. And that odor which, little by little, becomes an almost living physical entity, seems to interrupt the normal course of life in the body of the Indians. Its breath, attacking those little bodies covered in their light and filthy linen, seems to corrode them, forcing itself to sprout, to reach a human embodiment.

In that potent odor Muti Lal followed us humbly and anxiously. Every Indian is a beggar: even he who does not do it for a profession, if the occasion presents itself will not flinch from trying to extend his hand.

Our hotel rose up at the bottom of an overgreen lawn, dusty, wearing the sinister solemnity of a cure resort.

Moravia, having finished his little healthy walk which he had allowed himself in the midst of that "sea of rags," without any hesitation reached the hotel, the desperate prospect ahead of that enormous room furnished with desolate furniture, with the grey mosquito net and the dead roaches in the bath.

However I stopped at the entrance, on that peripheral road which had the aspect of a European street. I looked at Muti Lal, who was still smiling sadly, and exchanged a word with him. We introduced ourselves and he immediately told me everything about himself, as children do throughout the world. He came from Patyali in the province of Eata, where he had a family. He was working at Gwalior in a shop as a salesman. He was sleeping with some companions on the pavement. He was a Brahmin, as the associations of his name had already informed me. His skin was clear, almost white: and his features, a little unclear and delicate, were those of a bourgeois European boy. Indeed he knew how to read and write, and in fact he must also have attended a "high school": he lit up completely when he knew that I was a journalist, he wanted to know the name of the newspaper where I wrote my articles on India: and he asked me anxiously if I would also write the "story" of our evening. He was therefore a bourgeois.

It may have become clear that India has nothing mysterious about it, as the legends say. Basically one is dealing with a little country with only four or five big cities, of which one alone, Bombay, is worthy of the name; without industries, or almost; very uniform and with simple historical stratifications and crystallizations.

In substance one is dealing with an enormous agricultural sub-proletariat, blocked for centuries in its institutions by a foreign domination which has made certain that these institutions were preserved while at the same time, through the fault of a conservation so consistent and unnatural, that they degenerated.

In reality a country like India is easy to grasp intellectually. Although certainly one can go astray there, in the middle of this crowd of four hundred million souls: but one goes astray as in a rebus, in which one can arrive at the top with patience: the particulars are difficult, but not the substance.

One of the most difficult "particulars" in this world is the middle class. Certainly we Italians have a model which at present vaguely approximates to the Indian one, if we think of our Southern middle class: recent formation, imitation of another type of middle class, psychological imbalance with strong contradictions, ranging from a stupid and cruel pride to a sincere understanding of the people's problems, etcetera.

However in the Indian middle class there is something terribly uncertain, which gives one a sense of pity and of fear.

Obviously we are dealing with a disproportion that is almost inhuman in relation to the reality in which it exists, in which live the enormous mass of the sub-proletarian who surround it like an ocean. It is true that the Indian middle class is born into that inferno: in those unformed and hungry cities, in those villas constructed with mud and the dung of cows, amidst famine and epidemic. Because of all this, it seems traumatized by it. It is rendered speechless or at least voiceless by it. The owners of the shops, and the rare professionals always have a terrified look, almost stupefied. In comparison to the Europeans, who are still a model that seems unreachable to them, they have almost lost their tongue.

So they fix on family life, to which they give absolute priority: they are full of children whose gentility they cultivate: their own disturbed harmony is perpetuated in this tender model of children, and so the circle of gentility is closed, rather nastily and self-centeredly.

Whatever the Indian middle class is I have seen it above all in Africa, in Kenya, where there are some tens of thousands of Indians (brought there by the English to construct the railroad when the Africans were still unusable), who have become the lower middle class of the place. They have become completely washed-out. Unsympathetic to the Africans, they cultivate this family gentility around the shop which gives them the ease or even a little wealth to do so: while underneath lingers the pain of not yet being Europeans.

I remember that I was hurrying through the streets of Mombasa in a car when a silhouette crossed the street, unsure, risking being knocked down and my negro driver Ngomu hit his forehead with a finger, saying, as if one was talking of a habitual and natural topic: "Indian: stupid."

And another time I was walking through some little streets in Zanzibar at night, amidst piles of rubbish, and the two young negroes who were with me, Snani and Bwanatosha, said to me, with the same tone in their voice as they looked around: "Indian: dirty."

But it is not even accurate to speak of resignation and fatalism: because in the Indian middle class there is always a kind of anxiety, a sense of waiting, even if it is buried and useless.

Muti Lal wanted to take me to the theater. We met each other after supper, having spent some hours in the desperate room on the ground floor of the national hotel, which seemed to be specially made for the entry of cobras; and we went together through the now dark big street, deserted but for its vague and terrible scent.

We walked for a long time in between clusters of atrocious huts, little walls on fearsome meadows, and we arrived at a kind of fair: as usual, in the darkness and with the lights lit, everything appeared artificial, fantastic, worthy of *Thousand and One Nights*.

We walked amongst the illuminated tents for a good long way, between crowds in cloaks and girdles, with turbans wound round the most beautiful hair, black and wavy, in the world, and we arrived at the theater.

There was a large tent surrounded by a file of ragged people: some acting as guardians, others loitering and enjoying the music which floated violently, with frantic beatings of the drum, out of the tent.

Muti Lal bought the tickets and we entered.

One had to go down three or four steps of mud because the theater was a broad rectangle in fact scraped out of the yellow mud and covered over by the big tent.

Fifty or so rows of improvised seats filled it: and one saw from close by the lined faces of the Indians with their rags and their turbans. It was cold and everyone was trembling, covered with their light linen and with only a scarf around their head. A long row of spectators was also squatting along the edge of the rectangular pit, against the tent.

Some seats stood there on their own just below the stage, at least four to five meters from each other: they were the best places. Muti Lal happily guided me there, and I sat down between him and a bearded shopkeeper, who was already absorbed in the drama.

The podium in front of the stage had not been formed by digging out the mud; since it was attached to the apron of the stage, with some improvised steps on the side made of yellow mud. The instrumentalists were gathered above there: they were playing a kind of pianola, a drum, and a wind instrument which made a deafening noise, accompanying and underlining the

caressing, pathetic songs of the actors with unheard-of violence.

The actors were all fat or well nourished: they were enacting,
really, a drama of adventure with various *coups de théâtre*, with
refindings, deposed kings, robbers and unhappy loves: but they
were all as pink as piglets, with their full faces, their beautiful
penguin thighs. The essence of virility was represented in the
hero, by a pair of black whiskers which appeared to be false and
that stood out proudly from his pink face.

It didn't take me very long to notice that they were a disguise:
beneath the white and red face one saw the black hair of his neck
and his chest. The heroic and erotic idea of the Indians was one
of white coloring, endowed with a respectable rotundity.

In fact in all the little towns the advertisements for the cinema, depicted in a very simple and monotonous way, all represented endless processions of white protagonists with round
cheeks and a little bit of a double chin.

Now, all the Indians are minute, thin, with the little bodies of
children: they are wonderful until twenty years old, gracious and
full of pathos afterwards. How could such a monstrous ideal of
beauty ever happen? What a difference between those stocky,
puppyish heroes and my poor Muti Lal, sick, pallid, who was
drinking, trembling with cold, the boiling tea, which another like
him had offered him in some dirty cups.

Thus I learnt to recognize a certain type of Indian bourgeois:
which to be honest is still very rare. One finds him in some large
hotel or in the little waiting rooms of airports. He is massive,
corpulent, with hair which would have been beautiful, like that
of almost all Indians, if a clever barber had not made it similar
to two wings of a raven divided on the inclined skull: he has a fat

wife, dressed in a splendid pink and yellow sari, the features balanced on round cheeks, and a little hair on the upper lip: as well as a daughter clothed in the European style, curiously ugly, who laughs with the voice of a crackling gramophone.

It is the middle class which, still very discreetly, hurries to occupy the place left by the deposed but still very rich Maharajas (these are totally sold out in any case: I have seen one of them with his little court at the *Ritz*, which is the best, albeit only nightspot for the rich of Bombay: he seemed like a faded puppet, dressed in the European style, surrounded by European women with whom he was dancing the waltz).

In India the vigor possessed by that unpleasant institution called the Rotary Club is extraordinary. There was no hotel where we went (and the hotels of necessity had to be first class) where we did not find some people gathered for a cocktail. However they seemed to me reunions of the dead, who were embalmed with their beautiful flaring sari across them. I remember our arrival at Aurangabad, which was the first truly Indian town which we visited after Bombay. Before going to the hotel from the airport we wanted to pass through the center of the city, so voracious was our anxiety to look.

It was already night. Things appeared and disappeared like visions, encapsulated in clusters of lights by the indescribably "eastern" atmosphere: a mussulman arch, like a relic in the middle of a sea of huts, laid out like hunched backs, with the little shops offering materials or colored foods, and in front of them the whirling crowd of people with light blue or red bandages on their heads, absurd clothes of an epoch light years away from ours, goats, cows, rickshaws . . . Along the edge of the central street (which was like a long vivisection, with the walls of the little houses of one story leaning entangled one against the other, each one with an illuminated and crowded little shop in front) ran the ditches of the drains which passed under the shops, which one entered over a small rounded step . . . Observe the children who were collecting the dung of cows on the street, putting it into flat wide baskets . . . Observe the groups of young Mussulmans with their books under their arms . . . Observe a latrine, two high walls a half meter above the edge of the ditch, amongst which the Indians were urinating squatting, as is their habit . . . Observe the crows, always present throughout India with their purposeless scream . . . We crossed the entire city, which like all the Indian cities is only a big formless mass around a market. We left through another Mussulman archway and, across the country dotted with school buildings and barracks inherited from the English, we arrived at the hotel. This was a light construction of one story, most elegant, two long wings with the doors of the rooms giving onto a little portico, laid out in a large garden dotted with banjam trees and bougainvillea. As we entered into the little hall painted white with some little birds fluttering there freely, we didn't notice anything at first: but after an instant our attention was attracted by a crowd occupying this hall: gentlemen dressed in white and ladies in sari, all seated on some chairs laid out along the walls. Either they were silent or they were talking in a whisper. They were rich people, members of the Rotary Club in fact, perfectly inconceivable in the social circle which made up Aurangabad. After a few minutes they were eating at a very long table set out under the portico of one of the wings of the hotel, silent in the intense light which isolated them from the thick darkness of the country, one not without cobras, where thousands of miserable people were sleeping in their huts or on the rude earth, like a biblical dream.

And I remember also at Calcutta: this time it was not a matter of a Rotary Club meeting but of a cocktail party in honor of some actress or another, the usual fat piece with the made-up eyes: there had been a gloomy party with music and traditional dances in the dining room at the center of the hotel; then the guests had wandered out into the corridors and the waiting halls, with the great hangings and the huge ventilators suspended above the pink velvets and light woods of vast colonial elegance: they were all half drunk (the Indians get drunk easily: and in many states there is prohibition), lugubriously happy: but silent. They didn't know how to exchange conversation. And one understood that around their cocktail party extended Calcutta, the unconfined city where every human pain and suffering touches the extreme limit, and life is carried out like a funereal ballet.

The people in India that I have studied, whether they possess something or carry out that function one calls "governing," know that they have no hope: scarcely freed from the inferno by means of a modern cultural conscience they know that they will have to stay in that inferno. The horizon of even the most vague renaissance is not visible in this generation, nor even in the next, and who knows in which of the future ones. The absence of every realizable hope makes the Indian middle class, as I said before, enclose themselves in that little certainty they possess: the family. They huddle there in order not to see and not to be seen. They have a very noble civic sense: and their ideal heroes,

Gandhi and Nehru, are there to testify to it: they possess a quality which is absolutely rare in the modern world: tolerance. This, despite the impossibility of acting, forces them into a state of renunciation which reduces their mental horizon: but such modesty is infinitely more touching than irritating. And this is certain: it is never vulgar. Although India may be an inferno of misery it is wonderful to live there, because it almost totally lacks this vulgarity. Even the vulgarity of the "hero" with which the Indian identifies himself (the pink puppy with black whiskers) is in reality absolutely ingenious and comic, generally common to all peasant societies. The big puppies with their black whiskers, vulgar in the true sense of the word (be it in type contaminated by imitation of a foreign middle class, more precisely, by Americanism), are very rare. At Tekkadi, a place lost in the heart of the South, I saw two types of different middle-class people: exactly in proportion to their numbers.

Tekkadi is a tourist place: hotels are grouped on the boundaries of Kerala and the state of Madras, in the middle of a forest, on the banks of a large artificial lake. One goes there because they say there are some wild animals: indeed it is true that a tour by boat on the lake at dawn, the hour in which the animals go to drink is included in the tourist program. In reality we didn't see a single thing, and I had to seek the innocent pleasure of seeing wild animals roaming freely in Africa.

The day on which we arrived in Tekkadi was the day of the tenth anniversary of Indian independence. Throughout all the villages we crossed one felt this simple atmosphere of a noble national festival because, as I was saying, India is an extremely simple and provincial country. There were flags and bunting on the poor huts amidst the palm groves, columns of schoolchildren through the streets, and gatherings of people seated formally in the middle of dusty village squares.

Many groups had made an excursion to Tekkadi for the festival: but let's be clear, there was much simplicity and poverty. However the atmosphere was that of certain European tourist spots on a Sunday.

Evening was descending: the lake in front was fearsome in its primordial silence, inimical to man. But around us we heard voices, the laughter of groups.

Before supper Moravia and I went on a little walk along the road by the hotel which, with its rather Swiss aspect, rose up on a long promontory of the sad lake.

While we were walking a 1100, a black one (yes, a 1100, a Fiat, which is a very common car in India) came toward us, full of four or five rather fat young men, pink, with black whiskers: it pretended to come across our path, with an insolent hooting of the horn: nothing else. But this was the only pathetic, aggressive and vulgar act of our whole Indian stay: something worthy of Milan or Palermo. Heaven preserve that this is not the way of evolution of the scarcely formed Indian middle class. Certainly objectively there is a danger. The weak have a strong tendency to become violent, the fragile to become ferocious: it would be terrible if a population of four hundred million inhabitants, which at the moment carries such weight on the historical and political stage of the world, became westernized in this mechanical and degrading way. There is everything to wish for this people apart from the middle-class experience, which would end up being of the Balkan, Spanish or Bourbon type. However, those fat fellows with their whiskers were only four; nothing in comparison with the whole school with its teachers who we met a little while after as we were continuing our walk.

They were all dressed in white: but this time the cloth was really white and new, because it was a holiday, because it was the day of independence. The big sheet around the hips or held down as far as the ankles, or taken by the corners and tied on the stomach in such a way as to leave the leg bare, the little tunic or white blouse, the white turban bound round the black wavy hair, with its weight and curls so romantic and barbaric: all was clean and pure.

They were standing at the bottom of a grassy slope on the edge of the lake, which had already disappeared in the last blood-red colors of dusk.

We went to sit on the slope opposite them, and we began to look at each other a little timidly. What a difference to our students! These were behaving perfectly, almost silently, chattering amongst themselves or with their teachers almost in a whisper. However the happiness of the moment and of the occasion shone in their eyes, black and brilliant in their dark faces, those tender and modest features. They looked at Moravia and me, sometimes scarcely noticing us, other times giving us a full smile. But they didn't dare address us, and we were also silent, as if through fear of interrupting that current of sympathy, which although silent was so full. Also they seemed to have understood, teachers and students, that the best thing was to look and smile at us like that, in silence.

Five, ten minutes passed, a quarter of an hour. The light of dusk became ever more gloomy, and there we all were, opposite each other, looking: their clothes belonging to the ancient pagan world became ever whiter, their silent sympathy sweeter.

Then, after having exchanged some words almost in a whisper, one of them, who was nearer on the gentle slope, came forward to where we were sitting: his companions were seated around him, cross-legged on the dry grass; in his hand he held a recorder or a flute, I don't know, but a little wind instrument: almost hidden amidst the folds of his tunic. He was uncertain whether to play or not: and his companions smiled, encouraging him. Then he decided. He sat on the grass and, with his face turned toward us, began to play. It was an old Indian melody, because India is resistant to any kind of foreign musical influence: indeed I believe that the Indians may not even be physically capable of hearing music other than their own. It was a syncopated, muffled and doleful phrase, which always finished, as with every Indian air, in an almost guttural lament, a sweet, pathetic death rattle: but a kind of noble, innocent happiness was enclosed within this sadness.

The boy played his flute and looked at us. It seemed as if, by playing to us in that way, he spoke to us, he made us a long speech, for himself and his companions.

"Look at us here," he seemed to say, "poor little Indians, with these clothes of ours which scarcely cover our small bodies, naked and dark like those of animals, lambs or little goats. We go to school, it is true, we study. You can see our teachers around us. We have our ancient religion, complicated and a little terrifying, and in addition today we celebrate with flags and little processions the festival of our independence.

"But how far there is still to go! Our villages are constructed with mud and with the dung of cows, our cities are only markets without form, dust-ridden and impoverished. Illnesses of every kind threaten us, smallpox and plague are at home here, like snakes. And so many younger brothers are born for whom we cannot find a handful of rice to divide amongst them. What will happen to us? What can we do? However in this tragedy there remains in our souls something which, if it is not happiness, is almost happiness: it is tenderness, humility toward the world, it is love . . . with this smile of sweetness, you, lucky foreigner, when you have returned to your homeland you will remember us, poor little Indians . . ."

He continued to play and to talk like this, for a long time, in the anguished silence of the lake.

OCTAVIO PAZ

(1914–98)

Octavio Paz was born to an impoverished lawyer in Mexico City. He published his first collection of poems when he was nineteen. He visited Spain during the civil war in the 1930s, as a sympathizer for the Republican cause. He was influenced at the same time by French surrealists. In Mexico, he wrote more poetry and founded and edited literary magazines. In 1950, he published his influential study of Mexico, *The Labyrinth of Solitude*. He first visited India as a diplomat in 1951: a brief, tantalizing trip that ended before it began when Paz was transferred to Japan. In 1962, he returned as the Mexican ambassador in New Delhi. For the next six years he traveled extensively across the subcontinent. His "education in India," he wrote in *In Light of India* (1997), marked him deeply; and his record of it, contained in several poems and essays, present the rare spectacle of a Mexican sensibility examining with confidence what he called the "immense reality of India."

from A TALE OF TWO GARDENS

THE MAUSOLEUM OF HUMAYUN

To the debate of wasps
the dialectic of monkeys
twitterings of statistics
it opposes

(high flame of rose)
formed out of stone and air and birds
time in repose above the water)

silence's architecture

IN THE LODI GARDENS
for Claude Esteban

The black, pensive, dense
domes of the mausoleums
suddenly shot birds
into the unanimous blue

THE DAY IN UDAIPUR

White palace,
white on the black lake.
Lingam and yoni.

As the goddess to the god,
you surround me, night.

Cool terrace.
You are immense, immense—
made to measure.

Inhuman stars.
But this hour is ours.

I fall and rise,
I burn, drenched.
Are you only one body?

Birds on the water,
dawn on eyelids.

Self-absorbed,
high as death,
the marble bursts.

Hushed palaces,
whiteness adrift.

Women and children
on the roads:
scattered fruit.

Rags or rays of lightning?
A procession on the plain.

Silver running cool
and clanking:
ankle and wrist.

In a rented costume
the boy goes to his wedding.

Clean clothes
spread out on the rocks
Look at them and say nothing.

On the little island
monkeys with red asses screech.

Hanging from the wall,
a dark and angry sun:
wasps' nest.

> And my head is another sun,
> full of black thoughts.

Flies and blood.
A small goat skips
in Kali's court.

> Gods, men and beasts
> eat from the same plate.

Over the pale god
the black goddess dances,
decapitated.

> Heat, the hour split open,
> and those mangoes, rotten . . .

Your face, the lake:
smooth, without thoughts.
A trout leaps.

> Lights on the water:
> souls sailing.

Ripples:
the golden plain—and the crack . . .
Your clothes nearby.

> I, like a lamp
> on your shadow body.

A living scales:
bodies entwined
over the void.

The sky crushes us,
the water sustains us.

I open my eyes:
so many trees
were born tonight.

What I've seen here, what I say,
the white sun erases.

ALAN ROSS

(1922–2001)

Alan Ross was born in Calcutta and enjoyed an enchanted childhood in Bengal before being sent back, like many hapless colonial children, to bleak, unfamiliar England. He went to Oxford before serving in the Royal Navy. He emerged after World War II as one of the more flamboyant men of letters in Britain. He wrote poetry, travel essays, biographies, and memoirs; he reported on cricket matches for *The Observer*; but he was, above all, a keen connoisseur of good writing, painting, cricket, and Indian food. His friends included Ian Fleming, in whose spy novel *The Man with the Golden Gun* he featured as Commander Ross. Ross visited India regularly. He went horse racing in Calcutta and Bombay and sniffed around for local talent. Many of the Indian writers well known in the West today—Rohinton Mistry, Vikram Seth, Amit Chaudhuri—found their first tentative efforts showcased in the *London Magazine*, a prestigious literary quarterly Ross edited for over four decades. In this excerpt from his memoir, Ross remembers, with a fierce nostalgia, the idyll he was born into and from which he was then wrenched away.

from BLINDFOLD GAMES

Above my desk, two views of Calcutta, dated 1798; four years after the Daniells, uncle and nephew, had left India. Entitled

"Garden Reach" and "Hooghly" they show a similar sweep of river, that elbow of the Hooghly before it glides between the Botanical Gardens, with its Great Banyan Tree, and Kidderpore Docks. Soon it will straighten out past Fort William and the Racecourse, Eden Gardens and Strand Road. On the north bank the Grand Trunk Road, parallel to the river, leads out, behind Howrah station, to Belur Math, many-domed headquarters of the Ramakrishna Mission founded in 1897 by Vivekananda and so designed to resemble from different angles a church, a mosque and a temple. Not far off, at Chitpur, is the house where Tagore was born and where, in 1941, five years after the last of my childhood ties with India had been dissolved, he died.

What the engravings show are expanses of water under scattered cloud. Boats drift under lateen sails or are laboriously poled to new fishing areas. Lawns slope to the river edge. At intervals steep, narrow steps run down to bathing *ghats*. Landing stages glint behind clusters of bamboo and mango. Spindly mop-like palms shade the infrequent domed buildings, outposts of an invisible city. Between the huge sky and the wide waterway the land seems barely to have broken surface.

This same scene appears more elaborately in View of Calcutta from the Garden Reach, in the Daniells' *A Picturesque Voyage to India*. The river jostles with sailing vessels and small craft, and in the distance the skyline of Calcutta suggests Venice. The Garden Reach of East India Company princelings set its mansions to catch the breeze coming off the Hooghly, some far scent of the sea lost in its muddiness.

Thomas Daniell's drawings, particularly those of excavations, give India an Italian look. Doomar Leyna, or the ruins at Rameswaram, might be Pompeii, the Esplanade in Calcutta, Naples. The illusion derives from architecture divorced from climate.

The Calcutta that emerges from the engravings of late eighteenth-century travelers is white and stately, a far cry from Kipling's "City of Dreadful Night." That is how I remembered it, too, sheltered from its *bustees* and bustle. It does not matter how often I have experienced it to the contrary, I have only to look at a map of the skull-shaped city—the Hooghly running from temple to upper lip—for it to detach itself into a series of frozen images bereft of people: the Victoria Memorial; the Kalighat temple; South Park Street cemetery; the Ochterlony Monument; Dalhousie Square; the High Court; the Jain Temple; the Nakhoda Mosque; the Marble Palace. These are the conventional "sights" of Calcutta but they were nevertheless also the spoils of childish photographic expeditions that, so soon separated from the originals, were my only sources of comfort. They were "picturesque" views, just as the Daniells called their journeys "picturesque"—chosen for their suitability as subjects for pictures. From the ages of seven to twenty they had to stand in for me as icons.

The eyes open to the eyes of an ayah, lifting a mosquito net, become bridal. From downstairs the ebb and flow of talk as doors open, shut. Clink of glasses, smell of cigars. In a shaft of light beyond the bed a woman raises her dress to pee: silk stockings, band of bare flesh, dark triangle of hair. She gets up, pulls the plug, and before lowering the dress, a pale almost transparent green silk, examines herself in a mirror, turning this way and that, flattening her abdomen. Later I see her often, a friend of the family, but am conscious only of that moist delta, an image incongruously revived by any map of the Hooghly estuary.

The Sundarbans, where during monsoon tributaries of the Ganges and the Brahmaputra flood the estuaries between Calcutta and the sea, are haunts of the white tiger. On Sagar Island the Hooghly is fifteen miles wide and there, picnicking during the Daniells' visit, the heir to Sir Hector Munro was hauled headfirst into the jungle by a tiger. The Hooghly river pilots whom I knew as a child used to report on the number of tigers seen swimming between the islands. It was one of these pilots, Lew Borrett, who used to sing "Leaning" in his tenor voice when home on leave and staying with us in Cornwall. He was burly and good-natured, with black gleaming hair worn *en brosse*. There never was such a romantic-looking woman as his wife Anna. Years later, on my return to India for a holiday from school, I met her again on board ship; she had left her husband, married an Indian schoolteacher, thin, bespectacled, timid, and lived the genteel occluded life of those in her situation. I was traveling first-class; she was now in steerage, a nominal Indian. I could not bear it. Lew took to the bottle and picked up with a pretty Eurasian secretary who looked like Merle Oberon, herself a product of Eurasian Calcutta. Lew took me out from school in Falmouth, where I had been sent at the age of seven.

Childhood addresses: 7/1 Burdwan Road, 11 Camac Street, 22 Lee Road, 226 Lower Circular Road. It was in the last of these streets, in the Presidency General Hospital (now S. S. Karnani Hospital) that Surgeon-major Ronald Ross in 1898 developed the cure for malaria. A plaque records the fact, but not that

Mohamed Bux, Ross's servant, was sent out to catch mosquitoes in order that they could bite him. Ross was a good name to have in Calcutta.

These houses have merged in my mind into one house: a two-storied, porticoed building of grey stone, its wide verandah opening on to a neat lawn. There is a short sweep of drive, a compound to one side. An iron gate bars the entrance to the drive; beside it a hut for the doorman is festooned by some kind of creeper.

When my Indian childhood came to an end and I was sent to England—the first step in an alienation from all family life—it was for this composite house that I mourned. The bearers with whom secret alliances were joined against parental instructions, their lips stained with pan and betel as if they were bleeding; the mali alongside whom I would squat while he watered and weeded; the various drivers and kitmagars with whom I played cards on the verandah while increasing numbers of dependants would peer out from the compound. The authorized staff, including cooks and sweepers, amounted to about ten, their duties strictly delineated according to rank and caste. Trade Union members today have nothing on Indian domestic servants. In addition, platoons of relatives lurked in the shadows, swelling in numbers until the food bills grew out of all proportion. The servants' food always smelt more interesting than our own, and the nasal whine of Bengali popular songs never stopped. Every so often my mother would remonstrate and for a few weeks there would be a reduction in intake. Then, after a decent interval, they would drift back.

Sometimes curious antipathies and hostility would develop between various servants, presumably because of family encroachments or unfair shares of the spoils. Bearers would glide about with stony faces, doing the least they could get away with, or go unaccountably missing. Even the games with me would be reluctantly played. Then, without explanation, everything would be sweetness and light again. There was nothing to be done during these periods of tension: questioning resulted only in withdrawal. No one knew anything: heads would just be wagged from side to side in the familiar gesture.

It was this shifting, shiftless surrogate family whose loss I found most hard to bear in England. They appeared nightly among the squawks of mynahs and the flapping of crows. Their bare feet trod dry mango leaves and the sound of doves was drowned by the mali's mower. Calcutta came to me as a series of glints: glint of eyes and of hair and of saris, of cycles and rick-shaws, of cinema hoardings and punkahs, and always of the Hooghly. There was no heat or oppressiveness in these Bengal images. Discomfort had no part in that interior cinema whose colors were fusions of brown and green, the brown of bodies and water and earth, the green of palm trees and lawns, of the racecourse and Eden Gardens cricket ground, and the swarming maidan that contained both. Between now and then a thick glass pane muffles the misery. At the time it cracked and the splinters were embedded around my lungs.

I had a childhood in India and a brief period of adolescence there. What I left behind I came to understand less and less, but all the more to need. The childhood is real though scarcely remembered, as if memory itself was blindfolded. All the sounds of those years, jackals and pi-dogs howling into the dawn, the whistle of long-distance trains and shunt of engines at Howrah, the sirens of Hooghly steamers and tinkle of rickshaw bells, were melancholy, intimations of departures I had no part in. Through those boarding-school years what was most loved and familiar was oceans away, though it was the brown hands that I craved, and not the alternately distant and crowding affection of parents.

PAUL SCOTT

(1920-78)

Paul Scott first went out to India in his early twenties, during the turmoil of World War II, and, while immediately attracted by the landscape and people, he found himself alienated by the ignorance and racism of the British ruling class in India. He returned to India in 1964, after a successful career as a literary agent in London. His experiences on this trip—which included dinner parties with Anglicized Indians as well a paranoia-infected week at a village in southern India—gave him the inspiration for *The Jewel in the Crown* (1966). The book, so obviously superior to the novels, also with Indian themes, that Scott had previously written, was the first of the four novels that described the last days of the British Empire in India and came to be known as The Raj Quartet. In 1977, Scott published *Staying On*, a novel about British expatriates in independent India. Scott's reputation has grown since his premature death in 1978. A brilliant television adaptation of The Raj Quartet in 1984 introduced many new readers to the subtleties of Scott's vision of India: how he transmuted a seemingly commonplace affection for India into active sympathy and acute historical insight, and himself grew from a mediocre novelist into possibly the greatest fictional chronicler and analyst of the British Raj. In the following excerpt from *The Jewel in the Crown* he looks back at that great Anglo-Indian institution, the club, whose graveled driveways and high-ceilinged rooms are still found in the hundreds of towns the British created across India, along with its turbaned waiters and complex rituals of snobbery.

from THE JEWEL IN THE CROWN

The Mayapore district of the province is still administered in five sub-divisions as it was in the days of the British. It covers an area of 2,346 square miles. In 1942 the population was one and a quarter million. It stands now, in 1964, at one and a half million, 160,000 of whom live in the town of Mayapore and some 20,000 in the suburb of Banyaganj where the airport is. From the airport there is a daily Viscount service to Calcutta and a twice weekly Fokker Friendship service to Agra for the Delhi connection. The area in the vicinity of the airport has become the center of a light industrial factory development. Between Banyaganj and Mayapore there are to be found the modern labor-saving, whitewashed, concrete homes of the new British colony, and then, closer to town still, the old British-Indian Electrical factory, newly extended but still controlled by British capital. From the British-Indian Electrical the traveler who knew Mayapore in the old days and came in by air would find himself on more familiar ground as he passed, in succession, the red-brick Mayapore Technical College which was founded and endowed by Sir Nello Chatterjee, and the cream-stucco Government Higher School. Just beyond the school the railway comes in on the left with the bend of the river and from here the road—the Grand Trunk Road—leads directly into the old cantonment and civil lines.

Going from the cantonment bazaar which is still the fashionable shopping center of Mayapore, along the Mahatma Gandhi road, once styled Victoria road, the traveler will pass the main police barracks on his left and then, on his right, the Court house and the adjacent cluster of buildings, well shaded by trees, that comprised, still comprise, the headquarters of the district administration. Close by, but only to be glimpsed through the gateway in a high stucco wall, similarly shaded, is the bungalow once known as the chummery where three or four of Mr. White's unmarried sub-divisional officers—usually Indians of the uncovenanted provincial civil service—used to live when not on tour in their own allotted areas of the district. Beyond the chummery, on both sides of the road, there are other bungalows whose style and look of spaciousness mark them also as relics of the British days, the biggest being that in which Mr. Poulson, assistant commissioner and joint magistrate, lived with Mrs. Poulson. Almost opposite the Poulsons' old place is the bungalow of the District Superintendent of Police. A quarter of a mile farther on, the Mahatma Gandhi road meets the southeastern angle of the large square open space known as the *maidan*, whose velvety short-cropped grass is green during and after the rains but brown at this season. If you continue in a northerly direction, along Hospital road, you come eventually to the Mayapore General Hospital and the Greenlawns nursing home. If you turn left, that is to say west, and travel along Club road you arrive eventually at the Gymkhana. Both the club and hospital buildings can be seen distantly from the T-junction of the old Victoria, Hospital and Club roads. And it is along Club road, facing the *maidan* that the bungalow of the Deputy Commissioner is still to be found, in walled, arboreal seclusion.

At half-past six in the evening the sun has set behind and starkly silhouetted the trees that shelter the club buildings on the western side of the *maidan*. The sky above the *maidan*, colorless during the day, as if the heat had burnt out its pigment, now undergoes a remarkable transformation. The blue is revealed at last but in tones already invaded by the yellowing refraction of the sun so that it is awash with an astonishing, luminous green that darkens to violet in the east where night has already fallen and reddens in the west where it is yet to come. There are some scattered trees on the edge of the *maidan*, the homes of the wheeling sore-throated crows which Lady Chatterjee says were once referred to by an American woman as "those durn birds." Certainly, in India, they are ubiquitous. Driving slowly down Club road with Lady Chatterjee, in a grey Ambassador that belongs to a lawyer called Srinivasan whom one has not met but is about to, one might indulge in the fancy of a projection from the provable now to the hallowed then, between which the one sure animated connection is provided by the crows, the familiar spirits of dead white sahibs and living black inheritors alike. At this hour the *maidan* is well populated by an Indian middle class that enjoys the comparative cool of the evening. There are even women and young girls. They stroll or squat and talk, and children play games. But the overall impression is of the whiteness of men's clothes and caps and of boys' shirts, a whiteness which, like the brown of the grass, has been touched by the evening light to a pink as subtle as that of that extraordinary bird, the flamingo. There is a hush, a sense emanating from those taking the air of their—well, yes, a sense of their what? Of their self-consciousness at having overstepped some ancient, invisible mark? Or is this a sense conveyed only to an Englishman, as a result of his residual awareness of a racial privilege now officially extinct, so that, borne clubwards at the invitation of a Brahmin

lawyer, on a Saturday evening, driven by a Muslim chauffeur in
the company of a Rajput lady, through the quickly fading light
that holds lovely old Mayapore suspended between the day and
the dark, bereft of responsibility and therefore of any sense of
dignity other than that which he may be able to muster in himself, as himself, he may feel himself similarly suspended, caught
up by his own people's history and the thrust of a current that
simply would not wait for them wholly to comprehend its force,
and he may then sentimentally recall, in passing, that the *maidan*
was once sacrosanct to the Civil and Military, and respond, fleetingly, to the tug of a vague generalized regret that the *maidan* no
longer looks as it did once, when at this time of day it was empty
of all but a few late riders cantering homeward.

Not that the *maidan* did not find itself in those days—on certain occasions—even more densely populated than it is this
evening. The British held their annual gymkhana here, and their
Flower Show, and it was the scene of displays such as that put
on by the military complete with band in aid of War Week,
which Daphne Manners attended with other girls from the Mayapore General Hospital and several young officers from the military lines, which, like St. Mary's Church, are to be seen on the
far side of the *maidan*. The flower show is still held, Lady Chatterjee says; indeed until five years ago she exhibited in it herself; but the roses that used to be grown by Englishwomen
who felt far from home and had infrequent hopes of European
leave are no longer what they were and most of the space in the
marquees is taken up with flowering shrubs and giant vegetables.
The gymkhana, too, is still an annual event because Mayapore is
still a military station, one—that is to say—with a certain formal
respect for tradition. Cricket week draws the biggest crowds,

bigger even than in the old days, but then any event on the *maidan* now is bound to be more crowded, because although the British gymkhanas, flower shows and cricket weeks were also attended by Indians, that attendance was regulated by invitation or by the cost of the ticket, and the *maidan* was then enclosed by an outer picket of stakes and rope and an inner picket of poles and hessian (except in the case of the cricket when the hessian had to be dispensed with in the practical as well as aesthetic interest of the game)—pickets which effectively conveyed to the casual passerby the fact that something private was going on. Nowadays there are no pickets other than those—as at the gymkhana, for instance—whose purpose is to separate the spectators from the participants, and there are influential Indians in Mayapore, the heirs to civic pride, who feel that it is a mistake to leave the *maidan* thus open to invasion by any Tom, Dick and Harry. Last year's gymkhana [Lady Chatterjee explains] was ruined by the people who wandered about on those parts of the *maidan* where the gymkhana was not being held but got mixed up with the people who had paid for seats and even invaded the refreshment tents in the belief that they were open to all. So great was the confusion that the club secretary, a Mr. Mitra, offered to resign, but was dissuaded from such a drastic course of action when his committee voted by a narrow margin to reinstate the old system of double enclosure in the future. As for the cricket, well, on two occasions in the past five years, the players walked off in protest at the rowdyism going on among the free-for-all spectators, and the last time this happened the spectators invaded the field in retaliation to protest against the players' high-handedness. There followed a pitched battle which the police had to break up with *lathi* charges just as they had in the days when the battle going on was of a more serious nature.

From problems such as these the British living in Mayapore today naturally remain aloof—so far as one can gather from Lady Chatterjee (who, when questioned on such delicate matters, has a habit of sitting still and upright, answering briefly and then changing the subject). It is rare (or so one deduces from her reluctance to swear that it is not) to see any member of the English colony at a public event on the *maidan*. They do not exhibit at the flower show. They do not compete at the gymkhana. They do not play cricket there. There would seem to be an unwritten law among them that the *maidan* is no longer any concern of theirs, no longer even to be spoken of except as a short cut to describing something mutually recognizable as alien. Indeed, you might ask one of them (for instance the Englishwoman who sits with another in the lounge-bar of the Gymkhana club, turning over the pages of a none-too-recent issue of the *Sunday Times* Magazine—today's fashionable equivalent of *The Tatler* or *The Onlooker*) whether she went to the flower show last month and be met with a look of total incomprehension, have the question patted back like a grubby little ball that has lost its bounce, be asked, in return, as if one had spoken in a foreign language she has been trained in but shown and felt no special aptitude or liking for: "Flower show?" and to explain, to say then, "Why yes—the flower show on the *maidan*," will call nothing forth other than an upward twitch of the eyebrows and a downward twitch of the mouth, which, after all, is voluble enough as an indication that one has suggested something ridiculous.

Apart from this Englishwoman and her companion there are several other English people in the lounge. But Lady Chatterjee is the only Indian and she has only sat where she is sitting (bringing her guest with her) because the first person met, as the club was entered and found not yet to house Mr. Srinivasan, was an Englishman called Terry who had been playing tennis and greeted her gaily, with a reproach that she came to the club too seldom and must have a drink while she waited for her official host and so had led her and her houseguest to the table where the two English ladies already sat and then gone off to shower and change, leaving Lady Chatterjee wrapped in her sari, the stranger in his ignorance, and the table in awkward silence punctuated only by Lady Chatterjee's attempts at explanations to the guest of his surroundings and his attempts to engage Terry's waiting ladies in a small talk that grows large and pregnant with *lacunae*, for want of simple politeness.

A question arises in one's mind about the extent to which the club has changed since Daphne Manners's day. The servants still wear white turbans beribboned to match the wide sashes that nip in the waists of their knee-length white coats. White trousers flap baggily above their bare brown feet, and stir old memories of padding docile service. Perhaps in the decor of this particular lounge-bar, change of an ephemeral nature may be seen: the formica-topped counter instead of the old wood that needed polishing, glazed chintz curtains decorated with spiral abstractions instead of cabbage roses, and chairs whose severe Scandinavian welcome brings the old cushioned-wicker comfort gratefully back to the mind.

But it would be foolish to suppose that such contemporaneity is a manifestation of anything especially significant, or to jump to the conclusion that the obvious preference shown for this room by the handful of English members present proves, in itself, their subconscious determination to identify themselves only with what is progressive and therefore superior. This lounge-bar, giving on to a verandah from which the tennis can be watched, was always the favorite of the Mayapore ladies, and for the moment at any rate the only ladies in the club, apart from Lady Chatterjee, are English. If Indian ladies on the whole are still happier at home, who but they are to blame for the look the room has of being reserved for Europeans?

But then, why are there no Indian men in the room either? And why are some of the Englishmen not sitting with their own women in the lounge-bar but standing in the other room where drinks are served, talking to Indian men? And why do they manage to convey (even at a distance, in the glimpse you have of them between square pillars across the passage and through wide open doors to the old smoking-room) a sense of almost old-maidish decorum, of physical fastidiousness unnatural to men when in the company of their own sex? Why, whenever one of them breaks away, crosses the passage and enters the lounge-bar to rejoin his lady, is there presently a rather too noisy laugh from him and a shrug and secret little smile from her? Why does he now exude the aggressive, conscious masculinity that seemed to be held in abeyance in the smoking-room?

The arrival in the lounge-bar of a grey-haired, pale-brown man of some sixty-odd years puts only a temporary stop to such private speculations. Mr. Srinivasan is of medium height, thin, punctilious in manner. His skin has a high polish. He is immaculately turned out. The lightweight suit, the collar and tie, point another interesting difference. The inheritors come properly dressed but the Englishmen expose thick bare necks and beefy arms. Mr. Srinivasan makes a formal old-fashioned apology for being late, for having failed to arrive first and greet his guests. He also makes a joke (once current among the English) about Mayapore time which it seems is still generally reckoned to be half-an-hour in arrear of Indian Standard. One gets up to shake his hand, and meets the mild but penetrating gaze that reveals a readiness to withstand the subtlest insult that an experience-sharpened sensibility is capable of detecting. Lady Chatterjee who addresses him as Vassi, says, "You know Terry Grigson's wife, of course?" and Srinivasan bows in the direction of the Englishwoman who, still protectively immersed in the shallow enchantment of the *Sunday Times* Magazine achieves a token emergence by a slight lift of the head (which would be a look at Mr. Srinivasan if the eyelids did not simultaneously lower) and by a movement of the lips (that might be "Good Evening" if they actually opened more than a gummy fraction). Her companion, also introduced, nods, and being younger and less inhibited perhaps by ancient distinctions looks as if she might be drawn into the general conversation, but Mrs. Grigson, with a perfect sense of timing, turns the *Sunday Times* Magazine toward her and points out some extraordinary detail of Coventry Cathedral so that they are then both lost in the illustrated complexities of modern Anglo-Saxon art; and the uncharitable thought occurs that, for the English, art has anyway always had its timely, occupational value.

And it could occur to you, too, that Mr. Srinivasan is not at ease in the lounge-bar, that if he had only managed to conduct his affairs in accordance with Indian Standard instead of Mayapore time he would have been waiting at the entrance when his second best car, the Ambassador, drove up and deposited its passengers, and would then have taken them into the old smoking-room, not had to leave them to the jovial Terry Grigson whose wife finds nothing to laugh about but with whom Mr. Srinivasan and his guests are momentarily stuck, for politeness' sake, at least until Terry comes back from the showers and changing room—

—as he does, beaming and raw-faced, in a creased bush shirt and floppy creased grey trousers, but not before Mr. Srinivasan with a thin, almost tubercular finger, has summoned a bearer and asked everybody what they are drinking and sent the bearer off to collect it, having been answered even by Mrs. Grigson, and by her companion who taking her cue from Mrs. Grigson also said, "Nothing for me, thank you." Terry comes back between the sending away of the bearer with the curtailed order and his return with a tray of three lonely gins and tonics, by which time Terry has also been asked by Mr. Srinivasan what he will drink, thanked him, and said, "I'll go a beer." When the gins and tonics arrive and Srinivasan says to the bearer, "And a beer for Mr. Grigson," Mrs. Grigson pushes her empty glass at Terry and says, "Order me another of these, Terry, will you?" which he does, with a brief, almost private gesture at the bearer. The other woman, lacking Mrs. Grigson's nerve for studied insult, would go drinkless did Terry not say, while Srinivasan talks to Lili Chatterjee, "What about you, Betty?" which enables her to shrug, grimace, and say, "Well, I suppose I might as well." Since no money passes and no bills are yet presented for signing, one wonders who in fact will pay for them, but trusts—because Grigson looks almost self-consciously trustworthy—that he will see to it afterwards that Mr. Srinivasan's bar account is not debited with a charge it seems his wife and her friend would rather die than have an Indian settle.

And now, perhaps abiding by yet another unwritten rule, perhaps having even received some secret, clan-gathering sign, a dumpy Englishwoman at an adjacent table leans across and asks Mrs. Grigson a question which causes Mrs. Grigson to incline her angular body by a degree or two and with this inclination fractionally shift the position of her chair, so that by a narrow but perceptible margin she succeeds in dissociating herself from those with whom she actually shares a table. It is difficult to hear what it is that so arouses her interest, because Lili Chatterjee, Mr. Srinivasan and (to his lone, team-captain's credit) Mr. Grigson are also talking with animation, and the stranger can only observe and make possibly erroneous deductions: possibly erroneous but not probably. There is nothing so inwardly clear as social rebuff—a rebuff which in this case is also directed at the stranger because he has arrived with one Indian as the guest of another.

And in the momentary hiatus of not knowing exactly what it is that anyone is talking about, one may observe Terry Grigson's off-handsome face and see that old familiar expression of strain, of deep-seated reservation that qualifies the smile and points up the diplomatic purpose; a purpose which, given a bit more time, may not prevail against the persistence of his sulky segregationist wife. And this, perhaps, is a pity, considering all the chat that goes on at home about the importance of trade and exports and of making a good impression abroad.

"Well no," Terry Grigson says, in answer to Mr. Srinivasan's for-form's-sake inquiry whether he and his wife will join the trio of Srinivasan, Lili Chatterjee and her houseguest for dinner at the club, "It's very kind of you, but we're going on to Roger's farewell and have to get back and change."

The Roger referred to is, one gathers, the retiring managing director of British-Indian Electrical. Almost every month one more member of this transient European population ups stakes, retires, returns to England or moves on to another station. For each farewell, however, there is a housewarming, or a party to mark the occasion of a wife's arrival to join her husband in the place where for the next year or two he will earn his living. Whatever that living actually is—with the British-Indian Electrical, with one of the other industrial developments, or teaching something abstruse at the Mayapore Technical College, it will be earned by someone considered superiorly equipped to manage, guide, execute or instruct. He will be a member of that new race of Sahibs. He will be, in whatsoever field, an Expert.

"There is actually a most interesting but undoubtedly apocryphal story about the status of English experts in India nowadays," Mr. Srinivasan says in his rather high-pitched but melodious lawyer's voice when the party in the lounge-bar has been broken up by the quick-downing by Terry Grigson of his beer and by the ladies of their gin-fizzes, and their departure to change into clothes that will be more suitable for the purpose of bidding Roger Godspeed. Upon that departure Mr. Srinivasan has led Lady Chatterjee and the stranger across the lounge, through the pillared passage and the open doors into the comfortable old smoking-room that has club chairs, potted palms, fly-blown hunting prints and—in spite of the spicy curry-smells wafted in from the adjacent dining-room by the action of the leisurely turning ceiling fans—an air somehow evocative of warmed-up gravy and cold mutton. In here, only one Englishman now remains. He glances at Mr. Srinivasan's party—but retains the pale mask of his anonymity, a mask that he seems to wear as a defense against the young, presumably inexpert Indians who form the group of which he is the restrained, withheld, interrogated, talked-at center. It is because one asks Mr. Srinivasan who this white man is, and because Mr. Srinivasan says he does not know but supposes he is a "visiting expert" that the interesting but perhaps apocryphal story is told.

"There was," Mr. Srinivasan says, "this Englishman who was due to go home. An ordinary tourist actually. He fell into conversation with a Hindu businessman who for months had been trying to get a loan from Government in order to expand his factory. A friend had told the businessman, 'But it is impossible for you to get a loan from Government because you are not employing any English technical adviser.' So the businessman asked himself: 'Where can I get such an adviser and how much will it cost me seeing that he would expect two or three years' guarantee contract at minimum?' Then he met this English tourist who had no rupees left. And the Hindu gentleman said, 'Sir, I think you are interested in earning rupees five thousand?' The English tourist agreed straight away. 'Then all you will do, sir,' the Hindu gentleman said, 'is to postpone departure for two weeks while I write to certain people in New Delhi.' Then he telegraphed Government saying, 'What about a loan? Here already I am at the expense of employing technical expert from England and there is no answer coming from you.' To which at once he received a telegraph reply to the effect that his factory would be inspected by representatives of Government on such and such a day. So he went back to the English tourist and gave him five thousand rupees and said, 'Please be at my factory on Monday, are you by any chance knowing anything about radio components?' To which the English tourist replied, 'No, unfortunately, only I am knowing about ancient monuments.' 'No matter,' the Hindu gentleman said, 'on Monday whenever I jog your elbow simply be saying—"This is how it is done in Birmingham."' So on Monday there was this most impressive meeting in the executive suite of the factory between the Hindu businessman who knew all about radio component manufacture, the English tourist who knew nothing and the representatives of Government who also knew nothing. Before lunch they went round the premises and sometimes one of the officials of Government asked the Englishman, 'What is happening here?' and the Hindu gentleman jogged the Englishman's elbow, and the Englishman who was a man of honor, a man to be depended upon to keep his word said, 'This is how we do it in Birmingham.' And after a convivial lunch the Government representatives flew back to Delhi and the English tourist booked his flight home first class by BOAC and within a week the Hindu businessman was in receipt of a substantial Government loan with a message of goodwill from Prime Minister Nehru himself."

And one notes, marginally, that the new wave of satire has also broken on the Indian shore and sent minor flood-streams into the interior, as far as Mayapore.

PAUL THEROUX

(1941–)

Paul Theroux was born in Medford, Massachusetts. He joined the Peace Corps in Africa where he wrote his first novel *Girls at Play* (1969). He later moved to Singapore before making his home in London in 1971. He now lives in Hawaii, as prolific as ever. It has been his mixed fate to be better known as a travel writer despite having published such distinguished novels as *Saint Jack* (1973) and *My Secret History* (1989). This reputation began with *The Great Railway Bazaar* (1975), which described Theroux's four-month journey on rail through Asia. In this entertaining book, Theroux almost single-handedly reinvented the modern genre of travel writing: a writing that veers between brisk description and crankish irreverence—"Afghanistan," goes one not atypical sentence, "is a nuisance"—and establishes the author's iconoclasm in the reader's mind more securely than the passing scenery. In this excerpt he watches gypsies from a slow empty train, interrogates an American Buddhist monk, and judges the "sacredness of water" in a temple pond by "its degree of stagnation."

from THE GREAT RAILWAY BAZAAR

THE LOCAL TO RAMESWARAM

I had two ambitions in India: one was to find a train to Ceylon, the other was to have a sleeping car to myself. At Egmore Station in Madras both ambitions were fulfilled. My little cardboard

ticket read *Madras—Colombo Fort*, and when the train pulled out
the conductor told me I would be the only passenger in the car
for the twenty-two-hour journey to Rameswaram. If I wished,
he said, I could move to the second compartment—the fans
worked there. It was a local train, and, since no one was going
very far, everyone chose third class. Very few people went to
Rameswaram, he said, and these days nobody wanted to go to
Ceylon: it was a troublesome country, there was no food in the
markets, and the prime minister, Mrs. Bandaranaike, didn't like
Indians. He wondered why I was going there.

"For the ride," I said.

"It is the slowest train." He showed me the timetable. I borrowed it and took it into my compartment to study. I had been
on slow trains before, but this was perverse. It seemed to stop
every five or ten minutes. I held the timetable to the window to
verify it in the light.

Madras Egmore	11.00
Mambalam	11.11
Tambaran	11.33
Perungalattur Halt	11.41
Vandalur	11.47
Guduvanchari	11.57
Kattargulattur	12.06
Singaperumalkoil	12.15
Chingleput	12.35

And so forth. I counted. It stopped ninety-four times in all. I
had got my wish, but I wondered whether it was worth the
penalties.

The train gathered speed; the brakes squeaked; it lurched and stopped. It started again, and no sooner had it begun to roll easily than the brakes gave this metal wail. I dozed in my compartment, and each time the train stopped I heard laughter and the stamping of feet past my door, a muted galloping up and down the passage, doors banging and the ring of metal on metal. The voices ceased when the train was underway and did not start again until the next station, a commotion at the doors, shrieks, and clangs. I looked out the window and saw the strangest sight—children, girls and boys of anywhere from seven to twelve, the younger ones naked, the older ones wearing loincloths, were leaping off the train carrying cans of water. They were wild children, with long lank hair faded brown by the sun, with black shoulders and dusty faces and snub noses—like Australian aborigines—and at every station that morning they dashed into the sleeping car and got water from the sink in the toilet compartment. They raced with their cans to camps by the side of the track where thin older people waited, aged men with yellowing curly hair, women kneeling over cooking pots in front of crude lean-tos. They weren't Tamils. I assumed they were aborigines, like the Gonds. They had few belongings and they lived in this dry zone the monsoon had not yet reached. All morning they raided the sleeping car for water, skipping in and out, shouting and laughing, making their scavenging into a noisy game. I locked the inner door, preventing them from dancing down the corridor, but allowing them access to the water.

I had made no arrangements to eat and had no food with me. In the early afternoon I walked the length of the train but could not find a dining car. I was having a snooze at about two o'clock when there was a rap at the window. It was the conductor. Without a word he passed a tray of food through the bars. I ate Tamil-fashion, squelching the rice into a ball with my right hand, mopping the ball into the soupy vegetables, and stuffing the whole business into my mouth. At the next station the conductor reappeared. He took the empty tray and gave me a drowsy salute.

We were traveling parallel to the coast, a few miles inland, and the fans in the compartment gave very little relief from the pressure of humidity. The sky was overcast with clouds that seemed to add weight to the suffocating heat, and the train was going so slowly there was no breeze at the windows. To shake off my feeling of sluggishness, I borrowed a broom and some rags from the conductor; I swept out my compartment and washed all the windows and woodwork. Then I did my laundry and hung it on hooks in the corridor. I plugged the sink and sluiced myself with water, then shaved and put on my slippers and pyjamas. It was my own sleeping car, after all. At Villupuram the electric engine was replaced by a steam locomotive, and at that same station I bought three large bottles of warm beer. I plumped the pillows in my compartment and, while my laundry dried, drank beer and watched the state of Tamil Nadu grow simpler: each station was smaller than the last and the people grew increasingly naked—after Chingleput there were no shirts, undershirts disappeared at Villupuram, and further on *lungis* were scarce and people were running around in drooping loincloths. The land was flat, featureless except for an occasional storklike Tamil poised in a distant paddy field. The huts were as poorly made as those temporary ones thrown up in the African interior, where it is considered unlucky to live in the same hut two years in a row. They were of mud and had palm-leaf roofs;

the mud had cracked in the heat and the first of the monsoon would sweep those roofs away. In contrast to this haphazard building, the rice fields were cleverly irrigated by complex pumping systems and long canals.

The greatest annoyance that afternoon was the smoke from the steam engine. It poured through the windows, coating every surface with a fine film of soot, and the smell of burned coal—which is the smell of every Indian railway station—lingered in the compartment. It took much longer for the engine to build up speed, and the trip-hammer sound and the rhythmic puffing was transmitted through the carriages. But there was a gentleness in this power, and the sounds of the thrusting wheels gave a motion to the train that was not only different from the amplified lawnmower of the electric engine, but made the steam engine seem animal in the muscular way it moved and stopped.

After dark the compartment lights went out and the fan died. I went to bed; an hour later—it was 9.30—they came on again. I found my place in the book I was reading, but before I finished a paragraph the lights failed a second time. I cursed, switched everything off, smeared myself with insect repellent (the mosquitoes were ferocious, nimble with their budget of malaria), and slept with the sheets over my head, waking only at Trichinopoly (Tiruchirappalli) to buy a box of cigars.

The next morning I was visited by a Buddhist monk. His head was shaved, he wore saffron robes, and he was barefoot. He was the very picture of piety, the mendicant monk with his sweaty head, going third class on the branch line to Nirvana. He was, of course, so right for the part that I guessed immediately he was an American, and it turned out he was from Baltimore.

He was on his way to Kandy in Central Ceylon. He didn't like my questions.

"What do your folks think about you becoming a Buddhist?"

"I am looking for water," he said obstinately.

"Are you in a monastery or what?"

"Look, if there's no water here, just tell me and I'll go away."

"I've got some good friends in Baltimore," I said. "Ever get back there?"

"You're bothering me," said the monk.

"Is that any way for a monk to talk?"

He was really angry then. He said, "I get asked these questions a hundred times a day!"

"I'm just curious."

"There are no answers," he said, with mystifying glibness. "I'm looking for water."

"Keep looking."

"I'm dirty! I haven't slept all night; I want to wash!"

"I'll show you where the water is if you answer one more question," I said.

"You're a nosy bastard, just like the rest of them," said the Buddhist monk.

"Second door on your right," I said. "Don't drown."

I think the next ten miles were the most exciting I have ever traveled in a train. We were on the coast, moving fast along a spit of land, and on either side of the train—its whistle screaming, its chimney full of smoke—white sand had drifted into magnificent dunes; beyond these dunes were slices of green sea. Sand whipped up by the engine pattered against the carriages behind, and spray from the breakers, whose regular wash dramatized the chugging of the locomotive, was flung up to speckle the windows with crystal bubbles. It was all light and water and sand, flying about the train speeding toward the Rameswaram causeway in a high wind. The palms under the scudding clouds bowed and flashed like fans made of feathers, and here and there, up to their stupas in sand, were temples flying red flags on their crooked masts. The sand covered the track in places; it had drifted into temple doorways and wrecked the frail palm-frond huts. The wind was terrific, beating on the windows, carrying sand and spray and the whistle's *hooeeee*, and nearly toppling the dhows in full sail at the hump of the spangled horizon where Ceylon lay.

"Few minutes more," said the conductor. "I think you are sorry you took this train."

"No," I said. "But I was under the impression it went to Dhanushkodi—that's what my map says."

"Indo-Ceylon Express formerly went to Dhanushkodi."

"Why doesn't it go there now?"

"No Indo-Ceylon Express," he said. "And Dhanushkodi blew away."

He explained that in 1965 a cyclone—the area is plagued with them—derailed a train, drowning forty passengers and covering Dhanushkodi with sand. He showed me what remained, sand dunes at the tip of the peninsula and the fragments of black roofs. The town had disappeared so thoroughly that not even fishermen lived there any more.

"Rameswaram is more interesting," said the conductor. "Nice temple, holy places, and tombs of Cain and Abel."

I thought I had misheard him. I asked him to repeat the names. I had not misheard.

The story is that when Adam and Eve were driven from the Garden of Eden they went to Ceylon (Dhanushkodi is the beginning of the seven islands across the Palk Strait known as "Adam's Bridge"). Christ went there; so did Buddha and Rama, and so, probably, did Father Divine, Joseph Smith, and Mary Baker Eddy. Cain and Abel ended up in Rameswaram, which might be the true Land of Nod, east of Eden. Their tombs are not signposted. They are in the care of the local Muslims, and in this town of Hindus, the majority of whom are high-caste Brahmins, I had some difficulty locating a Muslim. The driver of the horse-drawn cab (there are no cars in Rameswaram) thought there might be a Muslim at the ferry landing. I said that was too far to go: the tombs were somewhere near the railway station. The driver said the Hindu temple was the holiest in India. I said I wanted to see the tombs of Cain and Abel. We found a ruminant Muslim in a dusty shop on a side street. He said he would show me the tombs if I promised not to defile them with my camera. I promised.

The tombs were identical: parallel blocks of crumbling stone on which lizards darted and the green twine of tropical weeds had knotted. I tried to appear reverential, but could not suppress my disappointment at seeing what looked like the incomplete foundations of some folly concocted by a treasonous clerk in the Public Works Department of the local mosque. And the tombs were indistinguishable.

"Cain?" I said, pointing to the right one. I pointed to the left. "Abel?"

The Muslim didn't know.

The Hindu temple, founded by Rama (on his way to Lanka, Ceylon, to rescue Sita), was an impressive labyrinth, nearly a mile of subterranean corridors, garishly lit and painted. The traveler J. J. Aubertin, who visited the Rameswaram temple (but not the tombs of Cain and Abel: maybe they weren't there in 1890?) mentions the "blasphemous" and "ugly" dances of the *nautch* girls in his book, *Wanderings and Wonderings* (1892). I looked. I saw no *nautch* girls. Five aged women were gravely laundering their shrouds in the sacred pool at the center of the temple. In India, I had decided, one could determine the sacredness of water by its degree of stagnation. The holiest was bright green, like this.

It was a three-hour trip across the Palk Strait on the old Scottish steamer, the T.S.S. *Ramanujam* (formerly the *Irwin*), from Rameswaram to Talaimannar at the top of Ceylon. Like everyone else I had met in India, the ship's second mate told me I was a fool to go to Ceylon. But his reason was better than others I'd heard: there was a cholera epidemic in Jaffna and it appeared to be spreading to Colombo. "It's your funeral," he said cheerfully. He held the Ceylonese in complete contempt, nor was he very happy with Indians. I pointed out that this must have been rather inconvenient for him since he was an Indian himself.

"Yes, but I'm a Catholic," he said. He was from Mangalore on the Malabar Coast and his name was Llewellyn. We smoked my Trichinopoly cigars on the deck, until Talaimannar appeared, a row of lights dimmed to faint sequins by what Llewellyn said was the first rain of the monsoon.

MARK TWAIN

(1835–1910)

Mark Twain, the pseudonym of Samuel Langhorne Clemens, was born in Missouri. His childhood on the banks of the Mississippi was made famous by such groundbreaking works of American literature as *The Adventures of Tom Sawyer* (1876) and *The Adventures of Huckleberry Finn* (1884). One of his first serious commissions as a journalist was to write comic travel letters, and his first bestselling book was *Innocents Abroad* (1869), which consisted of letters Twain wrote from Europe for the readers of the *New York Tribune*. He subsequently described his stagecoach journey across America in *Roughing It* (1872). For someone who now seems such a quintessentially American writer, Twain spent seventeen years of life abroad, traveling and lecturing. And for someone so commonly associated with humor, he had a dark vision of the contemporary world. He denounced American efforts to acquire the Philippines in 1898; he was one of the earliest critics of Belgian imperialism in the Congo. In 1895, financial difficulties forced Twain into accepting a commission for round-the-world travel. India bewildered Twain; it was like no other place he had ever seen. He made his usual jokes: He once learned, he said, all the 108 names of the Hindu god Vishnu by heart; sadly, he had forgotten all of them except John W. However, as the excerpt from *Following the Equator* (1897) shows, he was also curious about how the servants coped and was thrilled to be able to discuss Huck Finn with a Muslim prince.

from FOLLOWING THE EQUATOR

CHAPTER III

By trying we can easily learn to endure adversity.
Another man's, I mean.
—*Pudd'nhead Wilson's New Calendar.*

You soon find your long-ago dreams of India rising in a sort of
vague and luscious moonlight above the horizon rim of your
opaque consciousness, and softly lighting up a thousand forgotten details which were parts of a vision that had once been vivid
to you when you were a boy, and steeped your spirit in tales
of the East. The barbaric gorgeousness, for instance; and the
princely titles, the sumptuous titles, the sounding titles—how
good they taste in the mouth! The Nizam of Hyderabad; the
Maharajah of Travancore; the Nabob of Jubbulpore; the Begum
of Bhopal; the Nawab of Mysore; the Ranee of Gulnare; the
Ahkoond of Swat; the Rao of Rohilkund; the Gaikwar of Baroda. Indeed, it is a country that runs richly to name. The great
god Vishnu has 108—108 special ones—108 peculiarly holy
ones—names just for Sunday use only. I learned the whole of
Vishnu's 108 by heart once, but they wouldn't stay; I don't remember any of them now but John W.

And the romances connected with those princely native
houses—to this day they are always turning up, just as in the old,
old times. They were sweating out a romance in an English court
in Bombay a while before we were there. In this case a native
prince, sixteen and a half years old, who had been enjoying his
titles and dignities and estates unmolested for fourteen years, is

suddenly hauled into court on the charge that he is rightfully no prince at all, but a pauper peasant; that the real prince died when two and one-half years old; that the death was concealed, and a peasant child smuggled into the royal cradle, and that this present incumbent was that smuggled substitute. This is the very material that so many oriental tales have been made of.

The case of that great prince, the Gaikwar of Baroda, is a reversal of the theme. When that throne fell vacant, no heir could be found for some time, but at last one was found in the person of a peasant child who was making mud pies in a village street, and having an innocent good time. But his pedigree was straight; he was the true prince, and he has reigned ever since, with none to dispute his right.

Lately there was another hunt for an heir to another princely house, and one was found who was circumstanced about as the Gaikwar had been. His fathers were traced back, in humble life, along a branch of the ancestral tree to the point where it joined the stem fourteen generations ago, and his heirship was thereby squarely established. The tracing was done by means of the records of one of the great Hindu shrines, where princes on pilgrimage record their names and the date of their visit. This is to keep the prince's religious account straight, and his spiritual person safe; but the record has the added value of keeping the pedigree authentic, too.

When I think of Bombay now, at this distance of time, I seem to have a kaleidoscope at my eye; and I hear the clash of the glass bits as the splendid figures change, and fall apart, and flash into new forms, figure after figure, and with the birth of each new form I feel my skin crinkle and my nerve-web tingle with a new thrill of wonder and delight. These remembered pictures float past me in a sequence of contrasts; following the same order always, and always whirling by and disappearing with the swiftness of a dream, leaving me with the sense that the actuality was the experience of an hour, at most, whereas it really covered days, I think.

The series begins with the hiring of a "bearer"—native manservant—a person who should be selected with some care, because as long as he is in your employ he will be about as near to you as your clothes.

In India your day may be said to begin with the "bearer's" knock on the bedroom door, accompanied by a formula of words—a formula which is intended to mean that the bath is ready. It doesn't really seem to mean anything at all. But that is because you are not used to "bearer" English. You will presently understand.

Where he gets his English is his own secret. There is nothing like it elsewhere in the earth; or even in paradise, perhaps, but the other place is probably full of it. You hire him as soon as you touch Indian soil; for no matter what your sex is, you cannot do without him. He is messenger, valet, chambermaid, table-waiter, lady's maid, courier—he is everything. He carries a coarse linen clothes-bag and a quilt; he sleeps on the stone floor outside your chamber door, and gets his meals you do not know where nor when; you only know that he is not fed on the premises, either when you are in a hotel or when you are a guest in a private house. His wages are large—from an Indian point of view—and he feeds and clothes himself out of them. We had three of him in two and a half months. The first one's rate was thirty rupees a month—that is to say, twenty-seven cents a day; the rate of the others, Rs. 40 (40 rupees) a month. A princely sum; for the native switchman on a railway and the native servant in a private family get only Rs. 7 per month, and the farmhand only four. The two former feed and clothe themselves and their families on their $1.90 per month; but I cannot believe that the farmhand has to feed himself on his $1.08. I think the farm probably feeds him, and that the whole of his wages, except a trifle for the priest, goes to the support of his family. That is, to the feeding of his family; for they live in a mud hut, handmade, and, doubtless, rent-free, and they wear no clothes; at least, nothing more than a rag. And not much of a rag at that, in the case of the males. However, these are handsome times for the farmhand; he was not always the child of luxury that he is now. The Chief Commissioner of the Central Provinces, in a recent official utterance wherein he was rebuking a native deputation for complaining of hard times, reminded them that they could easily remember when a farmhand's wages were only half a rupee (former value) a month— that is to say, less than a cent a day; nearly $2.90 a year. If such a wage-earner had a good deal of family—and they all have that, for God is very good to these poor natives in some ways—he would save a profit of fifteen cents, clean and clear, out of his year's toil; I mean a frugal, thrifty person would, not one given to display and ostentation. And if he owed $13.50 and took good care of his health, he could pay it off in ninety years. Then he could hold up his head and look his creditors in the face again.

Think of these facts and what they mean. India does not consist of cities. There are no cities in India—to speak of. Its stupendous population consists of farm laborers. India is one vast farm—one almost interminable stretch of fields with mud fences between. Think of the above facts; and consider what an incredible aggregate of poverty they place before you.

The first Bearer that applied waited below and sent up his recommendations. That was the first morning in Bombay. We read them over; carefully, cautiously, thoughtfully. There was not a fault to find with them—except one; they were all from Americans. Is that a slur? If it is, it is a deserved one. In my experience, an American's recommendation of a servant is not usually valuable. We are too good-natured a race; we hate to say the unpleasant thing; we shrink from speaking the unkind truth about a poor fellow whose bread depends upon our verdict; so we speak of his good points only, thus not scrupling to tell a lie—a *silent* lie—for in not mentioning his bad ones we as good as say he hasn't any. The only difference that I know of between a silent lie and a spoken one is, that the silent lie is a less respectable one than the other. And it can deceive, whereas the other can't—as a rule. We not only tell the silent lie as to a servant's faults, but we sin in another way: we overprice his merits; for when it comes to writing recommendations of servants we are a nation of gushers. And we have not the Frenchman's excuse. In France you *must* give the departing servant a good recommendation; and you *must* conceal his faults; you have no choice. If you mention his faults for the protection of the next candidate for his services, he can sue you for damages; and the court will award them, too; and, moreover, the judge will give you a sharp dressing-down from the bench for trying to destroy a poor man's character and rob him of his bread. I do not state this on my own authority, I got it from a French physician of fame and repute—a man who was born in Paris, and had practiced there all his life. And he said that he spoke not merely from common knowledge, but from exasperating personal experience.

As I was saying, the Bearer's recommendations were all from American tourists; and St. Peter would have admitted him to the fields of the blessed on them—I mean if he is as unfamiliar with our people and our ways as I suppose he is. According to these recommendations, Manuel X was supreme in all the arts connected with his complex trade; and these manifold arts were mentioned—and praised—in detail. His English was spoken of in terms of warm admiration—admiration verging upon rapture. I took pleased note of that, and hoped that some of it might be true.

We had to have someone right away; so the family went downstairs and took him a week on trial; then sent him up to me and departed on their affairs. I was shut up in my quarters with a bronchial cough, and glad to have something fresh to look at, something new to play with. Manuel filled the bill; Manuel was very welcome. He was toward fifty years old, tall, slender, with a slight stoop—an artificial stoop, a deferential stoop, a stoop rigidified by long habit—with face of European mold; short hair, intensely black; gentle black eyes, timid black eyes, indeed; complexion very dark, nearly black in fact; face smooth-shaven. He was bareheaded and barefooted, and was never otherwise while his week with us lasted; his clothing was European, cheap, flimsy, and showed much wear.

He stood before me and inclined his head (and body) in the pathetic Indian way, touching his forehead with the finger-ends of his right hand, in salute. I said:

"Manuel, you are evidently Indian, but you seem to have a Spanish name when you put it all together. How is that?"

A perplexed look gathered in his face; it was plain that he had not understood—but he didn't let on. He spoke back placidly:

"Name, Manuel. Yes, master."

"I know; but how did you *get* the name?"

"Oh, yes, I suppose. Think happen so. Father same name, not mother."

I saw that I must simplify my language and spread my words apart, if I would be understood by this English scholar.

"Well—then—how—did—your—father—get—*his*—name?"

"Oh, he"—brightening a little—"he Christian—Portygee; live in Goa; I born Goa; mother not Portygee, mother native— high-caste Brahman—Coolin Brahman; highest caste; no other so high caste. I high-caste Brahman, too. Christian, too, same like father; high-caste Christian Brahman, master—Salvation Army."

All this haltingly, and with difficulty. Then he had an inspiration, and began to pour out a flood of words that I could make nothing of; so I said:

"There—don't do that. I can't understand Hindustani."

"Not Hindustani, master—English. Always I speaking English sometimes when I talking everyday all the time at you."

"Very well, stick to that; that is intelligible. It is not up to my hopes, it is not up to the promise of the recommendations, still it is English, and I understand it. Don't elaborate it; I don't like elaborations when they are crippled by uncertainty of touch."

"Master?"

"Oh, never mind; it was only a random thought; I didn't expect you to understand it. How did you get your English; is it an acquirement, or just a gift of God?"

After some hesitation—piously:

"Yes, he very good. Christian god very good; Hindu god very good, too. Two million Hindu god, one Christian god—make two million and one. All mine; two million and one god. I got a plenty. Sometime I pray all time at those, keep it up, go all time every day; give something at shrine, all good for me, make me better man; good for me, good for my family, dam good."

Then he had another inspiration, and went rambling off into fervent confusions and incoherencies, and I had to stop him again. I thought we had talked enough, so I told him to go to the bathroom and clean it up and remove the slops—this to get rid of him. He went away, seeming to understand, and got out some of my clothes and began to brush them. I repeated my desire several times, simplifying and resimplifying it, and at last he got the idea. Then he went away and put a coolie at the work, and explained that he would lose caste if he did it himself; it would be pollution, by the law of his caste, and it would cost him a deal of fuss and trouble to purify himself and accomplish his rehabilitation. He said that that kind of work was strictly forbidden to persons of caste, and as strictly restricted to the very bottom layer of Hindu society—the despised *Sudra* (the toiler, the laborer). He was right; and apparently the poor Sudra has been content with his strange lot, his insulting distinction, for ages and ages—clear back to the beginning of things, so to speak. Buckle says that his name—laborer—is a term of contempt; that it is ordained by the institutes of Menu (900 BC) that *if a Sudra sit on a level with his superior he shall be exiled or branded*[1] . . . ; if he speak contemptuously of his superior or insult him *he shall suffer death; if he listen to the reading of the sacred books he shall have burning oil poured in his ears; if he memorize passages from them*

---

[1]Without going into particulars, I will remark that, as a rule, they wear no clothing that would conceal the brand. —M.T.

he shall be killed; if he marry his daughter to a Brahman *the husband shall go to hell for defiling himself by contact with a woman so infinitely his inferior*; and that it is *forbidden to a Sudra to acquire wealth.* "The bulk of the population of India," says Buckle,[2] "is the Sudras—the *workers, the farmers, the creators of wealth.*"

Manuel was a failure, poor old fellow. His age was against him. He was desperately slow and phenomenally forgetful. When he went three blocks on an errand he would be gone two hours, and then forget what it was he went for. When he packed a trunk it took him forever, and the trunk's contents were an unimaginable chaos when he got done. He couldn't wait satisfactorily at table—a prime defect, for if you haven't your own servant in an Indian hotel you are likely to have a slow time of it and go away hungry. We couldn't understand his English; he couldn't understand ours; and when we found that he couldn't understand his own, it seemed time for us to part. I had to discharge him; there was no help for it. But I did it as kindly as I could, and as gently. We must part, said I, but I hoped we should meet again in a better world. It was not true, but it was only a little thing to say, and saved his feelings and cost me nothing.

But now that he was gone, and was off my mind and heart, my spirits began to rise at once, and I was soon feeling brisk and ready to go out and have adventures. Then his newly hired successor flitted in, touched his forehead, and began to fly around here, there, and everywhere, on his velvet feet, and in five minutes he had everything in the room "shipshape and Bristol fashion," as the sailors say, and was standing at the salute, waiting for

[2]Population today, 300,000,000.

orders. Dear me, what a rustler he was after the slumbrous way of Manuel, poor old slug! All my heart, all my affection, all my admiration, went out spontaneously to this frisky little forked black thing, this compact and compressed incarnation of energy and force and promptness and celerity and confidence, this smart, smily, engaging, shiny-eyed little devil, feruled on his upper end by a gleaming fire-coal of a fez with a red-hot tassel dangling from it. I said, with deep satisfaction:

"You'll suit. What is your name?"

He reeled it mellowly off.

"Let me see if I can make a selection out of it—for business uses, I mean; we will keep the rest for Sundays. Give it to me in installments."

He did it. But there did not seem to be any short ones, except Mousa—which suggested mouse. It was out of character; it was too soft, too quiet, too conservative; it didn't fit his splendid style. I considered, and said:

"Mousa is short enough, but I don't quite like it. It seems colorless—inharmonious—inadequate; and I am sensitive to such things. How do you think Satan would do?"

"Yes, master. Satan do wair good."

It was his way of saying "very good."

There was a rap at the door. Satan covered the ground with a single skip; there was a word or two of Hindustani, then he disappeared. Three minutes later he was before me again, militarily erect, and waiting for me to speak first.

"What is it, Satan?"

"God want to see you."

"*Who?*"

"God. I show him up, master?"

"Why, this is so unusual, that—that—well, you see—indeed I am so unprepared—I don't quite know what I *do* mean. Dear me, can't you explain? Don't you see that this is a most ex—"

"Here his card, master."

Wasn't it curious—and amazing, and tremendous, and all that? Such a personage going around calling on such as I, and sending up his card, like a mortal—sending it up by Satan. It was a bewildering collision of the impossibles. But this was the land of the Arabian Nights, this was India! and what is it that cannot happen in India?

We had the interview. Satan was right—the Visitor was indeed a God in the conviction of his multitudinous followers, and was worshipped by them in sincerity and humble adoration. They are troubled by no doubts as to his divine origin and office. They believe in him, they pray to him, they make offerings to him, they beg of him remission of sins; to them his person, together with everything connected with it, is sacred; from his barber they buy the parings of his nails and set them in gold, and wear them as precious amulets.

I tried to seem tranquilly conversational and at rest, but I was not. Would you have been? I was in a suppressed frenzy of excitement and curiosity and glad wonder. I could not keep my eyes off him. I was looking upon a *god*, an actual god, a recognized and accepted god; and every detail of his person and his dress had a consuming interest for me. And the thought went floating through my head, "He is worshipped—think of it—he is not a recipient of the pale homage called compliment, where-with the highest human clay must make shift to be satisfied, but of an infinitely richer spiritual food: adoration, worship!—men and women lay their cares and their griefs and their broken hearts at his feet; and he gives them his peace, and they go away healed."

And just then the Awful Visitor said, in the simplest way:

"There is a feature of the philosophy of Huck Finn which"— and went luminously on with the construction of a compact and nicely discriminated literary verdict.

It *is* a land of surprises—India! I had had my ambitions—I had hoped, and almost expected, to be read by kings and presidents and emperors—but I had never looked so high as That. It would be false modesty to pretend that I was not inordinately pleased. I was. I was much more pleased than I should have been with a compliment from a man.

He remained half an hour, and I found him a most courteous and charming gentleman. The godship has been in his family a good while, but I do not know how long. He is a Mohammedan deity; by earthly rank he is a prince; not an Indian but a Persian prince. He is a direct descendant of the Prophet's line. He is comely; also young—for a god; not forty, perhaps not above thirty-five years old. He wears his immense honors with tranquil grace, and with a dignity proper to his awful calling. He speaks English with the ease and purity of a person born to it. I think I am not overstating this. He was the only god I had ever seen, and I was very favorably impressed. When he rose to say good-bye, the door swung open and I caught the flash of a red fez, and heard these words, reverently said:

"Satan see God out?"

"Yes." And these mismated Beings passed from view—Satan in the lead and The Other following after.

CHAPTER IV

Few of us can stand prosperity. Another man's, I mean.
—*Pudd'nhead Wilson's New Calendar.*

The next picture in my mind is Government House, on Malabar
Point, with the wide sea view from the windows and broad balconies; abode of his Excellency the Governor of the Bombay
Presidency—a residence which is European in everything but
the native guards and servants, and is a home and a palace of
state harmoniously combined.

That was England, the English power, the English civilization, the modern civilization—with the quiet elegancies and
quiet colors and quiet tastes and quiet dignity that are the
outcome of the modern cultivation. And following it came a
picture of the ancient civilization of India—an hour in the
mansion of a native prince: Kumar Schri Samatsinhji Bahadur
of the Palitana State.

The young lad, his heir, was with the prince; also, the lad's sister, a wee brown sprite, very pretty, very serious, very winning,
delicately molded, costumed like the daintiest butterfly, a dear
little fairyland princess, gravely willing to be friendly with the
strangers, but in the beginning preferring to hold her father's hand
until she could take stock of them and determine how far they
were to be trusted. She must have been eight years old; so in the
natural (Indian) order of things she would be a bride in three
or four years from now, and then this free contact with the sun
and the air and the other belongings of the outdoor nature and
comradeship with visiting male folk would end, and she would
shut herself up in the zenana for life, like her mother, and
by inherited habit of mind would be happy in that seclusion

and not look upon it as an irksome restraint and a weary captivity.

The game which the prince amuses his leisure with—however, never mind it, I should never be able to describe it intelligibly. I tried to get an idea of it while my wife and daughter visited the princess in the zenana, a lady of charming graces and a fluent speaker of English, but I did not make it out. It is a complicated game, and I believe it is said that nobody can learn to play it well but an Indian. And I was not able to learn how to wind a turban. It seemed a simple art and easy; but that was a deception. It is a piece of thin, delicate stuff a foot wide or more, and forty or fifty feet long; and the exhibitor of the art takes one end of it in his two hands, and winds it in and out intricately about his head, twisting it as he goes, and in a minute or two the thing is finished, and is neat and symmetrical and fits as snugly as a mold.

We were interested in the wardrobe and the jewels, and in the silverware, and its grace of shape and beauty and delicacy of ornamentation. The silverware is kept locked up, except at mealtimes, and none but the chief butler and the prince have keys to the safe. I did not clearly understand why, but it was not for the protection of the silver. It was either to protect the prince from the contamination which his caste would suffer if the vessels were touched by low-caste hands, or it was to protect his highness from poison. Possibly it was both. I believe a salaried taster has to taste everything before the prince ventures it—an ancient and judicious custom in the East, which has thinned out the tasters a good deal, for of course it is the cook that puts the poison in. If I were an Indian prince I would not go to the expense of a taster, I would eat with the cook.

Ceremonials are always interesting; and I noted that the Indian good-morning is a ceremonial, whereas ours doesn't amount to that. In salutation the son reverently touches the father's forehead with a small silver implement tipped with vermilion paste which leaves a red spot there, and in return the son receives the father's blessing. Our good-morning is well enough for the rowdy West, perhaps, but would be too brusque for the soft and ceremonious East.

After being properly necklaced, according to custom, with great garlands made of yellow flowers, and provided with betel-nut to chew, this pleasant visit closed, and we passed thence to a scene of a different sort: from this glow of color and this sunny life to those grim receptacles of the Parsee dead, the Towers of Silence. There is something stately about that name, and an impressiveness which sinks deep; the hush of death is in it. We have the Grave, the Tomb, the Mausoleum, God's Acre, the Cemetery; and association has made them eloquent with solemn meaning; but we have no name that is so majestic as that one, or lingers upon the ear with such deep and haunting pathos.

On lofty ground, in the midst of a paradise of tropical foliage and flowers, remote from the world and its turmoil and noise, they stood—the Towers of Silence; and away below were spread the wide groves of cocoa palms, then the city, mile on mile, then the ocean with its fleets of creeping ships—all steeped in a stillness as deep as the hush that hallowed this high place of the dead. The vultures were there. They stood close together in a great circle all around the rim of a massive low tower—waiting; stood as motionless as sculptured ornaments, and indeed almost deceived one into the belief that that was what they were. Presently there was a slight stir among the score of persons present, and all moved reverently out of the path and ceased from talking. A funeral procession entered the great gate, marching two and two, and moved silently by, toward the Tower. The corpse lay in a shallow shell, and was under cover of a white cloth, but was otherwise naked. The bearers of the body were separated by an interval of thirty feet from the mourners. They, and also the mourners, were draped all in pure white, and each couple of mourners was figuratively bound together by a piece of white rope or a handkerchief—though they merely held the ends of it in their hands. Behind the procession followed a dog, which was led in a leash. When the mourners had reached the neighborhood of the Tower—neither they nor any other human being but the bearers of the dead must approach within thirty feet of it—they turned and went back to one of the prayer houses within the gates, to pray for the spirit of their dead. The bearers unlocked the Tower's sole door and disappeared from view within. In a little while they came out bringing the bier and the white covering-cloth, and locked the door again. Then the ring of vultures rose, flapping their wings, and swooped down into the Tower to devour the body. Nothing was left of it but a clean-picked skeleton when they flocked out again a few minutes afterward.

The principle which underlies and orders everything connected with a Parsee funeral is Purity. By the tenets of the Zoroastrian religion, the elements, Earth, Fire, and Water, are sacred, and must not be contaminated by contact with a dead body. Hence corpses must not be burned, neither must they be buried. None may touch the dead or enter the Towers where they repose except certain men who are officially appointed for that purpose. They receive high pay, but theirs is a dismal life, for they must live apart from their species, because their commerce with the dead defiles them, and any who should associate with them would share their defilement. When they come out of the Tower the clothes they are wearing are exchanged for others, in a building within the grounds, and the ones which they have taken off are left behind, for they are contaminated, and must never be used again or suffered to go outside the grounds. These bearers come to every funeral in new garments. So far as is known, no human being, other than an official corpse-bearer—save one—has ever entered a Tower of Silence after its consecration. Just a hundred years ago a European rushed in behind the bearers and fed his brutal curiosity with a glimpse of the forbidden mysteries of the place. This shabby savage's name is not given; his quality is also concealed. These two details, taken in connection with the fact that for his extraordinary offense the only punishment he got from the East India Company's Government was a solemn official "reprimand"—suggest the suspicion that he was a European of consequence. The same public document which contained the reprimand gave warning that future offenders of his sort, if in the company's service, would be dismissed; and if merchants, suffer revocation of license and exile to England.

The Towers are not tall, but are low in proportion to their circumference, like a gasometer. If you should fill a gasometer halfway up with solid granite masonry, then drive a wide and deep well down through the center of this mass of masonry, you would have the idea of a Tower of Silence. On the masonry surrounding the well the bodies lie, in shallow trenches which radiate like wheel spokes from the well. The trenches slant toward the well and carry into it the rainfall. Underground drains, with charcoal filters in them, carry off this water from the bottom of the well.

When a skeleton has lain in the Tower exposed to the rain and the flaming sun a month it is perfectly dry and clean. Then the same bearers that brought it there come gloved and take it up with tongs and throw it into the well. There it turns to dust. It is never seen again, never touched again, in the world. Other peoples separate their dead, and preserve and continue social distinctions in the grave—the skeletons of kings and statesmen and generals in temples and pantheons proper to skeletons of their degree, and the skeletons of the commonplace and the poor in places suited to their meaner estate; but the Parsees hold that all men rank alike in death—all are humble, all poor, all destitute. In sign of their poverty they are sent to their grave naked, in sign of their equality the bones of the rich, the poor, the illustrious, and the obscure are flung into the common well together. At a Parsee funeral there are no vehicles; all concerned must walk, both rich and poor, howsoever great the distance to be traversed may be. In the wells of the Five Towers of Silence is mingled the dust of all the Parsee men and women and children who have died in Bombay and its vicinity during the two centuries which have elapsed since the Mohammedan conquerors drove the Parsees out of Persia, and into that region of India. The earliest of the five towers was built by the Modi family something more than two hundred years ago, and it is now reserved to the heirs of that house; none but the dead of that blood are carried thither.

The origin of at least one of the details of a Parsee funeral is not now known—the presence of the dog. Before a corpse is borne from the house of mourning it must be uncovered and exposed to the gaze of a dog; a dog must also be led in the rear of the funeral. Mr. Nusserwanjee Byramjee, Secretary to the Parsee Punchayet, said that these formalities had once had a meaning and a reason for their institution, but that they were survivors whose origin none could now account for. Custom and tradition continue them in force, antiquity hallows them. It is thought that in ancient times in Persia the dog was a sacred animal and could guide souls to heaven; also that his eye had the power of purifying objects which had been contaminated by the touch of the dead; and that hence his presence with the funeral cortège provides an ever-applicable remedy in case of need.

The Parsees claim that their method of disposing of the dead is an effective protection of the living; that it disseminates no corruption, no impurities of any sort, no disease germs; that no wrap, no garment which has touched the dead is allowed to touch the living afterward; that from the Towers of Silence nothing proceeds which can carry harm to the outside world. These are just claims, I think. As a sanitary measure, their system seems to be about the equivalent of cremation, and as sure. We are drifting slowly—but hopefully—toward cremation in these days. It could not be expected that this progress should be swift, but if it be steady and continuous, even if slow, that will suffice. When cremation becomes the rule we shall cease to shudder at it; we should shudder at burial if we allowed ourselves to think what goes on in the grave.

The dog was an impressive figure to me, representing as he did a mystery whose key is lost. He was humble, and apparently depressed; and he let his head droop pensively, and looked as if he might be trying to call back to his mind what it was that he had used to symbolize ages ago when he began his function.

There was another impressive thing close at hand, but I was not privileged to see it. That was the sacred fire—a fire which is supposed to have been burning without interruption for more than two centuries; and so, living by the same heat that was imparted to it so long ago.

The Parsees are a remarkable community. There are only about sixty thousand in Bombay, and only about half as many as that in the rest of India; but they make up in importance what they lack in numbers. They are highly educated, energetic, enterprising, progressive, rich, and the Jew himself is not more lavish or catholic in his charities and benevolences. The Parsees build and endow hospitals, for both men and animals; and they and their womankind keep an open purse for all great and good objects. They are a political force, and a valued support to the government. They have a pure and lofty religion, and they preserve it in its integrity and order their lives by it.

We took a final sweep of the wonderful view of plain and city and ocean, and so ended our visit to the garden and the Towers of Silence; and the last thing I noticed was another symbol—a voluntary symbol this one; it was a vulture standing on the sawed-off top of a tall and slender and branchless palm in an open space in the ground; he was perfectly motionless, and looked like a piece of sculpture on a pillar. And he had a mortuary look, too, which was in keeping with the place.

GORE VIDAL

(1925–)

Gore Vidal was born in West Point, New York. His grandfather was a senator and his father, an adviser to President Franklin Delano Roosevelt. Vidal used his early proximity to the sources of power to brilliant effect in such novelized histories of America as *Burr* (1974) and *Lincoln* (1984). His political essays follow in the polemical tradition of Mark Twain, H. L. Mencken, and I. F. Stone. His literary essays, which have rescued a range of European and American writers from obscurity, are rather more difficult to place in any tradition. But Vidal is, above all, a connoisseur of the classical world, and particularly its pagan philosophical legacy. His novel *Julian* (1964) described the brief moment of royal apostasy in the post-Constantine Roman Empire. In *Creation* (1981), from which the following excerpt is taken, he set out to re-create the world at a crucial time in its history: the fifth century BC, which was privileged with the almost simultaneous presence of Socrates, Confucius, the Buddha, and Zoroaster. It is unlikely, Vidal said in a recent introduction to his novel, that one man could have met all of them. But it is what his Persian protagonist Cyrus does as he travels from Greece to China. To see these great men and their times through the eyes of a fifth-century Persian, as he is imagined by a twentieth-century American novelist, is often odd but never less than engaging. The section on India, where Cyrus meets the Buddha and is bewildered, shows that Vidal's research was thorough. And so riveting is Vidal's own curiosity that the few anachronisms—far from being the staple of classical Indians, curry was an Anglo-Indian invention—seem almost amusing.

from CREATION

This is what I think I know about the Buddha. At the time that I met him—more than a half-century ago—he was about seventy-two or -three years old. He was born in the Shakya republic, which is located in the foothills of the Himalayas. He came from a warrior family called Gotama. At birth, he was named Siddhartha. He was brought up in the capital city of Kapilavastru. At one time Gotama's father held high office in the republic, but he was hardly a king, as certain snobs at Shravasti and Rajagriha still like to pretend.

Siddhartha married. He had one son, Rahula—which means *link* or *bond*. I suspect that the child must have begun life with another name, but I never found out what it was. He certainly proved to be a bond with that world which the Buddha was to eliminate—for himself.

At the age of twenty-nine Siddhartha embarked upon what he called the noble quest. Because he was acutely conscious that he was "liable to birth because of self, and knowing the peril in whatever is liable to birth, he sought the uttermost security from this world's bonds—nirvana."

Siddhartha's quest took seven years. He lived in the forest. He mortified the flesh. He meditated. In due course, through his own efforts—or simply because he had evolved in the course of all his previous incarnations?—he understood not only the cause of pain but its cure. He saw all that was and all that will ever be. In a magical contest he defeated the evil god Mara, who is lord of this world.

Siddhartha became the enlightened one or the Buddha. Since

he had eliminated not only himself but the tangible world as well, he is higher than all the gods: they are still evolving and he is not. They continue to exist within a world that he has entirely dissolved. Since enlightenment is an end in itself—*the* great end—the now-eliminated world ought not to have concerned the Buddha. But the world that he had awakened from returned to him, as it were, when the high god Brahma came down from heaven and begged him to show others the way. But the Buddha was not interested. Why speak, he said, of what cannot be described? But Brahma was so insistent that the Buddha agreed to go to Varanasi and set in motion the wheel of the doctrine. He expounded the four truths; and he revealed the eightfold path. Yet at the same time, paradoxically, the entire exercise was—is—pointless because he had abolished this world and all other worlds, too.

"Everything subject to causation," the Buddha said, "is like a mirage." For him, human personality is something like a bad dream—to be got rid of, preferably, by waking up to . . . nothing? There is a point beyond which I cannot follow the Buddha. But then, he is enlightened and I am not.

In every way, the Buddha's teaching is opposed to that of the Wise Lord. For Buddhists and Jains, the world deteriorates; therefore, extinction is the goal of the wise. For Zoroaster, each man must make his way either toward the Truth or the Lie, and in eternity he will be judged for what he did or did not do in the course of only one life. Finally, after a time in heaven or hell, all human souls will share in the Wise Lord's victory over Ahriman, and we shall achieve a perfect state of being that is not so different from the Buddha's sunyata, or shining void—if that is the right translation of a word which explains so precisely the inexplicable.

For the Indians, all creatures are subject to constant reincarnation. Punishment and rewards in any given life are the result of previous deeds, in previous lives. One is totally subject to one's karma, or destiny. For us, there is suffering or joy in time of the long dominion and, finally, union with Ahura Mazdah in eternal time. For them, there is endless death and rebirth, only broken for a very few by nirvana, which is nothing, and sunyata, which is what it is if it is.

Democritus thinks that the two attitudes are not so far apart. I *know* that they are entirely unlike. Admittedly, there is something luminous if slippery about the Buddha's conception of sunyata; in fact, the more I think of his truths, the more I feel that I am trying to catch with two clumsy hands one of those swift eels that writhe at night in hot southern seas, ablaze with cold light. At the core of the Buddhist system there is an empty space which is not just the sought-after nirvana. It is perfect atheism.

To my knowledge, the Buddha never discussed any of the gods except in the most offhand way. He never denied them; he simply ignored them. But despite his formidable conceit, he did not set himself in place of the gods because, by the time he had set in motion the wheel of his doctrine, he himself had ceased to be, which is the ultimate stage of evolution. But while he still inhabited Gotama's flesh, he allowed others to create the sangha in order to alleviate for the chosen few some of life's pain.

At first only men could be admitted to the order. But then Ananda persuaded the Buddha that women should be admitted too. They would live in their own communities, and follow the eightfold path. Although the Buddha was complaisant, he did make a joke, much quoted by misogynists. "Had the order been made up only of men, Ananda, it would have lasted a thousand years. Now that women have been included, it will last only five hundred years." In either case, I suspect he was unduly optimistic.

Toward the end of the rainy season I accompanied Prince Jeta to the park which he may or may not have sold to the merchant Anathapindika for the Buddha's use. Here live a thousand monks, disciples, admirers. Many ascetics sleep out of doors, while pilgrims live in guesthouses and members of the order are quartered in a large building with a thatched roof.

Not far from this monastery, a wooden hut had been erected on a low platform. Here on a mat sat the Buddha. Since the hut was built without walls, he lived in full view of the world.

Sariputra welcomed us to the monastery. He moved like a boy, with a skipping step. He did not carry a parasol. The warm rain seemed never to bother him. "You're in luck. Tathagata is in a mood to talk. We're so glad for you. Since the full moon, he's been silent. But not today." Sariputra patted my arm. "I told him who you were."

If he expected me to ask him what the Buddha had had to say about the Persian ambassador, he was disappointed. I was ceremonious. "I look forward to our meeting." I used the word *upanishad*, which means not just a meeting but a serious discussion about spiritual matters.

Sariputra escorted Prince Jeta and me to the pavilion that had been built on a platform approached by eight shallow steps— one for each part of the eightfold way? At the first step, a tall heavyset yellow man greeted Sariputra, who then introduced him to us. "This is Fan Ch'ih," said Sariputra. "He has come from Cathay to learn from the Buddha."

"It is not possible *not* to learn from the Buddha." Fan Ch'ih spoke the Koshalan dialect even better than I, despite an accent that was rather worse.

Since Fan Ch'ih and I were to become close friends, I will only note here that he had not come to India to learn from the Buddha; he was on a trade mission from a small nation in southeast Cathay. Later he told me that he had come to the park that day in order to meet the Persian ambassador. He was as fascinated by Persia as I was by Cathay.

We followed Sariputra up the steps and into the hut, where all of those who had been seated rose to greet us except for the Buddha, who remained seated on his mat. I could see why he was called the golden one. He was as yellow as any native of Cathay. Not only was he not Aryan, he was not Dravidian either. Obviously, some tribe from Cathay had crossed the Himalayas to sire the Gotama clan.

The Buddha was small, slender, supple. He sat very straight, legs crossed beneath him. The slanted eyes were so narrow that one could not tell if they were open or shut. Someone described the Buddha's eyes as being as luminous as the night sky in summer. I would not know. I never actually saw them. Pale arched eyebrows grew together in such a way that there was a tuft of hair at the juncture. In India this is considered a mark of divinity.

The old man's flesh was wrinkled but glowing with good health, and the bare skull shone like yellow alabaster. There was a scent of sandalwood about him that struck me as less than ascetic. During the time I was with him, he seldom moved either his head or his body. Occasionally he would gesture with the right hand. The Buddha's voice was low and agreeable, and seemed to cost him no breath. In fact, in some mysterious way, he seemed not to breathe at all.

I bowed low. He motioned for me to sit. I made a set speech. When I was finished, the Buddha smiled. That was all. He did not bother to answer me. There was an awkward moment.

Then a young man suddenly asked, "O Tathagata, is it your view that the world is eternal and all other views false?"

"No, child, I do not hold the view that the world is eternal and all other views false."

"Then, is it your view that the world is *not* eternal and all other views are false?"

"No, child, I do not hold the view that the world is not eternal, and all other views are false."

The young man then asked the Buddha if the cosmos was finite or infinite, if the body was similar or not similar to the soul, if a holy man exists or does not exist after death, and so on. To each question the Buddha gave the youth the same answer or nonanswer that he had given to the question whether or not the world was eternal. Finally the young man asked, "What objection, then, does Tathagata perceive to each of these theories that he has not adopted any one of them?"

"Because, child, the theory that the world is eternal, is a jungle, a wilderness, a puppet show, a writhing, and a chain forever attached to misery, pain, despair and agony—this view does not contribute to aversion, absence of desire, cessation, quiescence, knowledge, supreme wisdom and nirvana."

"Is this Tathagata's answer to each question?"

The Buddha nodded. "This is the objection I perceive to these apparently conflicting theories, and that is why I have not adopted any one of them."

"But has Tathagata any theory of his own?"

There was a pause. I must confess that the blood was suddenly high in my cheeks, and I felt as if I had the fever. I wanted, desperately, to know the answer or nonanswer.

"The Buddha is free from all theories." The voice was mild. The eyes seemed to be looking not at us but upon some world or nonworld that we could not comprehend. "There are things, of course, that I know. I know the nature of matter. I know how things come into being and I know how they perish. I know the nature of sensation. I know how it is that sensation comes, and how it goes. I know how perception begins and ends. How consciousness starts, only to stop. Since I *know* these things, I have been able to free myself from all attachment. The self is gone, given up, relinquished."

"But Tathagata, are you . . . is the priest who is in such a state as yours, is he reborn?"

"To say that he is reborn does not fit the case."

"Does that mean he is not reborn?"

"That does not fit the case either."

"Then is he both reborn and not reborn?"

"No. Simultaneity does not fit the case."

"I am confused, Tathagata. Either he is the one thing or the other or even both things at the same time, yet—"

"Enough, child. You are confused because very often it is not possible to see what is right in front of you because you happen to be looking in the wrong direction. Let me ask you a question. If a fire was burning in front of you, would you notice it?"

"Yes, Tathagata."

"If the fire went out, would you notice that?"

"Yes, Tathagata."

"Now, then, when the fire goes out, where does it go? to the east? the west? the north? the south?"

"But the question is to no point, Tathagata. When a fire goes out for lack of fuel to burn, it is . . . well, it is gone, extinct."

"You have now answered your own question as to whether or not a holy man is reborn or not reborn. The question is to no point. Like the fire that goes out for lack of fuel to burn, he is gone, extinct."

"I see," said the young man. "I understand."

"Perhaps you *begin* to understand."

The Buddha looked in my direction. I cannot say that he ever looked *at* me. "We often hold this discussion," he said. "And I always use the image of the fire because it seems easy to understand."

There was a long silence.

Suddenly Sariputra announced, "Everything subject to causation is a mirage." There was another silence. By then I had forgotten every question that I had meant to ask. Like the proverbial fire, my mind had gone out.

Prince Jeta spoke for me. "Tathagata, the ambassador from the Great King of Persia is curious to know how the world was created."

The Buddha turned those strange blind eyes toward me. Then he smiled. "Perhaps," he said, "you would like to tell me." The

Buddha's bared teeth were mottled and yellow, disconcertingly suggestive of fangs.

I don't know what I said. I suppose I described for him the simultaneous creation of good and evil. Repeated my grandfather's doctrines. Observed those narrow eyes which were aimed—there is no other verb—in my direction.

When I had finished, the Buddha made a polite response. "Since no one can ever know for certain whether or not his own view of creation is the correct one, it is absolutely impossible for him to know if someone else's is the wrong one." Then he dropped the only important subject that there is.

The next silence was the longest of all. I listened to the sound of the rain upon the thatched roof, of the wind in the trees, of the monks chanting in the nearby monastery.

Finally I remembered one of the many questions that I had intended to ask him: "Tell me, Buddha, if the life of this world is an evil, why then *is* the world?"

The Buddha stared at me. I think that this time he might actually have seen me, even though the light inside the hut was now as dim and as green as pond water when one opens one's eyes below the surface.

"The world is full of pain, suffering and evil. That is the first truth," he said. "Comprehend that first truth, and the other truths will be evident. Follow the eightfold way and—"

"—and nirvana may or may not extinguish the self." There was a slight gasp from those present. I had interrupted the Buddha. Nevertheless, I persisted in my rudeness. "But my question is: Who or what made a world whose only point, according to you, is that it causes pain to no purpose?"

The Buddha was benign. "My child, let us say that you have been fighting in a battle. You have been struck by a poisoned arrow. You are in pain. You are feverish. You fear death—and the next incarnation. I am nearby. I am a skilled surgeon. You come to me. What will you ask me to do?"

"Take out the arrow."

"Right away?"

"Right away."

"You would not want to know whose bow fired the arrow?"

"I would be curious, of course." I saw the direction that he was taking.

"But would you want to know *before* I took out the arrow whether or not the archer was tall or short, a warrior or a slave, handsome or ill-favored?"

"No, but—"

"Then, that is all that the eightfold way can offer you. A freedom from the arrow's pain and an antidote to the poison, which is this world."

"But once the arrow has been removed and I am cured, I might still want to know whose arrow struck me."

"If you have truly followed the way, the question will be immaterial. You will have seen that this life is a dream, a mirage, something produced by the self. And when the self goes, it goes."

"You are Tathagata—the one who has come and gone and come again. When you are here, you are here. But when you go, where do you go?"

"Where the fire goes when it's gone out. My child, no words can define nirvana. Make no attempt to catch in a net of familiar phrases that which is and is not. Finally, even to contemplate the idea of nirvana is a proof that one is still on the near side of the river. Those who have achieved that state do not try to name what is nameless. Meanwhile, let us take out the arrow. Let us heal the flesh. Let us take a ride, if we can, on the ferryboat that goes to the far side. Thus we follow the middle way. Is this the right way?" The Buddha's smile was barely visible in the twilight. Then he said, "As the space of the universe is filled with countless wheels of fiery stars, the wisdom that transcends this life is abysmally profound."

"And difficult to comprehend, Tathagata," said Sariputra, "even for those who are awake."

"Which is why, Sariputra, no one can ever comprehend it *through* awakening."

The two old men burst out laughing at what was obviously a familiar joke.

I remember nothing more of that meeting with the Buddha. I think that before we left the park, we visited the monastery. I believe that I first met Ananda then. He was a small man whose life work was to learn by heart everything that the Buddha was reported to have said and done.

I do remember asking Prince Jeta if the Buddha had said anything to me that he had not said a thousand times before.

"No. He uses the same images over and over again. The only new thing—to me—was the paradox about awakening."

"But it was not new to Sariputra."

"Well, Sariputra sees him more than anyone else, and they tell each other complicated jokes. They laugh a good deal together. I don't know at what. Although I am sufficiently advanced that I can smile at this world, I cannot laugh at it just yet."

"But why is he so indifferent to the idea of creation?"

"Because he thinks it, literally, immaterial. The ultimate human task is to dematerialize the self. In his own case, he has succeeded. Now he has set up the wheel of the doctrine for others to turn as best they can. He himself is come—and he is gone."

Democritus finds these ideas easier to comprehend than I do. I can accept the notion that all creation is in flux and that what we take to be the real world is a kind of shifting dream, perceived by each of us in a way that differs from that of everyone else, as well as from the thing itself. But the absence of deity, of origin and of terminus, of good in conflict with evil . . . The absence of purpose, finally, makes the Buddha's truths too strange for me to accept.